Borderless Higher Education for Refugees

Also available from Bloomsbury

Citizenship Education in Conflict-Affected Areas, Bassel Akar
Comparative and International Education, David Phillips and Michele Schweisfurth
Continuing Professional Teacher Development in Sub-Saharan Africa: Improving Teaching and Learning, edited by Yusuf Sayed
Education and International Development, edited by Tristan McCowan and Elaine Unterhalter
Education and Disability in the Global South: New Perspectives from Africa and Asia, edited by Nidhi Singal, Paul Lynch and Shruti Taneja Johansson
Educating for Peace and Human Rights: An Introduction, Maria Hantzopoulos and Monisha Bajaj
Internationalization of Higher Education for Development: Blackness and Postcolonial Solidarity in Africa-Brazil Relations, Susanne Ress
Peace Education: International Perspectives, edited by Monisha Bajaj and Maria Hantzopoulos
Perspectives on Educational Practice Around the World, edited by Sue Hammond and Margaret Sangster
Picture Pedagogy: Visual Culture Concepts to Enhance the Curriculum, Paul Duncum
Postdigital Dialogues on Critical Pedagogy, Liberation Theology and Information Technology, Peter McLaren and Petar Jandric
Preparation and Development of School Leaders in Africa, edited by Pontso Moorosi and Tony Bush
The Bloomsbury Handbook of Global Education and Learning, edited by Douglas Bourn
Transnational Perspectives on Democracy, Citizenship, Human Rights and Peace Education, edited by Mary Drinkwater, Fazal Rizvi and Karen Edge

Borderless Higher Education for Refugees

Lessons from the Dadaab Refugee Camps

Edited by Wenona Giles and Lorrie Miller

BLOOMSBURY ACADEMIC
LONDON · NEW YORK · OXFORD · NEW DELHI · SYDNEY

BLOOMSBURY ACADEMIC
Bloomsbury Publishing Plc
50 Bedford Square, London, WC1B 3DP, UK
1385 Broadway, New York, NY 10018, USA
29 Earlsfort Terrace, Dublin 2, Ireland

BLOOMSBURY, BLOOMSBURY ACADEMIC and the Diana logo are trademarks of Bloomsbury Publishing Plc

First published in Great Britain 2021

Copyright © Wenona Giles, Lorrie Miller and Bloomsbury, 2021

Wenona Giles, Lorrie Miller and Bloomsbury have asserted their right under the Copyright, Designs and Patents Act, 1988, to be identified as Authors of this work.

For legal purposes the Acknowledgements on p. xviii constitute an extension of this copyright page.

Cover design by Charlotte James
Cover image by Harshil Gudka on Unsplash

All rights reserved. No part of this publication may be reproduced or transmitted in any form or by any means, electronic or mechanical, including photocopying, recording, or any information storage or retrieval system, without prior permission in writing from the publishers.

Bloomsbury Publishing Plc does not have any control over, or responsibility for, any third-party websites referred to or in this book. All internet addresses given in this book were correct at the time of going to press. The author and publisher regret any inconvenience caused if addresses have changed or sites have ceased to exist, but can accept no responsibility for any such changes.

A catalogue record for this book is available from the British Library.

Library of Congress Cataloging-in-Publication Data

Names: Giles, Wenona Mary, 1949– editor. | Miller, Lorrie, editor.
Title: Borderless Higher Education for Refugees : lessons from the Dadaab refugee camps / edited by Wenona Giles and Lorrie Miller.
Description: London ; New York, NY : Bloomsbury Academic, 2021. | Includes bibliographical references and index. |
Identifiers: LCCN 2021007634 (print) | LCCN 2021007635 (ebook) | ISBN 9781350151246 (hardback) | ISBN 9781350151239 (paperback) | ISBN 9781350151253 (ebook) | ISBN 9781350151260 (epub)
Subjects: LCSH: Borderless Higher Education for Refugees (Project) | Refugees–Education (Higher)–Kenya. | Dadaab Refugee Camp.
Classification: LCC LC3738.K4 B67 2021 (print) | LCC LC3738.K4 (ebook) | DDC 371.826/914096762—dc23
LC record available at https://lccn.loc.gov/2021007634
LC ebook record available at https://lccn.loc.gov/2021007635

ISBN: HB: 978-1-3501-5124-6
PB: 978-1-3501-5123-9
ePDF: 978-1-3501-5125-3
eBook: 978-1-3501-5126-0

Typeset by RefineCatch Limited, Bungay, Suffolk

To find out more about our authors and books visit www.bloomsbury.com and sign up for our newsletters.

Contents

List of Illustrations	vii
Notes on Contributors	viii
Acknowledgements	xviii
Introduction *Wenona Giles, Lorrie Miller, Philemon Misoy, Norah Kariba, Okello Mark Oyat*	1

Part One Putting a Project into Action

1 Historical and Political Contestations in the Dadaab Refugee Camps and North-Eastern Kenya *Mohamed Duale, Esther Munene and Marangu Njogu* 19

2 Gender Disparities in University Access in the Kenyan Kakuma Camps *Danielle Bishop, Hanan Duri and Grace Nshimiyumukiza* 35

3 The Challenges of Reciprocity and Relative Autonomy in North/South Partnerships *Josephine Gitome and Don Dippo* 49

4 Development of a Community Health Education Degree Programme through a North-South Collaboration: Lessons Learned *F. Beryl Pilkington and Isabella I. Mbai* 65

Part Two Students and Teachers: Inside the BHER Supported Classroom

5 Refugees Respond: Using Digital Tools, Networks and 'Production Pedagogies' to Envision Possible Futures *Abdikadir Abikar, Abdullahi Aden, Kurt Thumlert, Negin Dahya and Jennifer Jenson* 81

6 Technology and Flexibility: The Online Learning Experience of Teaching Assistants and their Students in the Dadaab Refugee Camps *Hawa Sabriye and Dacia Douhaibi, with contributions from Arte Dagane and Ochan Leomoi* 101

7 Out of Bounds: The BHER Bones of Teaching Geography Across
   Borders *Megan Youdelis, Dacia Douhaibi, Devin Holterman,
   Kamal Paudel, Valerie Preston, Tarmo K. Remmel,
   Elizabeth Lunstrum and Joseph Mensah*   115

8 Academic Philanthropy and Pedagogies of Resilience *Lorrie Miller,
   Graham W. Lea, Rita L. Irwin, Samson Nashon, Elizabeth Jordan,
   Kimberly Baker and Espen Stranger-Johannessen*   133

9 Refugee Students' Experience of Accessing English Language
   Learning in Dadaab, Kenya *HaEun Kim, Nombuso Dlamini,
   Dahabo Ibrahim, Seraphin Kimonyo and Johanna Reynolds*   151

10 A Gallery to Rethink and (Re)place the Anthropocene: Framing
   From A Place-based Borderless Higher Education *Steve Alsop
   and Roxanne Cohen*   167

   Afterword *Lorrie Miller and Wenona Giles with Fouzia Warsame,
   the Dean of Education, Somali National University, Mogadishu*   185

Notes   189
References   197
Index   219

Illustrations

Figures

i.1	Aerial view of the Dadaab camps, 2016, courtesy of Peter Murphy	2
i.2	BHER Commons Developmental Steps, courtesy of Wenona Giles	6
i.3	Map of Northern Kenya, including the location of Dadaab and Kakuma in relation To Somalia and Sudan, Map Data, 2020	8
i.4	Map of the Dadaab camps, 2016, courtesy of Joseph Mensah	10
8.1	View from within UNHCR compound, Dadaab 2017, courtesy of Lorrie Miller	134
8.2	Scenes on the road from Dadaab Town, 2017, courtesy of Lorrie Miller	138
8.3	Scenes on the road from Dadaab Town, 2017, courtesy of Lorrie Miller	138
8.4	Scenes on the road from Dadaab Town, 2017, courtesy of Lorrie Miller	138
10.1	BHER students in pursuit of the Anthropocene, December 2018, courtesy of Steve Aslop and Roxanne Cohen	167
10.2	Sample of images from our Anthropocene Gallery. Sources: Green Roofs for Healthy Cities 2013; Steffen et al. 2011; Belcourt 2015; Bottom Row: Noyle n.d.; author's personal photograph 2018; Woods n.d.	173
10.3	Greenbelt in Dadaab: Dagahaley Refugee Camp, 2015, Govt. Kenya & UNHCR. 2015.	176
10.4	Youth workshop, 2018, courtesy of Grace Nshimiyumukiza	177
10.5	Goats and Garbage, 2018, courtesy of Kassahun Tekalign Hiticha, Dahabo Abdi Ibrahim, Kiin Ahmed Mohamed, Salah Mohamud Maalin and Jeylani Hajji Abdullahi	179

Table

7.1	Geography Courses in the B.A. Geography Degree Offered Through BHER	116

Contributors

Abikar Abdikadir is a Master of Education candidate at York University, Canada, through the Borderless Higher Education for Refugees (BHER) program. He was a science, mathematics and technology teacher in Dadaab schools and is currently completing his Masters Research Project on professional learning communities in refugee contexts, while also mentoring new teacher candidates and graduate students in the BHER program, Dadaab, Kenya.

Abdullahi Aden is a Master of Education candidate at York University, Canada, through the Borderless Higher Education for Refugees (BHER) program. He has worked for twelve years as a senior high school instructor in the humanities and as a primary school administrator in the Dadaab camps. He is currently completing his Masters Research Project on education in Somalia and the Dadaab context.

Steve Alsop is Professor in the Faculty of Education at York University, Canada. He teaches courses and supervises graduate students in the fields of education, science and technology studies, and environmental sustainability. His research explores pedagogical articulations of scientific and ecological knowledge in selected educational settings, including North-South community-university partnerships, communities, science centres, schools, NGOs and youth organizations. His recent work has been located in contexts of emergency and ecological instability and shaped by a belief that education can helpfully join with others to assist in shaping more diverse, caring, peaceful, ecologically thriving and equitable worlds.

Kimberly Baker is a PhD candidate in the Department of Curriculum and Pedagogy at the University of British Columbia, Canada, and is a museum educator in the City of Richmond, British Columbia, Canada.

Danielle Bishop received her PhD from York University, Canada, and has ten years' experience working as a social worker and consultant in eleven countries across Asia, Africa and the Middle East with the UN and international NGOs in the areas of child protection, gender and protection, and commercial exploitation and sexual abuse in displacement and protracted crises settings. Her dissertation focused on how the violence of poverty, health inequity, food scarcity, and social and political marginalization is embodied and lived out in the everyday lives of both refugee young people and host Turkana young people working, and at times living, in the Kakuma refugee camps in north-western Kenya. From 2011 to 2014, Danielle worked with the Borderless Higher Education for Refugees (BHER) project as a graduate research assistant.

Roxanne Cohen is a PhD candidate in Education at York University, Canada. Her areas of focus are community-university partnerships, and youth leadership in climate change and place-based education. Her academic research intersects with her community and consultation work in urban full-cycle food security systems, youth and intergenerational democratic learning spaces for climate action-justice-healing-care.

Arte Dagane is a Master of Education candidate at York University, Canada, through the Borderless Higher Education for Refugees (BHER) program. He has worked as an English and History teacher in the Dadaab schools. He is currently finishing his Masters Research Project on girl-child education in Dadaab, while also working as a TA and mentor for the undergraduate students in the BHER program in Dadaab, Kenya.

Negin Dahya is an Assistant Professor at the University of Toronto Institute of Communication, Culture, Information and Technology and Faculty of Information, Canada. Negin's research in refugee education and technology has centred on applying socio-technical theory to understand the role of mobile phones and social media to support teaching and learning among refugees pursuing and enrolled in post-secondary training and higher education.

Don Dippo is University Professor in the Faculty of Education at York University, Canada. He co-directed the Borderless Higher Education for Refugees (BHER) project in Kenya, until 2019, when he became the lead Director. He serves on the Executive Committee of the Centre for Refugee Studies at York University, Canada, and is on the Board of Directors of Success Beyond Limits, a not-for-profit, community-based organization that supports high school age youth in Toronto's Jane/Finch community, Canada.

S. Nombuso Dlamini is an Associate Professor in the Faculty of Education at York University, Canada, and the Director of Youth in Politics. She also served as the inaugural Jean Augustine Chair in the New Urban Environment, York University, Canada. Her research includes youth projects that focus on civic engagements, and youth negotiation and production of diaspora identities; and, gender-based projects examining immigrant women's Canadian work experiences, immigrant women's production of social capital, and ethnic minority women's health and socioeconomic livelihood.

Dacia Douhaibi is a PhD candidate at York University, Canada. She spent five years working with the Borderless Higher Education for Refugees project and traveled to Dadaab as a teaching assistant and course director for the project. Dacia currently acts as the Research Coordinator for Justice Africa, an advocacy and research-based organization in South Sudan, and Research Advisor for aidx, a technology company working to develop peer-to-peer mobile applications to support systems of mutual aid amongst refugees. She also serves as Advisor to the Emerging Scholars and Practitioners on Forced Migration Issues (ESPMI) network, and Editor in Chief of the Refugee Review.

Mohamed Duale is a PhD candidate in Education and a Graduate Research Fellow with the Centre for Refugee Studies at York University, Canada. He is an interdisciplinary scholar currently researching refugee youth belonging, education and civic participation. His doctoral research examines the lived experiences of Somali refugee youth in the Dadaab refugee camps of north-east Kenya. He has been teaching in the Borderless Higher Education for Refugees (BHER) project to build the capacity of refugee and local teachers in Dadaab. Mohamed is also a researcher with the Local Engagement Refugee Research Network (LERRN), a SSHRC-funded international partnered research project.

Hanan Duri is a third-year PhD candidate in the Faculty of Education and holds an MA in Development Studies from York University, Canada. Since 2018, she has been a teaching assistant and course director with the BHER project in Dadaab, Kenya. Her research examines the role of higher education for refugee women living in camps, gender inequity, and access and barriers to higher education.

Wenona Giles is Professor Emerita and Senior Scholar in the Anthropology Department and Resident Research Associate of the Centre for Refugee Studies, York University, Canada, where she has taught and published in the areas of gender, forced migration, globalization, migration, education, nationalism and war. Her books include *Immigration and Nationalism: Two Generations of Portuguese Women in Toronto* (2002), *Development and Diaspora: Gender and the Refugee Experience* (1996), *Refuge on Gender Relations and Refugee Issues* (1995),

Refuge on Higher Education for Refugees (2010–11), *Feminists under Fire: Exchanges across War Zones* (2003), *Sites of Violence: Gender and Conflict Zones* (2004), *Refugees in Extended Exile: Living on the Edge* (2017) and *A Better Future: The Role of Higher Education for Displaced and Marginalised People* (2020). Giles co-founded and co-coordinated the International Women in Conflict Zones Research Network (1993–2004) and co-led the Borderless Higher Education for Refugees (BHER) project (2013–19) in the Dadaab refugee camps, Kenya.

Josephine Gitome is Senior Lecturer at Kenyatta University (KU), Kenya, and holds a doctorate in Religious Studies. She is a Founding Director of the former KU Centre for Refugee Studies and Empowerment and coordinated the establishment of the KU Dadaab Campus in 2012. Josephine coordinated the Borderless Higher Education for Refugees (BHER) project at KU (2011–18) and has vast experience in networking, partnership and collaborations. Her scholarly publications focus on Pastoral Youth Counselling, HIV and AIDS, and psychosocial challenges facing refugees.

Devin Holterman is a PhD candidate in the Faculty of Environmental and Urban Change at York University, Canada. Informed by the study of political ecology, his research focuses on the ever-growing intersections between biodiversity conservation and the extractive industries in Tanzania, Canada, and beyond. As a social scientist with a background in journalism, Devin is an avid environmental and human rights activist, and has experience working with various nongovernmental organizations around the world.

Dahabo Ibrahim is a first-year Master of Education candidate at the Faculty of Education, York University, Canada, through the Borderless Higher Education for Refugees (BHER) Project. She is also a program mentor for the current cohort of undergraduate certificate students in BHER related programs concerning teaching in elementary and secondary schools in the Dadaab refugee camps.

Rita L. Irwin is a Distinguished University Scholar and Professor of Art Education and Curriculum Studies at the University of British Columbia, Canada. She is an award-winning educator and scholar best known for her work in a/r/tography, teacher education, curriculum studies and socio-cultural concerns. As former Associate Dean of Teacher Education at the University of British Columbia, Canada, she co-coordinated the UBC portion of the Secondary Teacher Education Program in the Dadaab refugee camps as part of the Borderless Higher Education for Refugees project.

Jennifer Jenson is Professor of Digital Languages, Literacies, and Culture in the Faculty of Education at the University of British Columbia, Canada.

Elizabeth Jordan is an Emerita faculty member at the University of British Columbia, Canada. She has been a teacher for her entire career, in both a regular classroom and at the university level. Her particular interests have been in problem-based learning, pre-service education (both local and international), gifted education and the influences within a classroom environment that support creativity. She continues to be interested in the expanding developments and influence of teaching creativity on teachers and students.

Norah Kariba is the Programme Manager at Windle International Kenya, Dadaab, Kenya. She has more than ten years' experience working with the Kenyan government and NGOs in development and humanitarian work and has held a range of implementation, senior management and leadership positions in both the Kakuma and Dadaab refugee camps. She is responsible for overseeing the implementation of all Windle International Kenya programmes in Dadaab, Kenya.

HaEun Kim is the Program Administrator for the Borderless Higher Education for Refugees project. She is a certified secondary school teacher and has previously worked as an outreach worker running preventative programs for youth and families living in high priority communities in Toronto, Canada. She completed her MEd in Language, Culture and Teaching at York University, Canada. Her research interests include language and literacy education, forced migration and refugee studies, and understanding barriers that prevent access to learning in both urban contexts such as Toronto as well as settings considered to be education in emergencies.

Seraphin Kimonyo is a Master of Education candidate at the Faculty of Education, York University, Canada, through the Borderless Higher Education for Refugees (BHER) Project. He is also a program mentor for the current cohort of undergraduate certificate students in BHER related programs that concern teaching in elementary and secondary schools in the Dadaab refugee camps.

Graham W. Lea is an Assistant Professor of theatre/drama education at the University of Manitoba, Canada. His research interests include research-based theatre methodology, narrative in mathematics education, and theatre/drama in health and teacher education research. His doctoral research used research-based theatre to examine his mother's experiences as a CUSO teacher in Kenya in the 1960s and his as a student teacher in there in 2004. He is co-editor, with George Belliveau, of the book *Research-Based Theatre: An Artistic Methodology* (2016, Intellect) and *Contact! Unload: Military Veterans, Trauma, and Research-based Theatre* (2020, UBC Press).

Ochan Leomoi is a Master of Education candidate at York University, Canada through the Borderless Higher Education for Refugees (BHER) program. He has worked as a primary school teacher in Dadaab, Kenya. Ochan was a guest speaker at the 2019 Global Refugee Forum in Geneva, Switzerland. His Masters Research Project is an examination of cheating in secondary schools in Dadaab, Kenya. Ochan currently mentors and works as a TA for undergraduate BHER students in Dadaab, Kenya.

Libby Lunstrum is an Associate Professor in the School of Public Service at Boise State University, USA, where she teaches Environmental Studies and Global Studies. She was previously an Associate Professor of Geography at York University, Canada, where she was affiliated with the Borderless Higher Education for Refugees (BHER) project. She is a strong proponent of experiential and intercultural learning and had the privilege of exploring both during her teaching for the BHER project. Her research focuses on southern Africa and North America and examines the political ecology of conservation, including green militarization, conservation-induced displacement and illegal wildlife trade, along with the political ecology of international borders.

Isabella I. Mbai is Senior Lecturer and Founding (immediate outgoing) Dean of the School of Nursing at the Moi University, Kenya. She is a Kenya registered nurse, midwife and community health nurse. She holds a Diploma in Advanced Nursing and an MSc in Health Education/Promotion. Mbai has more than thirty years of nursing experience in education, administration and community-based service. She also has vast experience in networking, partnerships and collaborations. Her scholarly publications address community-orientated issues of the less fortunate in society.

Joseph Mensah is Professor and former Chair of Geography at York University, Canada. His research focuses on transnational migration, race and employment, and African development. Mensah received several competitive grants from the Social Sciences and Humanities Research Council of Canada (SSHRC), the Gates Foundation, and the Commonwealth Secretariat in London, UK. His publications include *Black Canadians: History, Experience, and Social Conditions* (2010) and *Boomerang Ethics: How Racism Affects Us All* (2017).

Lorrie Miller is Associate Director of The Institute for Veterans Transition and Education at The University of British Columbia (UBC), Canada, and teaches textile design and pedagogical approaches and art education for the Department of Curriculum and Pedagogy, in the Faculty of Education. She holds a PhD and an MA from UBC and a BEd from the University of Regina, Canada. She has worked in teacher education for much of this past decade. Lorrie was a Coordinator and Student Advisor at the Borderless Higher Education for Refugees (BHER) project in Dadaab, where she advised students who took UBC courses while they studied in Dadaab towards completion of their Diploma in Secondary Teacher Education.

Philemon Misoy is the Borderless Higher Education for Refugees (BHER) Project Liaison Officer based in Dadaab, Kenya. He holds a Bachelor of Education degree from Moi University, Kenya, and has served Dadaab refugee education programs in various capacities for more than ten years in secondary education, teacher training and tertiary education. His research interests include the monitoring, evaluation, accountability and learning in humanitarian projects.

Esther Munene is the Borderless Higher Education for Refugees (BHER) Academic Programs Officer, based in Dadaab, Kenya. She has worked for Windle International Kenya, served on the Dadaab refugee Secondary Education Program and worked as a teacher and a secondary school Deputy Principal in Ifo refugee camp in Dadaab, Kenya.

Samson Nashon is Professor and Department Head of the Department of Curriculum and Pedagogy at the University of British Columbia (UBC), Canada. His research includes the nature of science curriculums and instruction, the science learner and the deep meta-level mechanisms of science learning. He is one of UBC's lead participants and collaborators in the Borderless Higher Education for Refugees (BHER) project that brought together Kenyan and Canadian Universities to develop and implement a university-based Diploma in Teacher Education for refugee and host community student teachers in Dadaab, Kenya. He has a BEd from the University of Nairobi, Kenya, an MEd from the University of Leeds, UK, and an EdD in Education from the University of Toronto, Canada.

Marangu Njogu is the Chief Executive Officer of Windle International based in Oxford, UK, providing strategic leadership and bringing together the international and regional strategies for Windle. He has three honorary doctorate degrees from Guelph University, Canada, the University of British Columbia, Canada, and York

University, Canada. He is an internationally recognized leader in the development of refugee education and played a key role in the establishment of the Borderless Higher Education for Refugees (BHER) project in Dadaab, Kenya.

Grace Nshimiyumukiza is a Master of Education candidate at York University, Canada, through the Borderless Higher Education for Refugees (BHER) program. She is currently working as a Social and Emotional Learning Coordinator SEL, as well as facilitating the SEL Specialization course to the primary school athlete coaches in Kakuma, Kenya. Her thesis will focus on the role of multimodal tools and digital storytelling pedagogy in the Kakuma refugee camps.

Mark Okello Oyat is a graduate student at York University, Canada. He represents the Dadaab students in York University Graduate Students Council. In 2019, he participated in conferences concerning the World Refugee Day in Berlin, Germany, and Copenhagen, Denmark, where he represented Dadaab, Kenya. He won an undergraduate Writing Award and the Lillian Lermen Book Prize from the Faculty of Liberal Arts and Professional Studies at York University, Canada in 2017.

Kamal Paudel is a Geographic Information Systems (GIS) certified professional, currently working on his PhD within the faculty of Environmental Studies at York University, Canada. He also teaches GIS courses at the University of Toronto at Scarborough, Canada. He has degrees in Geography and Earth Sciences and Spatial Analysis from the USA, Nepal and Ryerson University, Canada. Kamal worked for fifteen years in the environmental sector and as a geography teacher and has recently co-led mapathons through the Humanitarian OpenStreetMap Team (HOT) in Toronto, Canada, after a serious earthquake in Nepal in 2015. He was a teaching assistant for the Borderless Higher Education for Refugees (BHER) course called Geoinformatics Introductions.

F. Beryl Pilkington is Associate Professor in the School of Nursing at York University, Canada. She has worked in maternal-child and women's health as a Registered Nurse before obtaining a PhD in nursing in 1997. Since 2014, she has been Coordinator for an interdisciplinary BA/BSc Global Health programme. Her research has explored a range of health-related experiences with women, seniors and marginalized groups. She is passionate about increasing access to higher education, especially in low- and middle-income countries.

Valerie Preston is Professor in the Faculty of Environmental and Urban Change at York University, Canada. An urban social geographer, her research and teaching focus on international migration, especially the varied economic and educational trajectories of the children of migrants, and inequalities in local labor and housing markets. Currently, she leads a partnership of academic researchers, community practitioners and government policymakers that is investigating a social resilience approach to inclusion of newcomers in contemporary cities. In addition to publishing numerous articles, she is co-author of *Everyday Equalities: Making Multicultures in Settler Colonial Societies* (2019).

Tarmo K. Remmel is Associate Professor in the Faculty of Environmental and Urban Change at York University, Canada, and is a GIScientist who uses and develops methods for remote sensing, GIS and spatial pattern analyses to quantify and compare dynamic landscape processes (primarily fire and harvesting disturbances). He holds a PhD from the University of Toronto, Canada, an MScF from Lakehead University, Canada, and a BES from the University of Waterloo, Canada.

Johanna Reynolds is completing her PhD in the Department of Geography, at York University, Canada. Her research focuses on discursive and spatial strategies of exclusion within Canadian refugee and border policies and practices. Her work is informed by feminist and political geography, critical refugee studies and critical border studies scholarship. Since 2018, Johanna is also a research coordinator for a SSHRC-funded project on refugee resettlement at York University's Centre for Refugee Studies. In 2013–2014, Johanna was a member of the BHER Student Group, created to offer a peer network for students who are part of the BHER program with the aim of providing peer-to-peer mentoring and support. Johanna is actively involved in refugee advocacy in all areas of resettlement, including access to education, and language acquisition.

Hawa Sabriye is a Project Development and Reporting Officer for the International Organization for Migration Somalia Mission in Mogadishu. She spent three years working with the Borderless Higher Education for Refugees (BHER) project as a York University Graduate Assistant and travelled to Dadaab, Kenya as a Teaching Assistant for the project. She has a Master Education from York University, Canada, and her graduate research documented the recruitment and retention of Somali female students accessing higher education in Dadaab, Kenya.

Espen Stranger-Johannessen is Associate Professor at Inland Norway University of Applied Sciences, Norway. He taught English and Communication Skills for secondary school teachers at the Borderless Higher Education for Refugees (BHER) project in Dadaab. His PhD in Literacy Education from the University of British Columbia, Canada, focused on teacher identity and the African

Storybook an online repository for traditional and contemporary African stories that allows users to read, write and translate children's stories.

Kurt Thumlert is Assistant Professor in the Faculty of Education at York University, Canada, and is an executive member in York's Institute for Research on Digital Learning (IRDL), Canada.

Fouzia Warsame is the Deputy Chief of Party – Policy, Curriculum and Government Liaison at Creative Associates International, Somalia, after seven years as Somalia National University's Dean of the Faculty of Education and Social Sciences, Somalia. Both her academic and professional work focus on the nexus between education, community and global connections, and how such connections can play a critical role towards systemic change, social justice and sustainable nation building in post-conflict Somalia. She holds a Master's of Education in International & Global Education from the University of Alberta, Canada.

Megan Youdelis is a Postdoctoral Research Fellow at the University of Guelph, Canada, and a Lecturer at the University of Toronto, Canada. Her research examines the political ecology of conservation and development, including nature-based tourism, coloniality and alternative political economies of conservation, with fieldwork experience in both Canada and Thailand. She is currently working with the Indigenous Circle of Experts (ICE) in Canada on a multi-year SSHRC-funded project to decolonize Canadian conservation and facilitate the implementation of Indigenous Protected and Conserved Areas.

Acknowledgements

We are very grateful to the BHER Guest Advisory Board: Don Dippo (York University), Josephine Gitome (Kenyatta University), Isabella Mbai (Moi University) and Samson Nashon (the University of British Columbia). We thank the funders of the BHER project: The Social Sciences and Humanities Research Council of Canada, the MasterCard Foundation, Global Affairs Canada, Open Society Foundation. And we are indebted to the generous financial and in-kind support for the BHER project from the following universities and organizations: Kenyatta University, Moi University, the University of British Columbia, Windle Trust International, the World University Service of Canada and York University. We would also like to thank those many individuals who worked for the BHER project at various moments and also generously offered advice and critique on aspects of this book: Aida Orgocka, Ron Srigley, Michele Millard and Don Dippo. There are numerous others, from Dadaab, Canada and elsewhere, who have worked for the project, some who contributed to the chapters herein, others who worked or volunteered their time over the years. The project and this book owe a large debt of gratitude to the Centre for Refugee Studies (CRS) at York University and particularly the several CRS Directors over the years who have hosted the BHER project to the present time: Susan McGrath, Jennifer Hyndman and Sean Rehaag. The former Dean of Education, Lyndon Martin, and the Faculty of Education generously co-hosted the project with CRS from 2018 onwards. The project and the book have benefitted from the wisdom and support of so many in Canada, Kenya and internationally.

Introduction

Wenona Giles, Lorrie Miller, Philemon Misoy, Norah Kariba and Okello Mark Oyat

The refugee camp as a university campus – that was the dream. This book tells the story of university partners in Canada and Kenya who collaborated in the development and delivery of tuition-free academic programs for refugees living in two of the largest refugee camps in the world, Dadaab and Kakuma (see Figure i.1). Was the endeavour successful? Was it worthwhile? And if so, for whom?

In this introduction and the chapters that follow, we analyse the inter-university partnership and the program development necessary to bring the Borderless Higher Education for Refugees (BHER) project into existence. A social justice approach that deems university education as a right for all undergirds this project, led by York University (YU), Toronto, in partnership with Kenyatta University (KU), Moi University (MU), The University of British Columbia (UBC) and Windle International Kenya (WIK).

Higher education (HE) is increasingly recognized as crucial for improving the livelihoods of marginalized populations, including refugees and displaced populations caught in emergencies and protracted crises, to enable them to engage in contemporary, knowledge-based global society. However, among refugee youths, only 1 per cent access scholarships for HE,[1] usually outside the country that hosts them (UNHCR, 2001–19a). Refugees in camps confront significant intersectional forms of discrimination that limit their access to HE, including economic deprivation, remote geographic location, racism, gender bias, ethnic and religious marginalisation and the remnants of colonial rule (Bhabha, Giles and Mahomed, 2020, p. 5). Many youths and adults caught in such situations would potentially access HE in countries where they live if programs were available to them. Such a 'systematic lack of access to HE and its benefits for some populations has a serious impact on life prospects and social justice' (Bhabha, Giles and Mahomed, 2020, p. 1).

Figure i.1 Aerial view of the Dadaab camps, 2016, courtesy Peter Murphy.

Recognizing the importance of HE, and the lack of access to it among refugees in long-term situations, the BHER project was designed to bring education to refugees *in situ* (blended on-line and on-site courses).[2] In 2010, primary education featured high in humanitarian appeals and limited or no attention was going to HE in the policy context. There was little research that examined the impact of a lack of access to HE for refugees or other marginalized populations of or from the Global South,[3] and until now, there is no research that takes a critical approach to existing HE development projects operating in humanitarian contexts (UNDP, 2019). We aim to do exactly that in this book, by focusing a lens on one of the first projects to bring HE to refugees in camps.

We direct this volume to at least two audiences. The first of these is women and men living in protracted or long-term refugee camp situations[4] who want to access accredited university programs. The limited number of HE scholarships that existed in 2010 mostly required refugees to leave behind their families and peer networks. Those scholarships result in such communities losing those with the best academic potential. Instead, the host country, where students study, benefits from their presence. In contrast, BHER, as one of the first initiatives worldwide to bring together a partnership of universities to offer accredited HE programs in refugee camps, offered a non-scholarship model that prepared students' capacities *in situ* and is conducive to students staying in the region or returning to their country of origin, where their upgraded knowledge, skills and university credentials are needed in countries' efforts towards peace and development.

Second, universities, particularly those that choose to offer HE in Global North-South partnerships will be interested in this volume. Drawing on the contributions of practitioners and scholars with a broad range of disciplinary and geographical expertise, our contributing authors explore the limitations, benefits and possibilities of offering HE through Global North-South partnerships that we recognize are characterized by various types of inequities. Over the lifetime of the project, we have held to social justice ideals, but nonetheless, it is likely that most of us would now concur with the statement that 'in the context of a Global North-South project, any partnership may be fraught with inequity, and the impact of these challenges is, perhaps inevitably, experienced most acutely by the Southern partners' (Kimari and Giles, 2020, p. 416). This book has much to say about the contextual inequities that we met in Dadaab, Kakuma and in the BHER partnership, and how we worked hard to learn from and overcome them.

Our Approach in This Book

Those who have contributed chapters to this book are mindful of the powerful and crucial critiques of postcolonial scholars concerning the tragedy of colonial and imperial forms of education (see Gregory, 2004; Hall, 1996; Jayawardena, 1986; Said, 1993; Spivak, 1988). And many of the same authors have experienced first-hand the ambivalent relationship of education to postcolonialism that Rizvi, Lingard and Lavia describe as follows: 'On the one hand, it [education] is an object of postcolonial critique regarding its complicity with Eurocentric discourses and practices. On the other hand, it is only through education that it is possible to reveal and resist colonialism's continuing hold on our imagination' (2006, p. 257; see also Giles and Dippo, 2019). We explore the argument by some scholars that North-South collaborations are not possible and will never produce good results in the Global South. Such an approach is aligned with ideas that schooling from the North is always 'bad' for the South and that 'Western' education inevitably exterminates traditional knowledge and culture (Black 2010).

Literature on partnerships (e.g. Baud 2002; Chernikova 2011; Hynie et al. 2014; Jazeel and McFarlane 2007; Ogden and Porter 2000; Clark-Kazak, 2019; Landau, 2019) refers to the challenges of developing ethical partnerships or networks between Global North and South participants. Chernikova's view that 'a successful partnership can support and meet different goals for the partners, but that success is contingent on the partnership valuing this diversity of goals' (2011 in Hynie et al., 2014, p. 6) is a key issue for this book. The dangers of unequal partnerships are taken up in this book by Gitome and Dippo, who raise concerns about 'the unidirectional transfer of capacity from the North to the South at the expense of mutual learning and responsiveness from both sides' (p. 51).

In this volume, chapter authors provide evidence that Global North-South partnerships can work well and do produce good results for both the South and North when the participating institutions are prepared to struggle through challenges rising from availability of resources and limitations of performance driven results, cultural and pedagogical differences at the institutional levels, and technological deficits in course delivery, among other issues. Contributors to this book also demonstrate that universities can be humanitarian and development actors; as evidence of this, we include chapters by 'emerging' refugee scholars who have begun to participate in and contribute to new knowledge about forced migration, as they achieve their undergraduate and graduate degrees. We write from a firm conviction that access to higher education, including to the resources provided by institutions of academic excellence, is a key tool for inequality reduction and social justice advancement. HE can provide refugees with the possibility of staying put or returning home with dignity.

Intersections of gender, race and culture have been shown to marginalize women from traditional and/or rural communities, where patriarchy prevails, for example in South Africa (Mabokela and Mawila, 2004). On the African continent generally, patriarchal norms and the political subjugation of women have also been said to militate against reforms in the higher education arena (Mama, 2003) and the provision of educational opportunities for marginalized or refugee women has destabilized negotiated gender and social relations of communities (Pittaway and Bartolomei, 2001; Grabska, 2011). While our authors engage in various critiques of gender relations, the chapter by Bishop et al. stands out in its perceptive analysis of how humanitarianism and the structure of refugee camps is systemically gendered against girls' and women's education and advancement.

Based on the idea that the neighbourhood in the world has changed, we take the approach that the responsibility of the university has thus also changed.[5] We build on the work of Hannah Arendt to argue for the development of worldly universities, rather than the constant striving among universities today to become 'world class'. And we stretch an interpretation of her ideas of worldliness that we consider to be a promotion of 'the development of individuals so that they too can join in the making of that world' (Giles and Dippo, 2019, p. 92). In the firm belief that ideas matter and are of consequence, the worldly university understands the problems, issues and affairs of the world as its own and accepts responsibility to think deeply about them and act.[6] In this book, we explore the role of the contemporary university as a development actor and a catalyst for change in development discourse. How can power dynamics be reshaped through higher education, especially as these pertain to gender and ethnic relationships and racialization? Is there a space for universities to be part of a changing humanitarian landscape, discourse and action in which a humanitarian-peace-development nexus informed by the Agenda for Humanity (UNOCHA, 2016)[7] is taking precedence over traditional charity-driven humanitarianism? By helping produce the human capital necessary to address fragility and conflict, can universities bridge the gap resulting from the siloed actions of humanitarians and development actors, the first concerned with life-saving interventions and the second with systems change?

The authors of this introductory chapter include a cross-section of members of the BHER project, including faculty, staff and a graduate student. Wenona Giles, an anthropologist, long-time anthropology faculty member and Resident Scholar of the Centre for Refugee Studies at YU co-led the BHER project with Don Dippo until 2019, when she retired from the university. Lorrie Miller, a lecturer and program coordinator in teacher education served as the UBC project coordinator during that university's engagement in the Teacher Education Diploma Secondary with the BHER project. Philemon Misoy, an educational administrator with experience in the management of refugee education was the Project Liaison Officer of the BHER project in Dadaab. He was in charge of all operations, staff supervision and support to students and instructors at the BHER Learning Centre in Dadaab. Norah Kariba, as the Program Manager for WIK in the Dadaab refugee camps, oversaw the implementation of education programs in the camps. Mark Okello Oyat studied at YU in the BHER program, from Dadaab in Kenya. He is among the first cohort of students to graduate with an M.Ed. in 2020.

The BHER Project and University Programs

The groundwork for our understanding of the need for, and feasibility of, a project like BHER and for the development of various degree programs began with research. In 2005, fieldwork and analysis in Dadaab on long-term displacement for refugees revealed a dearth of attention to higher education in extended exile (see Hyndman and Giles, 2017). Between 2009 and 2011, a request from WIK and the World University Service of Canada to develop and deliver university programs in Dadaab was followed up by visits of faculty to Dadaab. Pursuant to two visits in 2009 by UBC faculty (accompanied by MU faculty on the second visit), project feasibility reports were prepared for approval by the universities involved. Exploratory research in Dadaab by KU in 2010 reported on the possibility of building a university program there (Tumuti and Gitome, 2010). YU visits, a feasibility study and a video in 2011–13 revealed the possibilities as well as challenges related to the development and implementation of the BHER project (see Dippo, Orgocka and Giles, 2013; Murphy, 2012) and the various degree programs.

Figure i.2 is a visual depiction of the BHER Commons, which describes in detail the developmental steps of the project and makes available many of the tools and research gathered (see: http://bher.eecs.yorku.ca/[8]

Following the preliminary visits to sites in Dadaab, university representatives across all partners collaborated to design education, geography and public health degrees, diplomas and certificate programs that met the various academic and professional requirements at all the universities, and were acceptable for teacher certification in Kenya at both the primary and secondary levels. A primary teacher education program began with a one-year Certificate offered by York that laddered into a one-year Diploma offered by KU. A two-year Diploma for secondary teacher education was jointly offered by UBC and MU and the students were admitted and graduated with the diploma from MU. It was a Diploma, in each case, that was recognized for teacher certification. At both the primary and secondary levels of teacher education, it was critical that the students received their diplomas from Kenyan universities in order to meet the credentialing requirements from the regional authority of teacher education.

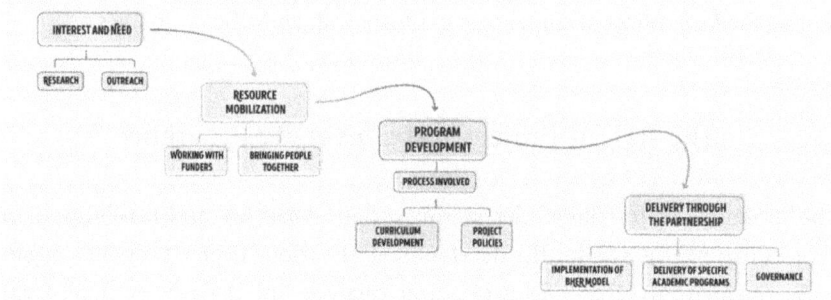

Figure i.2 BHER Commons Developmental Steps, courtesy of Wenona Giles.

Following receipt of two-year diplomas, students could progress into degree programs including a B.A. Geography (YU), a B.Ed. Science (KU), a B.Ed. Arts (KU) and a BSc in Community Health Education (MU).

Administrative staff in Dadaab were integral to the ongoing success of the BHER partnership and our ability to deal with the intricacies of programmatic and structural challenges. The Project Liaison Officer, Philemon Misoy, who is also a co-author of this chapter, managed operations at the Learning Centre and ensured staff supervision, as well as support to BHER instructors and students. An Academic Program Officer ensured that students were registered, received useful and correct advice on their programs, their academic records were maintained and mentorship programs ran well. An Information and Communication Technology (ICT) Officer played a key role in the set up and control of online course delivery sessions, providing constant technical assistance to students, ensuring that their tablets were uploaded with necessary course materials and that they were able to access online classes without challenges.

As of 2019, the BHER project began to contract in scope in response to the diminishing availability of funds[9] and by 2020 mainly focused in three areas: the completion of courses for students who were not able to conclude their undergraduate degree with their original cohort; an undergraduate teacher education cohort who were studying to be primary school teachers; and two cohorts of M.Ed. graduate students, formerly undergraduates in the BHER related undergraduate programs, who were completing on-line degrees offered by the Faculty of Education at York University. By 2019, the Lutheran World Federation had become a BHER partner that supported the training of primary school teachers for a possible third BHER cohort of students.

As we write this Introduction, in the spring of 2020, cases of COVID-19 are spreading in Kenya. The President has announced a total lockdown in Dadaab and Kakuma camps, whereby no movement of people is allowed into or out of the camps. He has also suspended learning in education institutions in the country and this has led to the closure of all education institutions in Dadaab, Kakuma and their camps. The BHER project field operations were modified in line with these government directives on social distancing and closure of learning institutions. Students who could no longer visit the Learning Centre were given the necessary resources to complete their online studies at home and BHER staff started to work from home. While most of the courses were already on-line, all courses in the project were subsequently offered online. Instructors, staff and students in the BHER project, long accustomed to daily challenges and crises of various kinds, have done their best to adjust.

The Dadaab and Kakuma Camp Context

Cognizant of the neo-colonial dangers of 'delivering' education, we understand context to be historically and culturally specific and, therefore, leading to different views on access to and content of education. However, we also maintain that comparative perspectives on context, pedagogy and methodology are indispensable to the 'education of university educators'. Hence, while camp situations may differ greatly, we believe that the experiences of the BHER project in Dadaab and Kakuma hold valuable lessons for university educators in other sites. A brief description of the contexts of the camps and the raison d'être of the BHER partnership follow and is deepened throughout the book, but especially in the first section of the book: 'Putting a project into action'.

The residents of Dadaab and Kakuma (see Figure i.3) have been arriving in the camps in these two locations since the early 1990s, decades of residence that contribute to the label long-term or protracted refugee situations. Those who live in the camps are supported by the UNHCR and nongovernmental agencies that implement UN programs; the much smaller numbers of Kenyans who live outside the camps, in the hinterland towns of Dadaab and Kakuma, receive marginal government support and are generally as impoverished as camp residents, or more so. Dadaab serves as a commercial hub connecting southern Somalia with north-eastern Kenya and Nairobi, and Kakuma is a link between South Sudan and Nairobi. In the early years of the camps, citizens from Somalia,

Figure i.3 Map of Northern Kenya, including the location of Dadaab and Kakuma in relation to Somalia and Sudan, Map Data, 2020.

Ethiopia, Sudan, Uganda and Eritrea fled clan based and civil wars as well as environmental crises in their home countries and arrived in the Kakuma and Dadaab UNHCR camps.

Dadaab currently comprises a small town and three camps, Dagahaley, Ifo and Hagadera, and is located about 100 km from the Somalia border. The population of these camps in north-eastern Kenya (see Figure i.4) in March 2020 was 217,511 people (UNHCR, 2020, p. 1). Of these, 96 per cent are Somali nationals (ibid.) and the majority of the Kenyan population in this region is ethnic Somali. The BHER Learning Centre where students come for lessons and tutorial sessions is located in the town of Dadaab (see Figure i.4). As stated elsewhere (Hyndman and Giles, 2017, p. 50), the Dadaab camps have been 'variously described as sites deeply rooted in violence and insecurity (Crisp 2000); as "non-communities of the excluded" (Hyndman 2000); as home to refugees whose livelihoods are transnational, rooted in but connected across many countries of asylum and settlement (Horst 2008); and as a transitional humanitarian space (Agier 2011 p. 199)'.

The number of the Dadaab camps' residents has waxed and waned over the two decades of the camps' existence; however, the population grew radically in 2011 to more than half a million people who were escaping increased violence and environmental degradation in Somalia (Hyndman and Giles, 2017). At the same time, a wave of insecurity impacted the camps at a scale previously unknown. Abductions of humanitarian aid workers, murder of security personnel and targeted killings of community leaders who were considered to have had close links to security personnel became common. Those residents who had fled conflict, invasion and famine found themselves embroiled in security crackdowns, curfews and the scaling back of operations by UNHCR and other partners.

While most of the research for this book and reflections on various aspects of the project are focused on Dadaab, some authors include reference to the Kakuma camps in north-western Kenya in their chapters (see especially Gitome and Dippo, Duale et al., Youdelis et al., Sabriye et al.), and the chapter by Bishop et al. is based almost entirely on research in Kakuma. The BHER project had not originally planned to operate in the Kakuma refugee camps, but the interrelated issues of insecurity and the emptying of the Dadaab camps over the past few years meant that non-Somali refugees from Dadaab were relocated to Kakuma and specifically to the Kalobeyei Settlement. Some of these camp residents were BHER students, and thus the project was prompted to begin operations in Kakuma. The BHER project maintains a limited presence in the Kakuma refugee

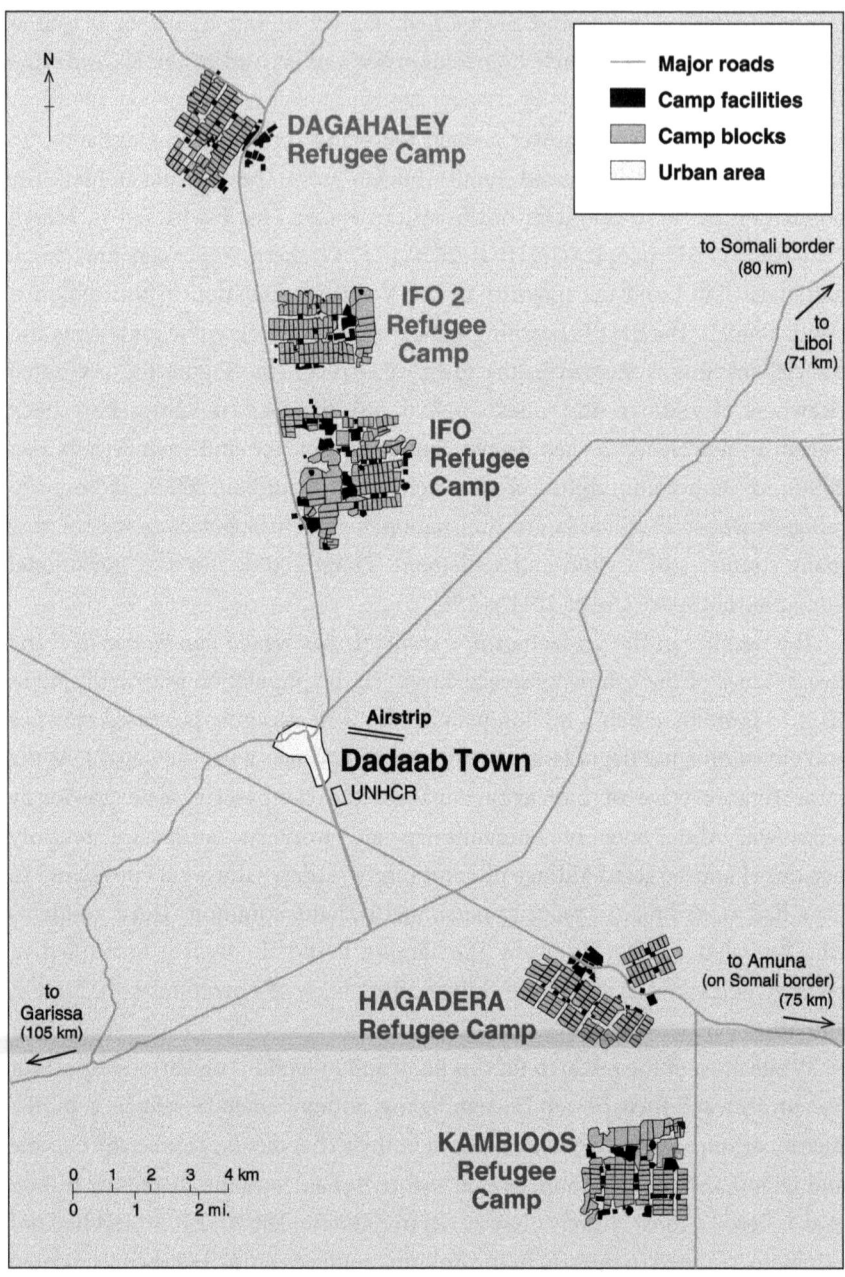

Figure i.4 Map of the Dadaab camps, 2016, courtesy of Joseph Mensah.

camps to facilitate the completion of university programs by BHER students. While Kakuma has not experienced the same kind of violence as the Dadaab camps, poverty in the camps and town, as well as the marginalization of the Turkana community, has created serious tensions between camp residents and the host community (Bishop, 2019).

The Book: Self-Reflection and Response

This book is an account of our successes and failures in overcoming the dangers inherent to neo-colonial forms of education. Chapters in this book document how a recognition of our position in relation to historical legacies of colonialism led us to develop a counter approach that 'emphasizes a learner-centred, curiosity-driven curriculum that includes local, traditional, and scientific/ academic knowledge, [and] a participatory, inquiry-based engaged pedagogy' (Giles and Dippo, 2019, p. 93). The two-way learning that instructors and staff experienced is also featured in a number of chapters. Professors realized early on that they had as much to learn from students as students did from them. The parallel learning that took and continues to take place on site in Dadaab reflects a commitment to social justice and takes a Freirean approach to teaching and learning where learning is deeply contextual and reciprocal (Freire, 1993).

Our book also responds to a need expressed by Sullivan-Owomoyela and Brannelly (2009) in their UNESCO document that 'accumulated institutional memories and knowledge in governments, agencies, and NGOs on education in emergencies are in danger of being lost due to both the dispersion and disappearance of documents, and to high staff turnover ... Most of the expertise is still in the heads of practitioners and needs to be collected, since memories fade fast' (p. 9). Authors in this book go beyond the call for documentation, to examine how and why aspects of the BHER projects succeeded or failed.

Today, there are several cohorts of students who have graduated with degrees, diplomas and certificates from one of the BHER partner universities and who are using their knowledge in various walks of life in Somalia, Kenya and elsewhere. Three hundred and forty-two students have graduated from the various programs (75 women and 267 men). Some have started new primary and secondary schools and many others are using their recently acquired skills as teachers. Others have found employment in NGOs and donor organizations or have started their own businesses. A number of graduates have taken up positions in the public health sector. And as mentioned above, some have gone on to graduate level studies in education.

As indicated in the previous paragraph, less than 30 per cent of the students graduating from the BHER related programs were women. The work accomplished in the BHER project indicates clearly that gendered forms of discrimination hindered women's access to higher education in the Dadaab and Kakuma refugee camps in Kenya. Those of us who taught in and led the BHER project were not as successful as we had hoped regarding the enrolment of women in the HE programs. Male and female children in refugee camps can usually access some form of education at the primary level. However, gendered inequities systemically embedded in the structure of refugee camps leads to girls' lack of access to secondary school education. Blame is normally defined (even by some of the authors in this book) as due to prevailing social-cultural relations, lack of childcare and travelling distance to schools. But understanding why young women are ill-equipped to pursue higher education requires a deeper and bolder analysis. Although there was an increase in youths attending secondary schools in the Dadaab camps from 4 per cent in 2011 to 10 per cent in 2017 (UNHCR, 2011; Giles and Orgocka, 2018), fewer young women than men from these camps accessed higher education in 2019. That same year only forty-nine (20 per cent) out of 234 students enrolled in HE in BHER project partner universities were women (WIK Scholarship program office, 2019). This gender disparity, as well as the impact of successful access to HE in women's lives, is examined in detail by Bishop et al., and in many of the chapters in Section Two of the book (see especially Kim et al.).

The 'MOOC'[10] *fantasy*, a pedagogical approach to teaching and learning, contends that making on-line courses available to refugees and other marginalized people leads to HE (higher education) accessibility. To the contrary, our hard-earned pedagogical success was principally due to the creation of a 'community of scholars' (Goodman, 1962), or cohorts of students who learned from and supported each other in ways that the institution of 'the university' cannot (see Sabriye et al. in this book). Throughout this volume, examples across programs and over the years of development and delivery of the BHER project illustrate the fundamental importance of on-the-ground learning that we find in place-conscious approaches, and with the development of solid and ongoing relationships. It is the adherence to an education that is rooted in a place and time, and which responds to the needs of the learners and their communities, that sets BHER apart from scholarship programs that take students away from their regions of origin. As academic institutions, we collectively 'delivered' programming in which we each held expertise. We also offered programming that responded to student needs – perceived and expressed – that were apparent at that time. Part of the overall project design encouraged the development of collegial communities amongst the students to support one another going forward and to increase the likelihood of the sustainability of quality higher education.

The way that this book has evolved is unique. Not only have all the contributors been involved in some way in the research, administration, teaching and learning that has led to the design, development and implementation of the BHER project over the past decade, but the authors gathered at York University in Toronto for an immersive workshop in May 2019, to reflect upon, discuss and develop the contents of the book. Synergies were identified amongst the group and individuals identified a number of writing partnerships across universities and among faculty, students and staff. As much as possible our contributors co-author in partnerships across the Global North-South divide. Junior and senior scholars and practitioners work together to address issues of concern. We believe that their contributions break new ground both theoretically and empirically. All of the authors have been involved in the implementation of the BHER project in Kenya, and thus, most have known each other for some years.

The book is divided into two sections, the first introduces the project and its context and the various types of resources, material, financial, relational and administrative that were necessary for the development and implementation of the BHER project. Setting the stage for readers, Duale, Munene and Njogu open this volume by presenting a concise history of the north-eastern region of Kenya and the relationships between the host and refugee communities in that area. Here, they tell how BHER is situated by assessing the social, political and historical complexities of the Dadaab camps. The chapter by Bishop, Duri and Nshimiyumukiza drills down into the critical area of gender disparity, in particular concerning access to university. Based on compelling primary data collected in the Kakuma refugee camps in north-western Kenya, the authors examine why, despite supportive programs (both governmental and NGO) to promote inclusiveness and gender equality in higher education, women refugees confront serious obstacles to accessing higher education. In chapter three, Gitome and Dippo, both professors involved in teaching and leadership of the BHER project from its inception, discuss some of the complexities of creating and sustaining a multi-university relationship. They lay bare some of the conflicts generated, while trying to honour reciprocity and the fundamental autonomy of the partner institutions. They provide valuable insight regarding how difficult but how valuable it may be for international collaborators to understand the impacts that the internal practices of each institution have upon each other's day-to-day operations in a joint project. From a more micro perspective, Pilkington and Mbai, bring readers to an examination of specific academic issues around the creation of an undergraduate degree in public health. The authors, from YU and MU, share their experiences of working together to create a Community Health Education undergraduate degree. Grounded in their own rich academic and experiential history, they also explore how a community health education program can be used to help mitigate the scarcity of human health resources in camps.

The second section of this volume takes readers inside the daily experiences of university students and teachers in programs associated with the BHER project. Authors explore innovative relationships and pedagogy within the course or classroom between and among instructors and students. Ethnicity, class and gender as well as various technologies impact the learning experiences of students and their professors and teaching assistants. This section opens with a chapter by Abikar, Aden, Thumlert, Dahya and Jenson who examine the use of digital tools and pedagogical impacts on a specific course. Digital innovations have been crucial features of higher education for the Dadaab students and have been used to help local actors foster the development of new ways of participating in academic, cultural and communicative practices. Authors Sabriye, Douhaibi, Dagane and Leomoi, who are both teaching assistants and students, discuss how an enhanced technology learning experience, through online courses alone, proved challenging. The periodic availability of course directors and teaching assistants in the Learning Centre in face-to-face interactions enabled students to share issues directly and overcome their isolation. Considerations of boundaries, borders and geography are raised by YU professors and teaching assistants Youdelis, Douhaibi, Holterman, Paudel, Preston, Remmel, Lunstrum and Mensah, who share their experiences in teaching geography to refugee students in Dadaab. They describe and analyse the very real challenges, but also successes of their courses, including teaching ill prepared learners in what was a difficult and unfamiliar learning environment for the geography instructors. Flexibility is described as crucial in the creation of a suitable pedagogy for these refugee students. In their chapter, Miller, Lea, Irwin, Nashon, Jordan, Baker and Stranger-Johannessen look to the experiences of the teachers, instructors and administrators from UBC. In this chapter, program instructors share their insights on teaching within this context and describe the impact of their Dadaab experience on their own pedagogical approaches in other learning sites. One of the co-authors, Lea, notes upon reflection of his experience in Dadaab, 'the learners called me to be with them, to learn with them, not to [just] teach them' (p.148). A final and compelling chapter by authors Alsop and Cohen tells us how they engaged their students in a unique course that considered the current Anthropocene epoch. They describe how learners connected activities in their locality with current global phenomena of climate change and global warming. The course led refugee students to rethink their flights from their countries of origin into exile, as well as their current impact on the Dadaab environment.

In a brief Afterword, we ask Fouzia Warsame, the former Dean of Education at the Somalia National University, to think forward to implications for other similar higher education projects, in parts of the world beyond Canada and Kenya. Dean Warsame offers insights about the hopes and impacts of academic opportunities for refugee and returning Somali students and on the importance of education for the rebuilding of a country torn apart by civil war.

This volume brings together many authors who have personal experience with the BHER project over a number of years, each of whom has their own grounding in post-secondary education in fragile contexts. The work described and analysed in the following chapters has one eye to the past and one to the future. We hope that our readers will be able to benefit from this collective effort in their own contexts.

Part One

Putting a Project into Action

1

Historical and Political Contestations in the Dadaab Refugee Camps and North-Eastern Kenya

Mohamed Duale, Esther Munene and Marangu Njogu

The contextual complexities and underlying humanitarian needs that gave rise to the Borderless Higher Education for Refugees (BHER) project are explored in this opening chapter. We present a history of the region and explore the nature of the relationship between host and refugee communities who live in or near Dadaab, a protracted refugee situation in north-eastern Kenya. We document what we have learned about the local context through our teaching, administrative work and research, and why we think the Dadaab camps are more than spaces of containment. It is our view that it matters how we think about refugee camps, and that this is particularly important for those who are interested in doing long-term educational work. If refugee camps are only places to warehouse refugees or sites of temporary containment for displaced people, then all of our work and efforts towards providing refugees with access to higher education cannot be considered a priority.

In order to understand what it is that can be done *with*, as well as *for* refugees and local host communities dwelling in and near the Dadaab camps, we begin by first setting out to understand the relationship between locals and refugees within the larger social, political and historical dynamics of these camps in Kenya's north-east. Over time, the proximity of refugees and locals, who are both largely ethnic Somalis, has enabled the establishment of amicable, though sometimes tense, host-refugee relations. In addition, we explore how the camps, as border spaces, are contested terrain in larger struggles over belonging, economic resources and the regional role of the Kenyan state. In the second part of this chapter, we describe how the camps attract refugees for their relative safety, prospects for resettlement and the availability of social supports such as education, which are often unobtainable in their war-torn countries. However, there are two sides to this story, as the camps are both enabling and disempowering.

They are ever changing social and political spaces that simultaneously offer refugees and locals new and hopeful beginnings, as well as precarious lives.

We would be remiss if we did not talk about our positionality within this discussion of the relationship between host and refugee communities in Kenya. This chapter was co-authored by two Kenyans, Esther Munene and Marangu Njogu, and a Somali Canadian, Mohamed Duale. We have many years of experience working or teaching in the camps and occupy different subject positions. Njogu came to work in the camps in the early 1990s as a humanitarian relief worker with CARE Kenya before joining Windle International Kenya (WIK) as its Kenya director. He is considered to have played an instrumental role in the establishment of the education system in Kenya's refugee camps. Munene came to teach in the Dadaab camps over seven years ago and has remained as field staff with WIK and the BHER project. She works closely with students to promote their success. Before coming to Dadaab, she expected to find a fenced camp with manned entry and exit points. There was a sense of fear fuelled by the stories in the media, family and friends about the Dadaab refugee camps. However, she quickly came to realize that this was not the case, and that refugees could move within and out of the camps, provided they received clearance from the Kenyan authorities. Duale also had similar initial concerns about going to an insecure space, but like Munene, has grown to appreciate the unique ways people in Dadaab have survived the hardships of protracted displacement. He fled Somalia as a child in the early 1990s and lived as a refugee in Kenya with experiences not unlike some of those in Dadaab.

As a result, co-writing about the camps as Kenyan, Somali and Canadian was sometimes challenging given our diverse personal experiences, different philosophical perspectives, varying professional commitments and the fact that we live and work in different parts of the world. We focus here on what the camps mean, not only to the people with whom we spoke (we conducted focus groups with ten refugee and host community members in Dadaab), but also to us as researchers and practitioners, who are neither locals nor refugees. Together, we feel a heightened sense of ethical responsibility to produce a nuanced work that attends to the social and political complexity of the Dadaab camps.

Contested Terrains

Through an exploration of the interplay between social and political conditions in the camps, this section discusses how a discourse about the Dadaab refugee camps as a 'security risk' is about more than actual dangers. It is also about who owns and who is entitled to benefit from economic resources in politically uncertain times in Kenya. The Dadaab refugee camps are borderlands where refugees and citizens live in close contact and are indistinguishable in terms of livelihood needs and, sometimes, nationality.

As the site of the Shifta War[1] of the 1960s, the region was militarized before the arrival of refugees, and its inhabitants were seen as disloyal and a threat to national security. As a result, local communities in the north-east have long held grievances about being marginalized by the Kenyan state. The establishment of refugee camps in the Dadaab sub-county added to these grievances as locals in Dadaab believed that the international community was doubly marginalizing them. For a long time, the local community was not part of the mandate of the humanitarian organizations that provide aid to refugee communities. Locals felt that the refugees led better lives than they did, with access to hospitals, schools, potable water and social services, and this occasionally created tensions with the aid agencies and refugees. Over time, a certain degree of personal integration occurred through close interaction.

Nonetheless, the prospect of large-scale refugee integration is opposed by the local community for several reasons. On the environmental front, locals fear the supposed impact of refugees on ecologically sensitive grazing land (see chapter by Alsop and Cohen). In addition, they are concerned about Somali clan demographics, which threaten local political power and finite financial resources. Furthermore, these local anxieties intersect with wider national concerns over security, including the suspected infiltration of the Al-Shabab terrorist group into the refugee camps. Economically, Kenyan elites are apprehensive about the Somali business community, which they accuse of benefiting from piracy, illicit imports and undercutting 'Kenyan' traders.

Securitization of the North-East and Al-Shabab

Known as the Northern Frontier District (NFD) during Kenya's colonial era, the north-eastern region of Kenya is ethnically Somali and was partitioned from other Somali territories, now part of Somalia, Ethiopia and Djibouti, and co-governed with Kenya as part of British East Africa. It was classified as a closed district by the colonial government and locals were later required to carry a permit to travel in and out of the district. On the eve of independence, Somalis in the NFD voted to join Somalia in an informal referendum, which was later discarded by the British colonial administration (Hyndman 1997, p. 15). After Kenya became independent in 1963, the Shifta War resulted in a declaration of a state of emergency that began in December of that year and continued until 1991. During this era, there were many human rights violations by the central government of Kenya (ibid.). The Shifta War thus cemented the status of the north-east, formerly the NFD, as part of the political periphery of Kenya. The region continues to be synonymous with insecurity, especially in recent years as a result of Kenya's intervention and war against the Al-Shabab terrorist group originating in neighbouring Somalia. At the same time, Kenya's north-east hosts the Dadaab refugee camps, one of the world's largest and most storied sites of protracted displacement. The camps are considered a security risk by the government.

Somali Kenyans may be part of the state, but they are not necessarily considered part of the Kenyan nation. An ethno-political geography of 'up Kenya' (the north-east) and 'down Kenya' (the rest of the country) is reinforced by racialized categories, which distinguish Somalis, who are called *warya* (or 'boy' in Somali) from non-Somali Africans, who the Somalis call *nywele ngumu* (or people with 'hard hair'). These racialized terms have their origin in European colonial rule in Africa, which categorized and governed the native population according to perceived racialized differences (Mamdani 2012, p. 74, 109, 115, 117, 123). Non-Somali Africans in Kenya complain of discrimination in the north-east, just as Somalis protest racialized profiling by police in the rest of the country. These terms also highlight the ways in which the Somali north-east is considered a nominal rather than a substantive and cultural part of the Kenyan nation.

In addition, the protracted war between the Kenyan government and Al-Shabab in Somalia keeps a political spotlight on the region. In 2011, Kenya sent an army to purportedly shore up its defences but, in the process, established a semi-autonomous regional state in Somalia's southern provinces. Kenya had not received consent from Somalia when it sent its army to intervene in their affairs, a move that continues to be a source of tension with the Somali Federal Government. The north-east has been reimagined as a front in Kenya's 'war on terror' where efforts to establish a buffer against extremist militancy in Somalia are focused. Initially, before refugees settled in the Dadaab refugee camps, banditry was the main threat in the north-east region of Kenya, particularly in the form of secessionist activities during the years of the Shifta War and emergency rule. Banditry was also seen in the form of intercommunal conflict over access to scarce water and pastureland (Whittaker 2012, p. 391–408).

During the most recent decade, a new threat posed by Al-Shabab has added to the longstanding perception of the north-east as an insecure borderland. There have been numerous attacks on Kenyan police and on communication masts. Humanitarian NGOs are also attacked for spreading 'Western' education as well as for more opportunistic reasons, such as the acquisition of vehicles and other equipment. There have been raids of NGO compounds within the camps as well as the kidnapping of aid workers (Sweeney 2012, p. 1), although there has not yet been an attack in the town of Dadaab. As a result of these increasing attacks, the BHER project, which had previously housed their staff within the BHER Learning Centre, in 2015 decided to relocate them to the more secure Dadaab NGO Compound.

After Al-Shabab attacked Nairobi's upscale Westgate Mall in 2013 (Blanchard 2013, p. 1) and Garissa University[2] in 2015, the Kenyan government identified the Dadaab camps as a sanctuary for the extremist group and demanded their closure (Allison 2015, p. 1). These terror attacks have hardened attitudes towards Somali refugees (New Humanitarian 2015, p. 1), though there is no evidence that refugees have been involved in the attacks. In 2013, Kenya concluded a tripartite agreement with the UNHCR and the Somali Federal Government to facilitate the camps' closure (UNHCR 2015, p. 6). Kenya hoped to shore up security in the north-east, which it considers a porous borderland, by repatriating Somali refugees, an aspiration that has yet to fully materialize despite the drastic decline in the number of registered refugees in the Dadaab camps.

The defeat of, or negotiations with, Al-Shabab still seem a long way off, and the group has sought to exploit ethnic, religious and regional divisions between Kenyans, often killing non-Muslims from 'down Kenya' in order to tempt an overreaction by the Kenyan government and society-at-large. The Kenyan government's responses to terror attacks have sometimes played into Al-Shabab's hands, particularly during the wide-ranging crackdown on Somalis in 2014 when police detained thousands of Somali refugees in Kasarani Stadium in Nairobi, called a 'concentration camp' by Somalis and drawing the ire of international human rights organizations (Sperber 2015, p. 1–2).

The establishment of the refugee camps in the predominantly Somali northeast was not an accident. Refugees were placed in a remote, economically marginalized and ethnically Somali part of the country that was already heavily surveilled. And as mentioned, the Dadaab camps are also the subject of multiple, sometimes contradictory, political contestations over local and national belonging, competition over resources and Kenya's role within the region. When the refugee camps were opened in the early 1990s, Dadaab was a small, isolated and under-resourced village without schools or clinics. Most of the community lived a pastoralist lifestyle and were often food insecure. As such, the socio-economic needs of local Kenyans and refugees were and are quite similar. However, for much of the 1990s, humanitarian agencies disregarded the social and economic needs of the local population, eventually resulting in resentment towards refugees (Kamau and Fox 2013, p. 4). The poor economic situation and lack of public services forced some in the local communities to register as refugees in order to access humanitarian support, including food and shelter materials from the United Nations High Commission for Refugees (UNHCR), which leads refugee operations in the camps (Callanan, 2006, p. 27–45). To avert political tension, humanitarian organizations started supporting local communities within a 25 km radius of the refugee camps. Subsequently, this saw the launch of local development projects such as vocational training and apprenticeship programmes, a medical laboratory and a secondary school (Milner 2009, p. 95). These supports somewhat improved the host community's access to job opportunities among other resources and assuaged some of the hostility towards refugees.

Local Integration Challenges

Despite differences in legal status, refugees and the host community have, to an extent, become socially integrated, with many intermarriages, business partnerships, and shared use of religious and cultural spaces. The process of integration is aided by a shared ethnicity, clan affiliations and a common Sunni Muslim faith. The non-Somali refugees have also intermarried with non-Somali Kenyans. Ali-Dhere,[3] one of our participants, highlighted how the border between the two countries belies close cultural ties between locals and refugees. He mentioned how 'so many people have intermarried. We are the same people. Same religion. On the other side, we are the same people. Even before they fled to this area, we had relatives on the other side.' Many Somali refugees in Dadaab have also learned Kiswahili to conduct business with Kenyans and to negotiate the challenges of dealing with Kenyan police and bureaucrats. This social and economic integration is inconsistent with national refugee policy, which seeks to make a clear distinction between citizens and refugees, particularly in a culturally homogenous and historically restive region.

Notwithstanding similar socio-economic conditions and close cultural and physical proximity, the differential way that the UNHCR, governmental and non-governmental organizations (NGOs) assist refugee and local communities creates livelihood disparities and competition for resources in the Dadaab area. Khalif, a member of the local community, insists that there continue to be barriers to accessing services for local Kenyans:

There's no student in the host community who goes to refugee schools, so that means they don't benefit from free education. But there are refugees who study in Dadaab public schools. About health, in fact, if you go to, in terms of emergencies, if you go to refugee camps, you will be assisted. But there are no services provided for [the] host community in Dadaab. If you go to the camps like Red Cross, MSF, etcetera, you will be assisted with a doctor's note, or if you know someone. The first thing they ask you is: are you [a] refugee? If not, you go to [the] host community hospital. You have three options: one, if you know someone inside the hospital; two, you're referred by a doctor with the Ministry of Health; three, if you have [a] ration card to show if you're a refugee. But you can't say I've fallen sick and have just come here. You will be told to go to a private hospital.

Though we spoke to several service providers in the camps who refuted Khalif's claims, his perspective nevertheless demonstrates continuing resentment at the way NGOs provide services to the host community. Amenities such as hospitals and schools built for refugees in the camps are considered to be better resourced than those for locals in Dadaab town (Government of Kenya 2018, p. 26). This disparity has created a perception among the local community that the national and county governments are not bothered by their lack of essential community services. However, refugee schools are also under-resourced, but unlike schools for the host community, they do not receive nor rely on government funding. The Teachers Service Commission (TSC) places a limited number of educators, mostly from 'down Kenya', throughout the north-east, due to the shortage of trained teachers in the region. These teachers often leave their posts due to insecurity, poor teaching conditions and the hardship of being away from family who live elsewhere. Both refugee and local schools have historically relied on uncertified local and refugee teachers, though the latter are not allowed to be registered with the TSC, nor are they paid the same salary as Kenyan teachers.

Despite close cultural relations between the host and refugee communities, worries about Somali clan demographics persist and these have been exacerbated as in the rest of Kenya by electoral politics since a transition to multiparty democracy. Khalif and Ali-Dhere reaffirmed how these concerns are based on present political realities in the country. The participants who we interviewed felt that they would not appreciate many non-Somalis permanently settling in the north-east, with one of them comparing it to the perceived untenableness of a Somali settling in central Kenya, where ethnic Kikuyus are the majority. Nevertheless, participants did not mind Somali refugees eventually settling in the north-east provided they lived with their clan community, as citizenship implied entitlement to the land. Khalif maintains, 'We don't mind Somalis being given citizenship. They can integrate into pre-existing clans here. There are not clans here who are not in Somalia.' This perspective was seen by some focus group participants as being important in keeping the peace. Ali-Dhere commented that since the refugee crisis of the 1990s, clan conflict in Somalia sometimes spills over the border and complicates local politics in Kenya's northeast. He said that 'before refugees, we never heard of tribe'.

In spite of that, Amos, a middle-aged South Sudanese refugee, told us that he found Dadaab more hospitable than Kakuma refugee camp in the north-west of the country:

> I have been living in two different camp environments. I came to Kakuma 15 years ago. The local community there in Kakuma is harsher. They cannot stand refugees and can beat you anytime. They have guns. But here you can walk from Ifo [one of the Dadaab camps] to town at night without worry. Even though I'm not Somali, I enjoy life here more.

Several other refugee participants confirmed Amos' claim, suggesting that local resentment toward refugees may not be anomalous to Dadaab and, in some respects, refugees might enjoy better relations with locals in Dadaab than in Kakuma.

Land Settlement and Food Security

Local preferences of integrating Somali refugees among the clans to which they belong runs contrary to global understanding of local integration, which often ignores local tensions. However, local integration, understood as the economic and legal incorporation of refugees into the host society, has a long history of practice among some host countries in the Global South. Regionally, local integration has periodically and for decades been a feature of refugee policy in Uganda (Ohanusi 2016, p. 1) and Tanzania, with the latter going as far as naturalizing some Burundian (Kuch 2018, p. 1) and Somali Bantu refugees (Bannon and Wolfcarius 2009, p. 1). Despite some social and economic integration in Dadaab, a number of local Somali Kenyans have misgivings about the statutory integration of refugees by means of potential permanent residency or rights to buy land. Ali-Dhere pointed out the impossibilities of global narratives in a local context of resource scarcity, explaining that 'there's competition over jobs and land between [the] local community'. The local community focus group seemed to agree that the legal integration of refugees would complicate contested ownership of land and access to pasture. For example, Ali-Dhere mentioned how the political class often takes land for themselves, sometimes at the expense of previous owners of the land. He described how '[the] governor[s] want this piece of land, and others will say we have been owning this piece of land over twenty years'.

The local community in Dadaab also complained that some refugees settled on land without the approval of the government. A few farmed on such pieces of land, raising fears about the permanence of the refugee presence. These unofficial settlements were famously known as the 'outskirts', and by enabling self-reliance, threatened to upend government and NGO control over the refugee population, and strained relations with the local community. The government stopped the refugees who had started to farm on land outside the designated camps. This had an impact on a few locals who wanted to learn agricultural skills from refugees – many of whom were farmers from Somalia's southern riverine regions – but could not, as refugees were not permitted to farm outside the camps. To provide access to a more varied diet and income generation, the UNHCR and the World Food Programme (WFP) supported some refugee and host community individuals to own kitchen gardens and multi-storey gardens between the years 2000 and 2005, before funding was discontinued (Callanan 2006, p. 25). Some refugees, especially those of non-Somali nationalities, still have small farms in the refugee camps located near water taps. They sell the vegetables that they grow to both the local and refugee communities, which is especially crucial as it supplements their diet. However, these initiatives cannot sustain the food needs of the two communities, and the closure of larger, refugee-initiated farms in the 1990s dealt a blow to food security in Dadaab.

Environmental Degradation

As locals are still predominantly pastoral, access to pastureland has been a point of tension with refugees. Host communities believe that refugees have caused environmental degradation by cutting down trees for fuel and shelter (Government of Kenya 2018, p. 25). Darfur village residents, close to Dagahaley refugee camp, reportedly refused to have refugees hosted near them, ostensibly to prevent environmental degradation as had happened to their neighbours. They also reported that refugees were responsible for hunting large wild animals like giraffes and destroying protected local forests. It is believed that, proportionally, the refugee population, which is roughly ten times the population of the local community, consumes in a year the natural resources the local community could have used for ten years. In this situation of competition for land and official corruption, local Kenyans view the permanent integration of refugees as problematic.

Challenging a Two-Tiered System

Although our participants emphasized the role of clan politics, local disquiet about refugee economic and political integration is also related to the economic marginality of Dadaab. Even though the refugee population has access to free social amenities like water, healthcare, food and education, local Kenyans must pay for access for most of these social amenities as NGO assistance to local communities remains minimal. This two-tiered system of supports causes resentment and a sense that locals are being left-behind. As macro-level or legal integration into Kenya is prevented by the country's encampment policy, at a micro level, some humanitarian actors in the Dadaab refugee camps have bowed to local pressure and opted to economically support local communities.

The BHER project, which was aware of the double marginalization of local Kenyans, adopted a similar approach towards local and refugee student recruitment. The strategy of ensuring that the local community benefit from BHER project resources was critical to gaining local political support for the project and securing land for the BHER Learning Centre prior to the delivery of university programmes. To a certain extent, this decision inoculated BHER from local grievances towards the humanitarian presence in Dadaab. For instance, some humanitarian programmes were temporarily interrupted in December 2017 by a prolonged local protest against the 'consolidation' of the Dadaab refugee camps, with complaints about the number of local Somali Kenyans who were made redundant by the downsizing of refugee programmes as a result of the closure of the Kambioos and Ifo 2 camps in 2017 and 2018. The reason given for the local job losses was the 'voluntary repatriation' of Somali refugees (UNHCR 2018, p. 2). Protesters blockaded the airstrip and the NGO compound, effectively curtailing refugee operations. However, the BHER Learning Centre remained open as a result of the employment of local community members who could more easily negotiate entry and navigate local politics. The architects of the BHER project also had a target of recruiting 25 per cent of its students from within local communities, an objective that was eventually surpassed to 30 per cent. The inclusion of students from local communities contributed to a general sense among the local community that they stood to benefit from the project.

The 2017 Dadaab protest illustrates the contradictory nature of local politics, where solidarity with refugees is tenuous, and dependence on refugee operations coexists with resentment and concerns about the long-term integration of refugees. Though refugees and locals have, thus far, peacefully coexisted, there remains low-level tension about the future of Dadaab, where locals want to decide the terms under which refugees will stay. Local anxieties about the future of Dadaab intersect with government policies that have securitized not only Somali refugees, but also Somali Kenyans themselves, making what Milner calls the 'everyday politics of the global refugee regime' locally complex and contested (2019, 0:45–51:12). In the following section, we extend this discussion, suggesting that refugee camps are socially and politically dynamic places that are both enabling and restrictive, offering a life of new beginnings as well as endless precarity due to the stigmatizing politics of refuge.

New Beginnings: Two Sides of a Story

Rather than merely a space of containment, the Dadaab camps also represent for most of their residents, locals included, a new start in difficult situations when the safety and services normally provided by the state are unavailable. But perceptions of the camps as a place to continue life projects (Turner 2015, p. 144) run contrary to conventional academic conceptualizations of refugee camps as mere states of exception, as in the work of Agamben (1998) and Agier (2010). During war and extreme marginalization, refugee camps can also offer the possibility of a better future through education and the chance of local integration or, for some, resettlement in a third country. In that sense, the refugee camp is what Turner (2015) calls 'a place of new beginnings', where 'social life, power relations, hierarchies and sociality are remoulded' (ibid.). This is particularly the case for women, children and castigated social groups whose marginality requires new forms of social protection by humanitarian actors.

Employment

Abdi, a young Somali male refugee, describes how living in the camp provided him opportunities for social mobility:

> I was nearly born here. This is where I started my life – in the refugee camp. I came here when I was three years old and went to primary and secondary school here. I have never left the camp, never went even to Garissa. I am presently a teacher in the camps and have gotten my education in the camps.

Though Abdi lives in a refugee camp in a remote part of Kenya, his story reveals the contradictory nature of refugee camps, which are concurrently places of containment and possibility. On the one hand, he received an education when most schools in Somalia were closed or destroyed during the conflict; on the other, although well-educated, he cannot earn the same salary as his certified Kenyan colleagues. We heard similar narratives about how coming to the refugee camp enabled people to reinvent themselves, but within limits. A female Somali refugee, Fatuma, who came to the camps in her late twenties, reveals how the Dadaab camps represent a kind of future-scape where one can resume life projects of self-improvement and social mobility:

> I came to this camp in 1992, and I started working in the field as a social worker. At the time, the salary [for refugee incentive work] was Ksh 750.[4] Then in 2002, I became a teacher first, then was promoted as a deputy headteacher. In 2009, I became a headteacher in primary school.

While employed as a social worker, Fatuma completed her education and applied to be a primary school teacher, and later became one of the first female refugee school administrators in Dadaab. She came to the focus group with Alia, a young Somali female refugee whom she had taught and mentored over the years. Alia recalled, 'I came here in 1994 as a one-year-old. I grew up in the camps and finished my primary and secondary education and have been teaching for seven years'. She emphasized how challenging it was to become a teacher, struggling against traditional gender norms and female underrepresentation in the teaching profession (see the chapter by Bishop et al. for a full discussion of gender relations). Despite gratitude for the opportunities offered to them, the two women expressed frustration about the ways in which their refugee status circumscribed their future trajectories.

Those who can find professional jobs with humanitarian organizations work for an 'incentive wage', typically $80–100 (USD) per month, a fraction of a Kenyan citizen's remuneration in the same position (Kamau and Fox 2013, p. 18). As incentive workers, refugee staff working with UNHCR and NGOs receive wages below the taxable salary in Kenya.

Mobility

Alia, as an ambitious young professional, felt suffocated by the legal constraints on refugee mobility and employment, a complaint that Fatuma shared:

> Refugees came here in Kenya in 1991 up to now, almost thirty years. We don't have freedom, but we can't blame the locals. If I want to go to Garissa, I cannot, unless, I go to DRA [Department of Refugee Affairs] and ask, which can take several days. There are people who are dying here without hospitals.[5] Before 1995, UNHCR used to give us travel documents, which would be taken to government, and taken back to us. But now, we have to approach DRA ourselves, and we are now in prison.

Like other focus group participants, Fatuma felt a desire for more freedom of movement and rights to move outside the camps without the possibility of arrest. Somali refugees are treated with suspicion upon arrival in the camps and are confronted with an encampment policy that takes away the normal rights to work and live like any other resident of Kenya. Before 1989, Kenya had an ad hoc open refugee policy that allowed refugees freedom of movement, the right to work and the possibility of protected status (Milner 2009, p. 85–6, 88). As Somalia's government faltered in 1991, Kenya reversed this posture. At that time, 400,000 Somalis fled to Kenya from internecine warfare and famine in their country, living in camps throughout Kenya (ibid., 87). Growing anxieties about Somali refugees in the mid-1990s led Kenya's government to close the various camps that dotted the country's map and mandated that refugees live in the refugee complexes of Dadaab in the north-east. In the early 1990s, both the UNHCR and the Kenyan government saw the crisis as temporary and tried several times to repatriate Somali refugees. This was abandoned as efforts to stabilize Somalia failed in the mid-1990s and the refugee crisis gradually morphed into a protracted refugee situation.

Although Somali refugees in Kenya live in relative peace with greater livelihood options as compared to those in parts of southern Somalia, many people still struggle to obtain necessities such as food, water, medicine and educational resources (Kamau and Fox 2013, p. 18, 27). As mentioned by Fatuma, refugees who want to travel outside the camp need special permission. Permission to travel is also limited to treatment for specialist medical care, school, or consular visits. These manifold restrictions render life in the camps more precarious because the task of 'imagining a future, planning one's life trajectory and acting accordingly in the present become seriously challenged' (Turner 2015, p. 145).

The dual nature of the camps as enabling and disempowering perhaps unsurprisingly reveals differences of opinion along generational lines. For Alia, growing up in the camps allowed her to achieve a level of education that was unavailable to most during the war in Somalia. Nevertheless, the restrictions on life in Kenya have made her consider the possibilities of making a future for herself in Somalia. Conversely, Fatuma, who remembers pre-war Somalia, felt despondent about returning to a country that has changed beyond her recognition and she would much rather live out her remaining years in Kenya with a greater sense of dignity. 'Me, I'm Somali,' she remarked, 'but at this moment, I'm more comfortable in Kenya. Because I forgot the area I came from. But if they give me Kenyan certificate or make my alien card strong, that would be good.' 'Not me,' Alia insisted, 'I would like to go to Somalia that I have not seen and help my community there.'

Conclusion

In a contradictory way, the camps offer and deny – at the same time – opportunities to refugees. For example, refugees can be educated in English and Kiswahili, the national languages, but are also deprived of a pathway to citizenship, a disappointment that reorients some refugees towards a better life in their home country. This was a point that was most clearly illustrated by Amos, who teaches refugee children and youths:

> What I have seen is that Somali refugees have adapted to this life because they have their own brothers who live in Kenya who share same culture and language. Ninety percent of refugees want to do local integration because majority did their schooling here and some even got Bachelors, and they are now willing to work here. Those who learn here are working with the agencies in Somalia. I know about a young man who wanted to go to US, but didn't, but completed his education here then went back to Somalia and [is] working for [an] international agency.

The Dadaab camps, then, offer an education and the chance of a better life elsewhere, outside of Kenya. Rather than a just an 'outplace', and 'an enduring present' where refugees live in a permanent state of waiting (Agier 2010, p. 79), current social realities in Dadaab are illustrative of Jensen's (2015) observation of refugee camps as connected spaces that draw people for humanitarian as well as developmental reasons, including a desire to secure and improve one's life chances in the aftermath of conflict and state collapse (Jensen 2015, p. 149–65). Jensen argues that in the absence of other sites of protection, we need to reconsider refugee camps 'as an option in a larger scheme of livelihood and economic possibilities' (ibid., 150). Terming these strategies as 'digging aid', he illustrates how camps attract people from the wider Horn and Eastern Africa regions. People come to the camps not only to access humanitarian assistance and educate their children, but also to find the protection of living further afield in southern Kenya or in a 'third country'. This is not an accident, Jensen suggests, as the social architecture of camps has long since 'moved from emergency mode to a phase of "care and maintenance" to include more developmental and empowerment programming' (ibid., 154). Abdi, also a teacher in the camps, contended as much, pointing out how parents send their children to be educated in Dadaab:

> There are many teachers from Dadaab that have gone to Kismayo [a town in southern Somalia] and opened schools; and therefore, people have seen [the] quality [of their teaching], and that [their children] can one day even become president. They are having discussions about harmonization [of schools in Kismayo and the Dadaab camps], and that is why parents send their kids from Somalia.

The pressure to close the Dadaab refugee camps, along with an increasing detachment of local Somali Kenyans from employment and other involvement in the camps suggests that the earlier appeal of the camps as a place of possibility may now be on the wane. The camps, currently undergoing gradual closure, might now represent the shuttering of old aspirations, and by the same token, the beginning of new chapters in the lives of their residents. This change in the character of the camps underscores the nature of the refugee camps as constantly evolving social and political spaces that are contemporaneous sites of possibility and precarity. The indistinct nature of camp life, where refugees and citizens mingle, and where the line between Somali and Kenyan is sometimes blurred, has heightened national anxieties about the Dadaab camps in a time of growing preoccupation with security as part of the 'war on terror'. Kenyan government discourse suggests the inability to tell Kenyans and Somalis apart in a region that is ethnically homogenous and 'insecure'. It is often lamented that in a porous borderland, one cannot distinguish 'terrorists' from blameless refugees, a problem which necessitates that the camps be shut, and the boundaries of the nation protected.

Understanding refugee camps requires that we attend to the relationship between local and refugee communities, and national policies and politics. In the Dadaab camps, local Kenyans and Somali refugees have a long and complex history that necessitates an analysis of the political, social and security interplays in the north-east region and the rest of Kenya, including the tensions created by the humanitarian system, given the differential way refugees and local communities have been served. Rather than focus exclusively on the refugee population, the BHER project sought to include local Kenyans from Dadaab town and neighbouring areas. The project has had a partnership with Windle International Kenya, Kenyatta University (KU), and Moi University for implementation and sustainability purposes, using land leased to KU by the county administration, and facilities given to and now owned by KU. It is hoped that if and when BHER ceases to exist, national and local education actors like our partners will take over programming. Currently, local Kenyans make up one-third of the project's student body and this integrative admissions approach has given the project local legitimacy and has simultaneously addressed the higher education needs of refugees and locals. The BHER project, in that sense, is an example of what is possible when we go beyond humanitarian thinking to address the coexisting needs and aspirations of refugee and host communities.

2

Gender Disparities in University Access in the Kenyan Kakuma Camps

Danielle Bishop, Hanan Duri and Grace Nshimiyumukiza

The Borderless Higher Education for Refugees (BHER) project aims to provide women and men who are living in the Dadaab refugee camps and town, and more recently the Kakuma refugee camps, equitable access to university courses and programmes. Among BHER's key principles is gender equity in university access, with emphasis on providing an inclusive and supportive environment for men and women students. Drawing from primary data collected from January to April 2019 in the Kakuma refugee camps in north-western Kenya with women university students, including BHER students, and community elders, this chapter explores the barriers that women confront in accessing or continuing in their chosen higher education programmes while living in the Kakuma refugee camps.

Our objective in this chapter is to further an understanding of women's access to higher education by looking at the complex relationship between all facets of the daily lives and the needs of the female students and their families living in a camp context that is known to be limited in availability of amenities and services, as well as restrictive in rights to work and move freely. We aim to move the discussion of gender equity in higher education in refugee contexts beyond an emphasis on how cultural norms present barriers to accessing education to a more holistic analysis that includes how encampment and the limited structural, social, material, and economic support provided to individuals and families by humanitarian agencies impede women university students' success in accessing or continuing in higher education. We argue that facilitating access to and/or ability to continue with higher education in refugee camps must first include unpacking and understanding unequal hierarchies of access to and participation of women at all levels, in all facets of their lived reality, not just education programmes. This includes taking into account how access to education is linked to gendered power-relations operating within the humanitarian sphere of a camp context. Linked to this, there is the more general inequality in access and participation women may have in making choices that exercise their agency and ability to meet every day needs, including childcare; in addition, there is their lived experiences as refugees residing in a camp exposed to heightened risks of gender-based violence, amidst restrictions on mobility, livelihoods and freedom.

Methods and Methodology

There are several reasons that our research is based on findings from the Kakuma camps. First of all, as described above, two of the authors have carried out research in Kakuma (Bishop and Nshimiyumukiza). Second, the Kakuma camps are home to refugees from a number of different countries, which allows for a potentially richer and more comparative study of gender relations than Dadaab, which is home to refugees from mainly one country, Somalia. Third, some of the BHER students from Dadaab were forced to relocate to the Kakuma camps in 2017[1] and an expansion of the BHER project has been discussed on and off since then. Finally, and perhaps most significantly, our research with mainly non-BHER students with whom we do not have teacher/staff-student relationships stands to result in less conflicted or subjective findings.

Our field methods included primary data collected from refugee women pursuing higher education programmes in Kakuma (BHER project courses, the Jesuit Worldwide Learning (JWL), InZone and South New Hampshire University [SNHU][2]). Fieldwork was conducted between the months of January and April 2019. Methods involved a small-scale qualitative study comprised of one-on-one interviews with twelve participants: three elderly women, four male elders and five women who attended a higher education programme at one time in their lives. One of the authors of this chapter was enrolled in the BHER project, in Kakuma. The participants were from various countries within the Kakuma refugee community: South Sudan, Uganda, Rwanda and Somalia. Most of the participants have been in the camp for more than 10 years.[3]

The research, analysis and focus of this chapter is informed by a critical review of literature on gender and education (Kirk, 2006; Plasterer and Wright, 2010; Bellino and Hure, 2018; Bellino, 2018; Dryden-Peterson and Giles, 2010; Dryden-Peterson and Dahya, 2017), and scholarship focused on refugee encampment and the limitations of humanitarian aid (Hyndman, 2000; Moret, Baglioni and Efionayi-Mader, 2006; Abdi, 2004; Chatty and Hundt, 2005; Harrell-Bond, 1986;

Horn, 2010; Grayson, 2017; Bishop, 2019). Indeed, the gradual decline in women's participation in education from primary to higher education in developing countries and refugee contexts has been the focus of a handful of scholars from disciplines in education, development, economics and women's studies (Stromquist, 1989; Hill and King, 1993; Olson-Strom and Rao, 2020; Chege and Sifuna, 2006; Jacobs, 1996). Though research emphasis is on barriers to *access*, our findings also reveal the significant barriers women face once they are accepted and/or enrolled into a higher education degree or certificate programme. If gender equity in BHER classrooms is going to be achieved, this is an important piece of research that needs elaboration.

The research, analysis and focus of the chapter is also informed by the personal and professional experiences of the authors, including their respective involvements with the BHER project. Danielle Bishop received her PhD from York University in Toronto in 2019. From 2010 to 2014, she was a graduate assistant to the BHER project, actively involved in curriculum development and the literature reviews required to inform the structure of the programme. Between 2013 and 2016, Danielle spent fourteen months conducting qualitative field research in Kakuma, Turkana County and Nairobi for her PhD dissertation, focused on young people's navigation of insecurity and precarity in the Kakuma camps and among the Turkana host community. Hanan Duri is a third-year PhD student in the Faculty of Education at York University. She is the oldest of three siblings and the first female in her family to pursue post-secondary education. Her parents are refugees from Ethiopia who fled from political instabilities. Her research interests in gender equity in higher education and access to higher education in Ethiopia have developed from this history. Hanan has been a Teaching Assistant and Course Director to the BHER project since September 2018. Grace Nshimiyumukiza was born in Ngara refugee camp of Tanzania, the first of seven siblings. In 2000, Grace and her parents moved to Nairobi, Kenya and were subsequently moved by UNHCR Nairobi to the Kakuma refugee camp. After completing Form Four (final year of secondary school) in 2014, she completed a diploma with JWL, followed by an Applied Arts Certificate with InZone, a BA, and then an online MEd with York University, a key partner of the BHER project. Since graduating, Grace has worked with the Lutheran World Federation (LWF) Child Protection Unit as a community caseworker and is currently working for InZone as a Social and Emotional Learning (SEL) Coordinator. Her experiences and the challenges she faced in these three programmes are what drive her to focus her research on the theme of women's access to higher education in protracted refugee situations.

The Camp Context

Kakuma is located in the north-western region of Kenya and hosts one of the largest populations of refugees in the world. The camp was originally established in 1992 as a response to the large influx of young Sudanese people fleeing the civil war. Ethiopians, also among the largest groups of refugees in Kakuma, arrived after the fall of the military dictatorship of Mengistu Haile Mariam. The camps are located outside the town of Kakuma, in Turkana County. In 2013, after renewed conflicts in South Sudan, overpopulation in the Kakuma camps required that additional land be allocated near Kalobeyei Township for refugees. According to the United Nations High Commissioner for Refugees (UNHCR), the settlements of Kakuma and Kalobeyei currently house 188,794 refugees. The camp's population is made up of refugees from twenty-two different nationalities (UNHCR, 2019): 'Ongoing conflict and instability, as well as drought and famine, pushed young people out of their homes in Congo, Ethiopia, Somalia, Sudan, South Sudan, Uganda' (Bellino and Hure 2018, 48). Today, approximately 55.5 per cent of the population is under the age of seventeen years old. Twenty-four per cent are young unaccompanied orphaned children who have been separated from their parents after fleeing their conflict-affected home countries (Lutheran World Federation, 2015; Bellino and Hure, 2018).

A number of educational projects have been established in Kakuma to provide education to refugees, from primary education to tertiary education. However, many of the teachers in the camps have little to no teacher training. According to data from education partners in Kakuma and Kalobeyei, 38 per cent of the 1095 teaching staff are deemed qualified. Nine hundred and nine or 83 per cent are refugees recruited from the camps, 25 per cent of whom are deemed qualified.[4] The latter are called 'incentive teachers' and most have only completed up to a secondary school level of education (Abdi, 2016). Yet there is 'broad consensus … that "teacher quality" is the single most important school variable influencing student achievement' (OECD, 2005, p. 2; Darling-Hammond, 2000; Schwille et al., 2007). Given that a qualified teaching workforce is crucial for the effective functioning of any education system (Abdi 2016, 24), the lack of prioritization of teacher training inevitably leads to poor quality of education.

There is also a disproportionate number of male teachers in the Kakuma's camp schools, which has created a male-dominated environment that further contributes to the small number of women completing secondary school. Female students do not have role models to motivate them to persist and often complain about not receiving the same attention and support in the classroom as their male peers (Douhaibi et al., 2020). It is within this context that the BHER project seeks to build the capacity of the teachers in the Dadaab and Kakuma camps through gender equitable teacher education. The aim is that both female and male students, who are already teachers within the camps, will take these new university qualifications with them should they return to their country of origin and gain employment as teachers, thus helping to rebuild their country's educational system.

Finally, as noted by humanitarian agencies in the camp, learner retention is often tied to structural challenges that schools in a refugee camp setting confront, such as overcrowded classrooms, scarce resources and poor infrastructure (LWF, 2015; Lowe, 2019; Abdi, 2016; El Jack, 2010). As a result of these structural challenges and gender inequalities pervasive in camp situations, research on refugee contexts shows that, overall, only 40 per cent of refugee girls in Kakuma even attend primary school. By the time they enter secondary school, the number is reduced to 22 per cent. At the postsecondary level, the participation of women dwindles to less than 1 per cent (UNHCR Kakuma, 2017). This is important, as completion of secondary school is a key determinant of access to higher education. However, even for those refugees who have completed secondary schooling in Kakuma, higher education is considered by donors and the humanitarian community as a longer-term development project (Mendenhall et al., 2015) and thus, tertiary educational programmes and teacher education are not a high priority area in humanitarian contexts due to the perception that refugee camps are temporary sites of emergency response.

When it is offered and available, the space of higher education in refugee situations is a site wherein gender inequalities play out. For instance, and despite the efforts made by the BHER project and other organizations and their partners offering tertiary education programmes to promote gender equity and enrol as many qualified women as possible,[5] the overall participation of women across higher education programmes in Kakuma is 26 per cent compared to 74 per cent of men enrolled in higher education programmes. From 2013 to 2019, the four universities affiliated with the BHER project admitted 120 female students (fifty-four from the Kenyan host community and sixty-six refugees from Dadaab and Kakuma) into various programmes out of a total of 463 engaged students (26 per cent of the total number of students). A total of seventy-five women have so far graduated with undergraduate certificates, diplomas and degrees out of 342 graduates (22 per cent of the total number of students).

These statistics may be the result of the gradual decline in girls' participation and completion of secondary school more generally. In addition, however, and drawing from primary data collected from the interviews in Kakuma, the following section also explores intersecting cultural, social, structural and material barriers that women face not only when trying to access higher education programmes, but also when trying to continue with and graduate from their studies in higher education.

Gender Disparities and Barriers to Access and Retention in University Programmes

Living conditions in refugee camps are extremely difficult and have been found to violate refugees' rights (Hyndman, 2000; Moret, Baglioni and Efionayi-Mader, 2006; Abdi, 2004; Chatty and Hundt, 2005; Harrell-Bond, 1986). Verdirame and Harrell-Bond (2005) in *Rights in Exile*, outline the human rights abuses refugees living in refugee camps face in Uganda and Kenya. They found violations in 'the right to work and to freedom of movement, insecurity, reduced legal recourse for refugees, arbitrary arrests and detentions and constraints on political activities and freedom of expression and association' (71). Refugee rights to adequate living conditions (food, clothing and housing) are also severely challenged.

To this end, some of the participants in our interviews suggested that it is not simply the poor quality of secondary education in the camps that has made it difficult for women to be well equipped to pursue higher education. Rather, women students and male elders in Kakuma revealed to us that women students also face a great number of day-to-day barriers in accessing and continuing in higher education linked to macro circumstances of limited rights and restrictions on movement. These include shifting cultural norms, domestic violence, family obligations, the lack of childcare centres, the distance to the learning centres or schools, financial crises at home and lack of adequate support from the NGOs to allow married women with children or single mothers to attend classes, such as lactation rooms or day-care facilities. These factors reflect the gendered experiences of living in a refugee camp more generally, and gender equity in higher education specifically. They also reflect how accessing higher education is inextricably linked with how humanitarian assistance and encampment policies impact on and shift the social and material relations of refugees, the opportunities they have, and the physical, mental and social well-being of individuals, families and communities.

Cultural Barriers and Gender Discrimination

Refugee life within a humanitarian structure creates conditions that become exacerbated in displacement, especially when it is protracted. Socio-economic life in refugee camps and the lack of resources for refugees to generate sustainable incomes is one of the sources of ongoing frustration for refugees (Carlson, 2005). Poverty is amplified due to the lack of employment opportunities available. Kenyan government policy requires that refugees must remain in one of the two camp sites, Dadaab and Kakuma, and cannot take up formal employment. According to Horn (2010), the loss of the role of providing economically for a family, leading to a sense of loss of household status, can be a challenge for male refugees. While females may maintain traditional roles as wives and mothers, men may find that it is difficult to maintain a role of provider and protector in the face of socio-economic difficulties, and may compensate such a loss of power by instigating marital conflict and violence (Carlson, 2005; Yick, 2001; Giles, 2013). In addition, the humanitarian structure present in Kakuma operates on an 'ideology of equality', which promotes specialized programmes and opportunities for women to generate an income. This has led some refugee women to find more employment opportunities than men, thus becoming the primary providers in the household. Women taking on these additional responsibilities shift traditional gender roles and this, too, may exacerbate tensions in the home.

Displacement also intensifies discrimination against women and may lead to gender-based and sexual violence (Horn, 2010; Giles, 2013). Our findings confirm that one of the key obstacles that continues to hinder women from attending or remaining in university programmes in Kakuma is gender discrimination rooted in shifting sociocultural norms and customs, and unequal gender relations at the individual, household and community levels. Indeed, cultural factors often prove difficult to address because they manifest themselves as static customs and norms developed and practiced over a long period of time. When humanitarian organizations define women, girls and gender relations in a camp in static homogenous categories, as dependent, vulnerable and victims, they are supporting and reproducing gender inequalities in refugee camps (Giles, 2013).

The stressors of life in refugee camps due to the loss of employment opportunities, coupled with years of limitations on mobility may also lead to low self-esteem, resentment, frustration and anger of men towards women (Loescher and Milner, 2008; Giles, 2013). The participants interviewed noted a pervasive perception that a woman should not be educated to a higher level because the moment they go to university, they are the same people who 'bring trouble' to the community. For this reason, women and girls are not often given equal opportunities to receive an education in comparison to boys or men in Kakuma. The education of women in the circumstances outlined above, is not only met with resentment but also seen as challenging traditional social norms that identify women as rightly preoccupied by work in the home. Reportedly, due to perceptions and societal expectations of marriage and maintaining subservience to men, the young girls and young women who attend primary and secondary education are rarely given the chance to pursue higher education. Male elders from the South Sudanese community in Kakuma refugee camp further elaborated in their interviews on why men feel conflicted with having women from their communities participate in higher education programmes. For instance, they said that when a woman comes back from school with the knowledge of human rights and women's rights, she brings with her ideas of equality between men and women. According to the elders interviewed, 'we [the men in the community] have never known what equality means, we were brought up knowing that men are superior, and no women should argue with us' (group of male Sudanese elders). Very few young women in the Kakuma camps are adequately prepared to safely stand up against such discrimination and enrol in a higher education programme from this community.

For some women, however, unequal power relations do not automatically end once they participate in a degree or postsecondary certificate programme. Grace's experience as the only woman enrolled in the BHER programme in Kakuma testifies to the isolation and loneliness some female students may feel once enrolled in a programme that is dominated by male students:

> My experience as the only female BHER student in Kakuma ... it has not been easy. I was the only female student among my colleagues in Kakuma, and the gender dynamic made me feel distant and alone. The other three were married men with lots of family responsibilities. While it was not possible for me to attend tutorials on Sabbath (Saturday), they were not in a position to help me during the weekdays. The fact that I had no other woman to support me on the ground made it even worse because I felt very lonely and misplaced. What made it even more challenging is that I had to be the teaching assistant for my male colleagues. I needed to understand content very well so I could later on clarify to them. I lacked the support from my classmates and had to work harder on my own.

Gender-Based and Domestic Violence

Rooting the gender disparities in higher education in context-specific social expectations around gender roles and the patriarchal cultural norms pervasive to certain contexts is important for a further understanding of the social and cultural milieu that operates in a particular time and place. However, cultural norms are often symptomatic of and/or *intersect* with political, socio-economic and structural constraints to exacerbate other gendered social factors indicative of pervasive inequality, including gender-based violence, that impact on access to or continuance in higher education, or even secondary schooling. For instance, the intersections between material poverty, gender-based violence, exploitation and education are gaining increasing attention in research and policy reports (Kirk, 2010; Moletsane, 2005; Fawole, 2008).

When discussing key determinants of attending higher education, the barriers to secondary school were a major topic amongst interviewees. A group of male South Sudanese elders reported that when family material or economic resources are limited, there may be situations, for instance, where the education of sons is favoured so that the daughters can assist their mothers with household duties. Like many other refugees living in protracted camps situated in remote areas with no right to movement or employment, many families living in Kakuma are very poor and dependent on humanitarian aid, such as the provision of food and non-food items. The only way to reduce poverty is to work for an NGO in the camp, or to set up an informal income generating activity, which may not be sustainable over the long-term. In addition, '[g]irls may leave [secondary] school earlier than their male counterparts due to early marriages' (Namarome, Ugandan woman student), as marriage can provide a much-needed bride-price payment.

The story of Rebecca, a former student of the JWL programme in Kakuma, speaks to the difficulties of accessing or remaining enrolled in a post-secondary education programme in a refugee context due to intersecting risks and factors related to early marriage. During the time of her interview, she had already dropped out of the programme. Rebecca is a South Sudanese woman who successfully completed high school in Kakuma. Due to her high academic performance, she was awarded a scholarship to a Kenyan university. Yet, her family denied her the opportunity to leave Kakuma refugee camp to further her education. Instead, they wanted her to marry a wealthy Sudanese man from the United States, thinking marriage would give her and them a more fruitful life. Within a month of receiving the acceptance letter from the university, Rebecca was forced to marry the man with whom the family had an agreement, who in turn, paid a substantial bride price. Fearing they may be reported to the authorities, as forced marriage is illegal in Kenya, Rebecca's family quickly fled to South Sudan, leaving Rebecca behind. But Rebecca took action against her family and reported the case to the Kenyan authorities. She was rescued from her marriage by the authorities and was able to commence her studies at the university that had offered her a scholarship.

According to Carlson, 'the nature of the refugee camp ... plays a role in creating the conditions that facilitate domestic violence' (2005, 11), and this is reflected in Horn's argument that community and family structures that used to protect women from violent spouses have broken down in the Kakuma camps (2012, 363). One participant said that domestic violence is pervasive in Kakuma, but often goes unreported (Namarome, Ugandan woman student). Another participant from JWL explained how difficult it is for a student to attend classes with a swollen eye, the result of a beating from a husband. Participants said that women simply drop out due to the fear that someone at the university programme will report their abusive husband to the police. This fear is compounded by the fact that there are few safe places to escape from violent spouses, and few support services to turn to in the camps.

Marriage was also described by some participants as a hindrance to completing a university programme because the domestic responsibilities that accompany marriage in Kakuma generally fall disproportionately on women's shoulders. Some women students in the university programmes in Kakuma who were pregnant or have a child or children reportedly dropped out because there are no childcare supports in place at the university learning sites. There is also the difficulty of balancing childcare with their studies at home. Single mothers face additional challenges, with fewer childcare options. Women in one programme in Kakuma have adopted a collective childcare option, alternating childcare responsibilities with one another.

Finally, distance to a learning site also hinders women in Kakuma from accessing or continuing their studies as they fear experiencing violence and abuse on their way to the classroom and do not have funds for transport. As a result, our participants told us that some women decide to drop out in order to avoid dangerous road travel.

Some of the barriers to accessing higher education described above are what one might describe as challenging and are confronted by women the world over as they try to balance home life with university studies. However, a number of the obstacles are unquestionably extreme and life-threatening, raising serious questions about how to introduce university programming into a refugee camp community, without causing serious harm to women. Despite the challenges and even dangers involved, the participants we spoke to were enthusiastic about the benefits of a university education in their lives.

'Higher education has driven us into choosing career pathways' (Namarome, Ugandan woman student): The Benefits of Higher Education for Women, Their Families and Communities

Participants reported that higher education has given them the ability to envision alternative choices or pathways and hope that their opportunities for employment and mobility may be expanded. This finding from our interviews is aligned with other research on the importance of empowering or expanding 'people's ability to make strategic life choices in a context where this ability was previously denied to them' (Kabeer 1999, 437). In addition, accessing higher education and being able to complete the courses also opens doors for further educational opportunities and alternative pathways beyond the camp context. Enrolment in a B.A. programme through the BHER project, for instance, encouraged Grace, a co-author of this chapter, to move forward with an online Education M.A. graduate programme at York University.

According to one interviewee, participating in higher education programmes has also increased social cohesion between the different refugee communities as well as between refugee and host communities. A female participant noted that '[Pursuing] higher education has driven us into interacting with people [of] different calibres' (Aladit, Sudanese woman graduate). Specifically, being part of a higher education programme has introduced refugee women students to other refugees in the camps from different ethnicities and nationalities. This exposure has, according to some interviewees, led to opportunities to create meaningful relationships and interactions, which lead to mutual learning and increased cultural sensitivity.

Displacement separates people from their community and family members, leading to isolation and loss of social support. Often overcrowded, refugee camps are spaces where refugees may only know a few people and are mixed with people from other ethnic groups, leading to loneliness and an inability to relate (Horn, 2010; see also Andrade et al., 2001). Community groups such as women's church and youth groups are destabilized during displacement and the loss of social support is exacerbated. Even when entire communities are relocated, they may no longer function as a community (Horn, 2010; Wessells and Monteiro, 2004).

Social capital theory posits that engagement in the formation of social networks and voluntary organizations can be a source of confidence, a consistent source of reciprocal support and coping mechanisms (Putnam, 2000). Beyond increased social interactions and communication in the spaces of postsecondary education, women students interviewed in Kakuma reportedly also gained confidence through their engagement in post-secondary education programmes to create community groups outside the school. One participant expressed how she has developed leadership skills as a result of her studies: 'With higher education many are now able to run their own community-based organization in the refugee camp of Kakuma' (Zigashana, DRC woman student). Being connected with one another and able to create meaningful groups outside of the learning centres is also linked to a more existential finding that women who were enrolled in post-secondary education programmes say that they have gained the ability to think critically about their lives. When asked about the benefits of having access to higher education, one participant explained:

> [C]ritical thinking/problem-solving skills: in higher education, you are really required to think, as we are always [trying to] find the solutions to our problems. And through innovation, we are able to discover much each day.
>
> Mary, Rwandan, woman graduate

This finding is quite striking as it has been argued that social capital in refugee contexts is normally quite limited for women because they have 'few opportunities to develop social interaction and integration that would foster adaptation and assimilation in the host country' (Boateng 2010, 390). However, higher education through the BHER project, InZone, or JWL programmes has evidently offered a unique opportunity for women students to enhance their social capital within the camps. To this end, our results validate the perspective that tertiary education not only builds self-reliance and empowerment, but also equips refugees with the skills to come up with durable solutions for their communities (Zeus, 2010; Zeus and Chaffin, 2011). Indeed, there is a famous proverb in Kinyarwanda[6] that speaks to the significance of community problem-solving: *umutwe umwe ntiwigira inama*, which translates as, *one head cannot advise itself* (Sengupta and Blessinger, 2018).

Increased social cohesion and an increased sense of community responsibility towards solving problems or changing the status quo also relates to attempts to reduce gender discrimination and unequal gender relations, gender-based violence, and the mitigation of risks, as well as efforts to change social and cultural norms through sensitization processes. Our findings show that higher education spaces have given refugees that sense of support and community. Through an increase in access to support groups, they have been able to discuss issues such as gender-based violence and shift sociocultural norms. As one female participant noted: 'higher education has acted as a safe ground of sharing taboo issues such as domestic violence, female genital mutilation and other forms of violence' (Abir, South Sudanese woman graduate). According to another participant, more than anything, higher education has created a platform for women to discuss issues that impact their daily lives and has given them an opportunity to challenge cultural norms in a safe space.

Conclusion

In *Children of the Camp: The Lives of Somali Youth Raised in Kakuma Refugee Camp Kenya,* Grayson (2017) asserts that refugees in Kakuma are left in a state of limbo, with extremely limited opportunities for improving their livelihoods and that granting refugee rights is critical in order to improve their social, economic and political standing in society. We have illustrated in this chapter how a lack of rights to mobility, the inability for self-employment outside the camps and employment with a liveable income is not only gendered, but also extends to issues of and equity in access to higher education for refugee women in the context of Kakuma. While culture may be one of the contributing factors that impacts women's access to and continued enrolment in higher education, displacement and the politics of humanitarian aid and its limitations also contribute to the gender disparities in education access in contexts such as Kakuma.

This chapter has also shown that access to and participation in higher education is fundamental to overcoming and challenging the structural limitations that are endemic to protracted refugee situations, especially in camp contexts where rights and mobility are severely restricted. Higher education equips refugee women students with skills that can lead to better decision-making capabilities and skills that can transfer into improved livelihoods and numerous careers (Clark-Kazak, 2010). This is important for refugee women and their families, whether they return to their country of origin, or resettle in countries other than their own, to which they carry qualifications gained from education towards future training and new employment opportunities (El Jack, 2010; Plasterer and Wright, 2010; Zeus, 2010). There is also evidence from our participants that education spaces that promote gender equity (e.g. mixed classes of men and women; teaching practices that encourage women's active and informed participation), such as is found in the BHER project, also lead to a lessening of gender-based violence in a community.

3

The Challenges of Reciprocity and Relative Autonomy in North/South Partnerships

Josephine Gitome and Don Dippo

Contemporary and progressive approaches to establishing formal working relationships among universities for research and teaching purposes stress the importance of mutuality and reciprocity as foundational principles (Halvorsen and Nossum, 2017; Karim-Haji, Roy and Gough, 2016; Downes, 2013). At the same time, universities are heavily invested in preserving and protecting institutional autonomy, which is seen as one of the hallmarks of higher education (Bergan and Harkavy, 2019; Eastman, Jones, Begin-Caouette, Li, Noumi and Trottier, 2018; Shore and Taitz, 2012; Gutmann, 1983). In this chapter, we explore some of the challenges of establishing and maintaining a multi-university partnership, which grow out of the tensions sometimes created when trying to uphold both the principles of reciprocity and relative autonomy.

We begin by examining the global experiences of partnerships between the North and the South. Whereas BHER partnerships focus on higher education for refugees, other similar partnerships have focused on research, health and development (Yarmoshuk, Cole and Mwangu, 2019; Umoren, James and Litzelman, 2012). A few universities in the south including Moi and Kenyatta Universities have partnered with other humanitarian institutions to provide higher education and those experiences are considered here to give a comparative perspective on the BHER experience (see also Pilkington and Mbai in this volume). In the two sections that follow, we highlight structural impediments we confronted as partners, including challenges brought about by funding structures, and offer suggestions for future programs. As we then describe, partnerships of the kind in which we engaged need a prior understanding of each organization's institutional policies that are likely to affect the day-to-day running of the programs. For example, what became pertinent to our BHER partnership included academic assessment, the valuation of test scores and the use of tuition waivers, along with the question of religious affiliations and appropriate accommodation.

Unlike partnerships in many other Global South locations, Dadaab was a highly securitized site. In the latter part of the chapter, we try to shed light on the shifting social and political position of the refugee teacher in Dadaab. A context of insecurity and instability influenced not only the budget, but also each institution's capacity to deliver quality educational experiences to the student teachers enrolled in our programs.

Finally, the chapter concludes with a consideration of the place for personal commitment to the partnership and the creation of a collegial community of academicians with similar aims and interests in contributing positively to a durable, mutually beneficial North/South partnership. As faculty members at Kenyatta and York Universities, respectively, with BHER related teaching and administrative responsibilities, we have spent many hours over the years in formal meetings and less formal settings discussing the myriad of partnership related challenges that seemed, at times, about to threaten the viability of our work together. Yet in spite of these challenges, we are both of the view that our involvement in the BHER project ranks among the most meaningful and most satisfying experiences we have had as teachers and scholars. We offer these comments in the hope that they will encourage others to invest the time, effort and energy it takes to create partnerships to do the work that only partnerships can do.

What We Know about North/South University Partnerships

University partnerships are relationships among universities and other groups where members agree to collaborate in order to enhance their basic institutional mandates of teaching, research and community outreach. Universities stand to benefit from partnerships through student and faculty exchange programs, joint research projects, conference presentations and publications, as well as increased opportunities for international funding (Blessinger and Cozza, 2016; Chernikova, 2011; Giles and Dippo, 2019). While the benefits of cross-sectoral and inter-institutional partnerships might seem self-evident, their creation and continuance depend on finding ways to ensure that reciprocity remains mutual and that respect for autonomy is maintained.

Blessinger and Cozza (2016) assert that 80 per cent of any country's research is influenced by collaboration with researchers in other countries and that individual performance and institutional capacity are both enhanced through partnerships. The very concept of partnership has, however, been challenged by many scholars who note the structural imbalances that come with them (Nakabugo, Barrett, McEvoy and Munck, 2015; Downes, 2013; Ishengoma, 2016). Despite contributing immensely towards international development, building education capacity and helping to bridge the higher education knowledge divide, these partnerships have tended to operate on the assumption of a unidirectional transfer of capacity from the North to the South at the expense of mutual learning and responsiveness from both sides (Landau, 2012).

Downes (2013) provides a critical analysis of North/South educational partnerships in development contexts where he argues that the type of partnerships that should be promoted are founded on conditions such that authentic dialogue is possible. In horizontal relationships, he envisions actors who recognize each other as equals and participate in exchange relations considered mutually useful and enriching to both sides. Ishengoma (2016) notes that higher education partnerships are posited as instrumental and strategic in institutional capacity building, yet to date they have not significantly contributed to the strengthening of higher education in the South because of the inherent structural imbalances and inequalities embedded in such partnerships. However, as we begin to define the BHER project in the section that follows, we assert that reciprocity and mutuality are indeed achievable, but only in a context of respectful engagement that acknowledges the possibility of irreconcilable difference (see also Giles and Dippo, 2019).

Funding Assumptions and Reciprocity Challenges

In the beginning, BHER was supported by grants from the Social Sciences and Humanities Research Council of Canada (SSHRCC) and the Mastercard Foundation to develop our partnership and to conduct a feasibility study (Dippo, Orgocka and Giles, 2012). Funds that enabled BHER operations to begin, including the construction and equipping of the BHER Learning Centre, and the admission of a cohort of students, came from Global Affairs Canada (GAC), the international development arm of the Canadian federal government. Its mandate is to support poverty reduction initiatives in so-called 'developing countries' (Global Affairs Canada, 2019). GAC funds, which are defined as 'development funds', are understandably expected to be spent on materials, resources and activities that benefit people outside of Canada in poorer regions of the world.

Appreciative of the challenges described above, BHER took as a founding principle a commitment to reciprocity and mutual respect. Our project was conceptualized as a project where all parties would contribute and all parties would benefit. Canadian partners would contribute financial resources, administrative oversight, curriculum content, pedagogical approaches, library access and collegiality. Kenyan partners would contribute national reputation and credibility, physical infrastructure and personnel resources, local knowledge, curriculum content, pedagogical approaches, library access and collegiality. Such a working partnership would enable institutions, North and South, to reconsider vision, mission and mandate. It would enable programs at all partner universities to review core-offerings and programme requirements. It would enable faculty members to refresh the content of their courses and innovate in their approaches to pedagogy. The intent was that students in both Kenya and Canada would be the ultimate beneficiaries of such collaboration.

Such a vision of mutuality, however, does not fit easily into the assumptions that underpin most institutional approaches to international development. References to Canadian benefits in our foundational BHER documents (concept notes, draft proposals, etc.) were unusual, but vitally important. While the project is described in GAC project documents (annual and semi-annual reports) as one where Canadian expertise is employed to 'build capacity' in our Kenyan partners, there is also the recognition among members of the BHER consortium that the capacity of Canadian partners to deliver high quality, online learning opportunities will be enhanced in the process. The members of the BHER partnership, all experienced in other Global North/South partnerships, knew from the outset that if they were to work at developing genuine reciprocity and mutual benefit, foundational document templates that rest on counter-assumptions would have to be contested.

In the BHER partnership, we spoke openly and honestly about this issue at the outset of the BHER project. We reaffirmed our collective commitment to work together in ways that were honourable and ethical and that were premised on the assumption that each partner in the consortium would contribute to, and would benefit from, our work together. Historical, structural, institutional, cultural, political and interpersonal challenges notwithstanding, our aims and purposes were ambitious, and we needed each other to achieve them. Ultimately, the language and assumptions of the funding agreement, while imperfect, were not consequential enough to undermine our sense of collective purpose. Understandings worked out among members, however, are not always easily translated into practice.

Financial Arrangements and Institutional Autonomy

Faculty and staff from each of the partner institutions and organizations met in person or by videoconference throughout the year and regularly found solutions to the programmatic, curricular and operational problems that inevitably arose over the course of weeks or months. However, staff and administrators at each of our institutions who were not so directly involved in day-to-day BHER operations did not have the opportunity to develop an appreciation of the amount of flexibility, creativity and willingness to compromise that was necessary to keep this very complex project running smoothly. The expectation of strict adherence to each institution's own procedures and protocols was often the source of internal and inter-institutional tension. For example, because Global Affairs Canada does not consider tuition to be an eligible cost for tertiary education programs, the BHER funding model was based on the principle of cost-recovery. This approach to budgeting was very new to partner universities in both Canada and Kenya. We note, however, that cost-recovery modelling within higher education carries several options. In the broadest sense, there are typically three main categories of financing higher education: private financing, state financing and shared financing (Nkrumah-Young and Powell, 2011). However, according to Nkrumah-Young and Powell (2011), what is most important in implementing different cost-recovery models is being made aware of the contextual influences affecting higher education institutions (e.g. expense types, private donorship, or sole-state-providing). This message is further backed up by Bellino and Hure (2018), who examine financial support systems in the refugee camps in Kakuma, Kenya. They stress the importance of establishing clear timelines and procedures regarding financial matters, which all parties understand and agree to observe, to avoid negative consequences for refugee students.

In the case of the BHER project, the grant 'holder', York University (YU), assumed fiduciary and administrative responsibility for the distribution of funds to each of the partners. The process of meting out funds required certain deliverables having been met. However, this proved to be somewhat challenging since each institution had its own processes for providing deliverables and receipts. The usual procedure for distributing funds is that partner institutions are given an 'advance' to run programs. They can only request another advance after 80 per cent of the previous advance has been accounted for, or 'cleared', by providing receipts. If receipts are not provided, funds are not advanced and operations come to a halt (see also Kimari and Giles, 2020). In terms of creating and maintaining productive North/South relations, this structure presents on-going challenges. As holder of the grant and distributor of the funds, YU was often positioned as an inflexible and controlling partner using its financial authority to pressure other partners. On the other hand, YU sometimes saw their partners as irresponsible and unaccountable when it came to the management of funds.

For the university partners in Kenya, the requirement and processes of the funding agreement created many thorny experiences. The Kenyatta University (KU) financial systems were forced to adapt to another financial system, which was unfathomable to most of the university's financial officers, causing disputes at every stage of the process. These disputes and the related requirement to account for up to 80 per cent of the previous disbursement before new funds could be made available resulted in delays in students starting programs at the beginning of every semester. Thus, learning materials for the BHER students were often not available to them until weeks into semester activities (Kimari and Giles, 2020). In the next paragraph, we further unpack the case of KU in this regard.

The cost recovery model, a component of the funding agreement, meant that students would not pay individual fees, but instead, the donor would pay for learning equipment and instructional expenses. Ordinarily, KU focuses on an individual student's apportioned fees, and the University financial clerks and auditors do not have a policy or practice that allows them to consolidate students and apportion a tranche of money received as fees.[1] Furthermore, it is only after a student's fee has been sent to the individual student's account that the student can receive learning materials and access to the online module platform where they can interact with the lectures online.[2]

To further complicate matters, some of the required KU student fees, for example, the alumni fee or what is termed 'caution money', are not eligible under the GAC funding agreement. The financial implementing teams from both Kenyatta and York Universities had to work intensively to arrive at an agreement as to how both the requirements of GAC and KU could be met. In addition to these challenges, personnel changes at KU often meant that previously agreed to arrangements and understandings had to be repeatedly re-explained and renegotiated.

Taken together, these challenges meant that KU student access to course materials and their learning platform was frequently delayed, sometimes by months, because the BHER project financial officer at YU had to wait for receipts from KU to confirm expenses from the previous disbursement. While these were standard accounting procedures for North American universities, they were seen to be overly bureaucratic and somewhat superfluous by our Kenyan partners. Delayed registration often meant that BHER students had the additional challenge of catching up with course assignments past the deadlines of KU instructors. Given that online students are distant from the KU campus and do not have routine access to lecturers, the only opportunity to explain the complications of their predicament to an instructor would be on those occasions when KU instructors visited the Learning Centre in Dadaab. Incompatible requirements, by the donors, the Canadian host university and KU routinely put BHER students' success in their courses in jeopardy. These procedures delayed students' academic progress and were frequently cited by students as the primary reason for dropping out of the program. In addition, these persistent difficulties added a significant measure of counselling, liaising and advocacy work for the KU faculty and staff who supported the BHER initiative.

When we found ourselves in the 'no funds without receipts, no programs without funds' conundrum, students suffered, and project faculty criticized each other's institutions for being inflexible and unreasonable. 'Why,' KU faculty would ask, 'can't YU just release the funds so that we can open the portal for students? YU knows the receipts will be forthcoming.' 'Why,' YU faculty would respond, 'can't KU just open the portal for students? KU knows the funds will be forthcoming.' A measure of trust on the part of finance departments at both KU and YU might have led to a quick and lasting resolution of this persistent irritant, which constantly threatened to undo any goodwill that had been re-established among colleagues since the last occurrence. But instead, institutional partners at YU and KU acted as if receipts might not be forthcoming or funding might be withheld. So that while project partners (e.g. BHER faculty and staff) worked continuously at building trust and mutual respect, institutional partners (e.g. university finance and accounting departments) seemed unable to move beyond mutual suspicion.

The experiences described above are not uncommon. Projects are created with ambitious curricular, pedagogic and programmatic goals in mind. Financial arrangements are not ordinarily the stuff of dreams, and fiscal safeguards may unfortunately not be accorded the time and attention they deserve. Commenting on collaboration in international development projects, Bailey and Dolan (2011) emphasize the importance of establishing 'respect, trust, reciprocity and transparency' (p. 34) in partnership matters. Woldegiorgis and Scherer (2019) reflect on another partnership troubled by financial issues by examining the Mwalimu Nyerere mobility programme in Tanzania, which was a pioneering attempt to create higher education partnerships among African institutions. The programme began in 2007, and by 2008 was facing challenges associated with unanticipated growth. A proposal to cut costs by waiving tuition for students in their host university was suggested by the funder, but was dismissed by partners as being ineffective in that programmes such as these are dependent on student fees for financial viability. Woldegiorgis and Scherer conclude that there are no simple answers to the challenges of financing partnerships in higher education (Woldegiorgis and Scherer, 2019).

It would be a mistake to underestimate the threats to project viability that financial challenges caused to our partnership, particularly toward the end of the GAC funded project when it became clear that KU students had not yet satisfied requirements for graduation and yet funds were coming to an end. Issues to do with financial process and controls, with who has the power to release or withhold funds, with jurisdictional issues defining where one institution's financial control begins and ends, are issues that need thorough discussion before funding agreements can be concluded and implementation commences. In their discussion of intrinsically unequal power relations in international partnership development, Bailey and Dolan (2011) stress that it is important that partners openly address the issue of power in terms of project ownership, decision-making, funding, planning and evaluation, as well as the power relations of partnership management and practice. This, they argue, should be discussed and resolved well before implementing a project, so that solutions can be found to potential problems where institutions have policies that do not concur with the donor's expectations. These are, of course, good suggestions, but in our experience good planning and a thorough airing of partnership power relations are no guarantee that such issues will not re-emerge in an on-going way throughout the life of a project. More important may be structures of routine engagement and embedded systems of formative assessment that help clarify expectations, assist in the creation of greater levels of mutuality, and develop basic institutional, cross-cultural structures and procedures of operation. While financial challenges impact overall project administration, there are other kinds of structural impediments, discussed below, that complicate day-to-day project operations.

Student Access, Inclusion and Accommodation

The Kenya Certificate of Secondary School Education (KCSE)

Students in Canada certainly take exams, but there is no exam in Canada quite like the Kenya Certificate of Secondary School Education, commonly known as the KCSE. Strict adherence to access to higher education based on KCSE scores was difficult for Canadian partners to understand, especially in the context of Dadaab, where admission based on KCSE scores had such a profoundly negative effect on access to higher education for women. Our collective aspirations regarding gender equity for women and girls were routinely and inevitably undermined by strict adherence to the test score policy. In Canada, we did not understand the significance of this exam in Kenyan thinking about access to higher education. We routinely tried to convince our Kenyan colleagues that the exam was an unreliable measure of a student's potential to succeed in higher education. We pointed out the obvious gendered implications of using KCSE scores as the sole basis for admission to the programmes we were intending to offer in Dadaab. We emphasized the challenges such an admissions process would pose to our collective BHER commitment to gender equity. Ultimately, we had to invoke the importance of respect for institutional autonomy in North/South relations to justify institution-specific admissions processes that we all understood as clearly inequitable and contrary to overall project goals. Yet the picture is even more complex.

The KCSE is regulated by the Kenyan National Examination Council (KNEC). This replaced the East African Certificate of Education (EACE), a secondary school examination taken by students in the last class of secondary school. KCSE was established in 1989 as the new entrance requirement for entry to Kenyan Universities. It can be compared to the General Certificate of Secondary Education (GCSE) level of education taken in England, Northern Ireland and other previously colonized British territories.

KCSE results became significant to the BHER Partnership because the Kenyan accrediting body, which is the Commission for University Education (CUE) standards, regulate admission criteria and whoever does not have the qualification for either certificate, diploma, or degree admission is simply not admissible, no matter what grades the applicant may have gathered after KCSE. The Kenyan Universities' admission officers' hands are rigidly tied to CUE criteria with no alterations allowed whatsoever (for critique of this issue see the chapter by Abikar et al. in this volume). While the programmes offered through all four universities linked to the BHER project included many highly qualified students, students with lower KCSE grades than allowed by CUE were also admitted. This meant that a curriculum model had to be developed that would enable students who were capable, but deemed inadmissible to Kenyan universities, to find admission to university programmes – in this case, at YU. Programmatically, this was an adequate solution insofar as it meant that all BHER students who were successful in their courses could continue to study and progress towards a degree. It did, however, undermine efforts to develop clearly articulated partnership principles and practices, especially related to gender equity.

Often refugee students in Dadaab have yet another challenge when it comes to admissions and credit waivers/recognition. Some bring secondary school certificates from their home countries, which are supposed to be KCSE equivalent, but these certificates need equivalency ratification through the Kenyan National Examination Council (KNEC). The Council has guidelines for equivalencies for local and foreign applicants, but some of the requirements do not accommodate the refugee situation, especially where the applicant's home country examination regulating body does not respond to KNEC request for equivalency procedures. This leaves some refugee students, especially those from racial and ethnic minorities, ineligible to apply for admission to Kenyan diploma and degree programmes offered through Moi University and KU. These policies, once again, raise legitimate questions about the depth of the BHER Partnership commitment to admissions equity.

The KCSE standard regulation posed a challenge to the principle of credit transfer (Canada), credit waiver (Kenya) and credit recognition.[3] The tensions created over questions of 'transferability' of credits from one BHER partner institution to another BHER partner institution served to threaten the viability of the partnership. The principle of credit transfer and credit recognition was one of the foundational principles of the BHER partnership. Yet often results of transfer/waiver negotiation and renegotiation stalled or even derailed the process of graduation. Despite the agreement in principle, each student's grades had to be reconsidered in view of previous certificates that determined admission in the first place and had a bearing on the number of credits to be transferred or waived. As much as BHER students had a common policy applied to them, the process of qualifying for admission or credit waiving was done individually as per grades acquired at KCSE level. It is a rigorous process, overseen by the Registrar, and refugee students whose documents come from elsewhere or who have credits for courses they were later deemed ineligible to take (based on KCSE scores) have issues and questions that complicate matters even more. Consideration of processes of admissions, credit transfer and credit recognition requirements by each partners' governing policies may appear to be well understood at the early stages of partnership development. In our experience, it is important to have those principled understandings in writing and endorsed by senior officials at each partner university. Over the course of a multi-year project, it is likely that at least a few of those senior university officials will move on and take their understandings and commitments with them. A document that attests to those commitments will be invaluable when it comes to reaffirming the principles that underpin the partnership in response to changing circumstances and contexts.

Religious Rights

Among the potential threats to viable university partnerships in general, and North/South partnerships in particular, is the assumption that one partner institution has correct (or better) policies and procedures, which ought to be adopted by the other partners. This is complicated when matters in question are 'legal' and particularly delicate, as when they have to do with human rights. Across Canada, the Charter of Rights and Freedoms and various provincial human rights codes seek to ensure that no person experiences discrimination based on age, ancestry, citizenship, colour, creed, disability, ethnic origin, family status and marital status, place of origin, race, record of offenses, sex, or sexual orientation (Ontario, 1962). Schools, colleges and universities are expected to make reasonable accommodations that would enable students to satisfy course and programme requirements.

In the context of Dadaab, activities are organized in a way that accommodates mid-day prayer for the majority Muslim population. There are very few activities on Sunday to accommodate the largely Christian NGO staff. Among the BHER student population, there are also Seventh Day Adventist students who worship on Saturday. To accommodate these students, group-work, tutorials, video screenings, etc. were often scheduled on alternative days. Examinations were another matter. At KU there is a prohibition against scheduling alternatives to regularly scheduled exam days, the thinking being that the content of the exams would be 'leaked' by the students if they sat the exams before everyone else, or 'leaked' to the students if they see the exams after others have done it. This is not an unreasonable concern, but one that might be addressed and accommodated if there was a policy of reasonable accommodation. The strain on North/South relations comes about when we, in the North, expect compliance from our Southern partners to *our* regulatory regimes. In this instance, the Adventist students had no choice. If they wanted to study, they would have to enrol in programmes offered by Canadian universities. In that sense, they were accommodated in the BHER project for their coursework. But it speaks once again to the issues of authenticity, mutual trust and respect, willingness on the part of partners to accommodate each other's autonomy, institutional independence, priorities and commitments.

The universities in Kenya are obliged to listen to the students' religious needs, but only to the extent that befits the general policy of the university on solving the problem. Universities are not obliged to provide religious accommodation. In this case, all BHER students undertook an Online, Distance and E-Learning (ODEL, n.d.) mode of study whose activities in KU in all ODEL centres were carried out over the weekend. This meant that on any of the days from Friday to Sunday there would be students missing classes or exams because each of the three are worship days for either Seventh Day Adventist (SDA), Muslim, or Christian students.

The Kenyan students and faculty normally forego worship to attend classes in the event that the activity falls on their day of worship. In Dadaab, there were cases of students who worshiped on Saturday and could not bring themselves to come and sit exams after worship. This was one of those experiences observed to be challenging to the KU administration in the experience of BHER in Dadaab. This was mainly because the exams for an ODEL course are set for many students, not just students in Dadaab, and specifications to set the SDA students on Friday or Sunday did not quite fit the university schedule because in any one exam period, several students had to sit the exam. All other ODEL students whose exams were set on their day of worship managed to sit the exams despite the worship day. Unfortunately, every time a solution for an alternative exam was set, some of the SDA students' exams were held on a Saturday. KU expects students to appreciate the urgency of sitting the exam on a weekend and considers it a short term and one-off process after which students could go back to routine religious observance. At least that is what happens to all other KU students in similar circumstances.

This matter of examination days was not the only challenge to providing religious accommodation to our students. Other issues came up during Physical Education lessons whereby female students would not remove the hijab even for swimming lessons. The swimming instructor also had to be female. In similar classes at KU in Nairobi, female Muslim students routinely remove their hijabs, change into swimsuits and accept the instructor regardless of gender. Their compliance does not rule out the need for a policy on accommodating students' religious requirements. At the end of the day, with or without a policy, the BHER women were accommodated in their Physical Education classes by being permitted to participate wearing the hijab, including in the pool.

Returning to the themes of reciprocity and autonomy, the idea of 'partnership' assumes that two or more autonomous agents (or institutions) will come together to explore ways in which to collaborate, to learn from each other, and to benefit from mutual engagement. For this to happen, parties to the partnership agreement must be prepared to question and be questioned about current practices, the assumptions that underpin them and their implications. If KU had a clear policy on religious accommodation, the SDA students would have had a base from which to argue further for their case for examination day accommodation; furthermore, the accommodation made for the swimming students would be the rule rather than the exception.

A Shifting Social and Political Landscape

The smooth running of a North/South partnership is also affected by local social and political contexts and dynamics. The BHER partnership had to rethink its aims, purposes and especially its public profile when a tripartite agreement between Kenya, Somalia and UNHCR was signed in 2013. The agreement announced plans for the imminent closure of the Dadaab refugee camps. The majority of BHER students are Somalis, and the tripartite agreement assumed a systematic and orderly, voluntary repatriation of Somali refugees. In addition, the Kenyan government had initiated a process whereby all non-Somali refugees would be relocated to the camps in Kakuma in northwest Kenya. There was discussion among the partners as to the appropriateness of such a response to security concerns in the region. There was discussion about the 'voluntary-ness' of repatriation in practice. There were questions raised among partners about if and how BHER should respond to the impacts of the agreement on our students. Canadian partners and Kenyan partners were not of a single mind. What we all understood was that if BHER was seen as an obstacle to implementation of the agreement to close the Dadaab camps, we could easily be asked to shut down operations there. So rather than raise our collective voice regarding our concerns about the agreement, we instead put in place programme structures and technologies that would enable students who moved from Dadaab to Kakuma, or to parts of Somalia, to continue their studies. In addition, KU negotiated MOUs (memoranda of understanding) with two universities in Somalia, whereby examinations could be administered without requiring students in Somalia to return to Dadaab.

On other occasions, sociopolitical events and resulting decisions posed challenges to BHER budget forecasting and programme support and threatened to derail study progress. An example was the response of the Kenyan federal government after the Al-Shabab attack on Garissa University College on 2 April 2015. The government gave instructions that enhanced armed security must be provided for all institutions in Garissa County whenever classes were held. This demand required partners to reorganize their budgets, often cutting support for programmes to accommodate the new security expenses. In the case of BHER, the field staff could no longer use the accommodation facility built for them in the BHER Learning Centre and instead needed to be relocated inside the UNHCR compound. Again, the project budget had to be adjusted to provide for their safety and partners had to come to an agreement as to where to make cuts to programme support.

Personal Commitments and the Creation of a Collegial Community

Those engaged in the BHER project share a responsibility to work to maintain the smooth functioning and integrity of the partnership, and by so doing remain committed to the political and pedagogical vision that is sustaining our North/South collaboration. In these efforts, the significance of the interpersonal dimensions of our work together cannot and should not be ignored. Over the nearly ten years that we have worked together, faculty, staff and teaching assistants have acted under tremendous pressure, have forged ahead with work that needed doing despite floods, sickness, security incidents, labour disputes and more, and have developed an appreciation for each other's contributions and a pleasure in each other's colleagueship.

We have enjoyed each other's company at work in the field, in meetings, travels and conferences. This is an indicator of the health of collegial relationships as confirmed by Blessinger and Cozza (2016), who note that effective partnerships start with valuing the opinions and contributions of all participants. They note that when partners engage in caring and thoughtful dialogue, they gain understanding and appreciation of the differences in people (Blessinger and Cozza, 2016). Partnerships continue to grow as the project is growing. We have strengthened our relationship with Lutheran World Federation (LWF), the implementing partner for all primary schools in Dadaab, and the Somali National University (SNU) in their efforts to rebuild public schooling in Somalia. We note that in our experience of working together and reaching out to new partners who share our aims and purposes, we have also developed a collective resilience to working in a fragile context, and an understanding of refugee students not only as individuals, but also as members of communities with cultures to be recognized, respected and engaged.

'Collegial community' implies a certain quality of social relationships involving participants from different viewpoints, roles and regions. Like North/South institutional partnerships, collegial communities are built on the expectation of, and commitment to, reciprocity and mutual benefit while respecting the autonomy of individual members. The BHER partnership fostered collegiality by giving every individual member a chance to speak in meetings, and to play their role in the field without interference from other partners even when it was evident the approaches were different from one partner to another (for further discussion of this issue, see the chapter by Miller et al. in this volume). This enabled members to develop and maintain respectful relations among participants.

We can say that, in our experience, North/South partnerships are based on collaborations that cultivate collegial relationships that help to demystify any power differences among partners and between partners. With social mediation at BHER, leaders were able to bring together people from different backgrounds to not only work together towards common goals efficiently, but also to develop interest in, and scholarship about, the field of refugee education. This is an area that was non-existent in KU's curricular and programme offerings, yet it was and is now covered in the university's strategic plan objectives. The BHER partnership has inspired other scholars and humanitarian groups to see and respond to the need to form similar higher education for refugee partnerships across the globe. Such groups include the Connected Learning in Crisis Consortium (CLCC) established in 2015, the Local Engagement Refugee Research Network (LERRN), which is in its initial stages of formation, and many others. The interest in higher education for refugees among the humanitarian and development organizations has become more pronounced through the efforts of BHER and others and we now expect more and more improvement in the lives of refugee youth globally.

Conclusion

Despite the above-mentioned challenges, partners in the BHER consortium remain committed to working together. We view our ten-year collaboration as a remarkable achievement. We are reminded daily, in small and profound ways, that the work we do together is consequential. We are gratified to have pioneered this type of partnerships. We have demonstrated that balancing reciprocity and autonomy, while difficult, is not impossible. More and more institutions of higher learning have built on the BHER partnership structure and established similar partnership to address higher education gaps among the refugees in camps[4] as well as urban settings.

We have seen, over time, a significant improvement in the quality of teaching and learning in schools in Dadaab. We see our work with teachers as contributing to the overall safety, security and well-being of children, their families and their communities. As our students complete their studies and assume leadership positions in schools, community organizations, international NGOs and the emergent civil society in Somalia, we see our work as supporting efforts to establish peace and sustainable prosperity in the region.

4

Development of a Community Health Education Degree Programme through a North-South Collaboration: Lessons Learned

F. Beryl Pilkington and Isabella I. Mbai

Introduction

This chapter presents the authors' experience of a collaboration between their two academic institutions (York University and Moi University) during the development of an undergraduate degree programme in Community Health Education (CHEd) at Moi University (MU) that would be accessible to students living in the Dadaab refugee camps and the surrounding host community. We describe the gestation of the programme idea and how it was brought to fruition through our intensive collaboration between 2014 and 2016. The idea of this community health education initiative was conceived in 2012, when, along with several colleagues from the Borderless Higher Education for Refugees (BHER) project, we connected via Skype to explore the possibility of collaborating to develop a health-related programme to add to BHER programme offerings. Inspired by the BHER project, we envisioned a programme that produced graduates who in turn could improve Dadaab refugee and host communities' access to basic health services. Moreover, the education model could be used in other settings that host refugees. Our purpose in this chapter is to reflect on the successes, challenges and lessons learned from this North-South[1] collaboration to create a community health education programme with the hope of informing others considering such an undertaking elsewhere.

The original aim of the BHER project was to offer access to higher education to refugees serving as teachers so that they could obtain teaching credentials, which would ultimately improve the quality of primary and secondary school education in Dadaab. However, early on, a feasibility study conducted by Dippo,

Orgocka and Giles (2012) showed that not all refugee-teachers necessarily wanted to pursue teaching as a career. Hence, the leaders of the BHER project began seeking other programme options. In 2011, one of us (Pilkington) was invited to join the project to work on a health option. Initially, nursing was considered; however, while medical and nursing education programmes would have been welcome, both require health infrastructure and educational resources not available in the Dadaab area. The Dadaab refugee camps are a protracted displacement situation with an acute shortage of health professionals and limited resources and infrastructure. The host community members who live in the area around the camps, including in the town of Dadaab, experience similar conditions to the refugees. In the camps, basic health services are mostly provided by humanitarian nongovernmental organizations (NGOs) that utilize refugee incentive workers[2] trained as community health workers (CHWs). However, their training is quite limited and does not adequately prepare them to deal with the challenges arising in this context.

From the outset, our unique positions enabled us to see the potential contribution of a community health education programme to the BHER project. We are both faculty members in university Schools of Nursing: Pilkington at York University (YU), Toronto, Canada and Mbai at Moi University (MU), Eldoret, Kenya. Mbai has a background in community health and a graduate degree in health education/promotion, while Pilkington has a background in maternal-child and women's health and coordinates an interdisciplinary undergraduate programme in Global Health. As such, both of us recognized the intersection of community health and education as fields of study as well as practice. Moreover, we believed that a community health education programme could help to address the scarcity of health human resources in the camps by preparing graduates who could assist with the provision of basic health services and, in the longer term, provide leadership for the development of health services on their return to the country of origin (for most, Somalia).

In the sections that follow, we begin by reflecting on our positions as co-leaders in the development of a community health education programme. Next, we describe and contemplate the successes and challenges we encountered while conducting a collaborative research project in Dadaab that led to the community health education programme at MU, with team members located on separate continents and in different time zones, with limited internet connectivity and financial constraints. Finally, we summarize key lessons learned. We hope that our exploration of the successes and challenges experienced and how we overcame the challenges will help to inform future North-South initiatives.

Reflection on Our Positionalities

The term 'positionality' is used in qualitative research to indicate the researcher's stance or position in relation to the social or political context of a study (Coghlan and Brydon-Miller, 2014). It involves 'reflexivity', that is, critical reflection upon one's thoughts, actions and biases, which in turn arise from one's identities, roles and experiences, and influence how one approaches and participates in research and other scholarly endeavours (Agee et al., 2011). Here, we disclose aspects of our respective identities, roles and experiences to provide readers with additional context for understanding the North-South collaboration discussed in this chapter. To aid clarity, we refer to ourselves in the first person.

I (Pilkington) am a white, female, second-generation Canadian of English heritage, educated in Canada and the United States (PhD). As such, I am a member of the European settler class whose history includes subjugation of colonized peoples and appropriation of their resources and lands. My academic and professional background is in nursing (maternal-child and women's health) and includes a practice position under the auspices of CUSO in Nigeria in 1992. This was a formative experience that heightened my awareness of issues of equity and social justice in health and health care. More recently, as a tenured professor at YU, I was able to obtain funding for our project from Canada's International Development Research Centre (IDRC), which was administered by YU. Reflection on my biographical situation reveals unearned privilege and unequal access to power through my European ancestry, academic position in a developed country, and as the holder of the grant that funded our project. Keeping this power imbalance in mind prompted me to focus on seeking equity and sharing power throughout the project.

I (Mbai) am a black African female of Kenyan origin and citizenship, educated in both Kenya and the United Kingdom (MSc). I am a nurse experienced in both nursing and midwifery education, administration and collaborative research, currently a senior lecturer at Moi University, Kenya. In various capacities, I was able to direct several research projects that are community-oriented that target disadvantaged members of the community, including orphans, street children and, most recently, the refugee population. This experience is what enabled me to engage in the partnership with YU that facilitated the development of the first higher education health-related programme in a refugee setting in Kenya. Aside from this, my passion for healthcare and healthcare education, particularly for the less fortunate in the community, drew me to this project, as I expected that it would result in higher education being available to an otherwise unreachable population.

Theoretical Foundations

The research project that informed the CHEd Programme development (see Pilkington, Mbai and Abuelaish, 2016) was informed, in part, by research and theoretical literature on the concept of partnership. Accordingly, the partnership between YU, MU and several NGO stakeholders in this project (the Kenya Red Cross, Windle International Kenya (WIK) and the International Rescue Committee) became a key component in the evaluation of our work together. For the purposes of evaluation, we utilized and adapted a version of the Partnership Assessment Toolkit (PAT) developed by the Canadian Coalition for Global Health Research with support from IDRC (Afsana et al., 2009). The PAT was developed through consultations with colleagues in Africa, South Asia and Latin America, drawing on a review of literature and project outcomes. It was created 'to openly and candidly address the persistent problems facing health research partnerships', while facilitating partnerships that are equitable, mutually beneficial and 'lead to increased health equity' (Afsana et al., 2009, p. 4–5). We selected the PAT based on its congruence with the assumptions underpinning our collaboration and because it can be utilized to guide continuous monitoring and evaluation. We assumed that to be effective, our health research partnership would not only require completion of our research project but also all parties would be engaged in ways that were just and beneficial and the research would lead to increased health equity. Outcome indicators for evaluation purposes included symmetry between partners in building research and health education capacity, challenge mitigation (i.e. of challenges foreseen and unforeseen), and the quality of communication among the research partners at MU and YU.

A second focal topic in the project was that of community health worker (CHW) education. How CHWs should be educated raises questions around gender equity, health equity, health system sustainability and more (Bhutta et al., 2010; Ehiri et al., 2014; Ingram et al., 2012). CHWs are used in many countries, especially in rural settings and in low- and middle-income countries, to assist with delivery of primary health care (Bhutta et al., 2010). Usually women and members of the community without formal training, CHWs are assigned to specific primary health care centres or small populations. In Africa, CHWs mainly work under the supervision of community extension workers who are trained professionals. Research aimed at evaluating the utilization of CHWs globally suggests that their impact on health outcomes varies depending on how they are trained, supervised and utilized, and the status of the respective countries' health and economic systems (Bhutta et al., 2010). There has been limited research on the capacity of refugees and internally displaced persons living in camps to provide health services to others living in the camps (Ehiri et al., 2014). In the research conducted during this project, we investigated the utilization of refugees as CHWs to provide basic health care services in Dadaab, including current training and gaps in training (Mangeni et al., 2016). The purpose of the research was to inform the development of an education programme and model for building health care capacity in disadvantaged communities in Kenya (and ultimately, Somalia) by utilizing the cross-sector experience and expertise of Canadian and Kenyan universities and NGOs (Pilkington et al., 2016).

Successes

Below, we describe our key successes: obtaining funding, completing the collaborative research project, and developing the new Bachelor of Science in Community Health Education (BSc CHEd) degree programme. We then reflect on the things that made these successes possible.

Obtaining Funding

The purpose of our collaboration was to develop a community health education programme to add to the degree offerings available under the BHER project. However, the BHER funding envelope did not include development of a health education programme, but rather aspects of the implementation of the degree. Therefore, we looked to the IDRC for research funding under its 'Small Grants for Innovative Research and Knowledge-Sharing' programme (no longer available). Our first application in September 2013 was unsuccessful, but a resubmission in March 2014 (titled 'Researching the Gap between the Existing and Potential Community Health Worker Education and Training in the Refugee Context: An Intersectoral Approach' – hereafter, 'feasibility study') was successful, and we were awarded CA$60,000 for two years. This award covered an MU Research Consultant/Coordinator (Judith Mangeni), Research Assistant (RA) (Cosmas Apaka), four community researchers (CRs), two workshops (before and after the fieldwork), travel and accommodation to attend the workshops, and related research expenses. It also covered the cost of an independent evaluation of the MU-YU project and partnership, the findings of which we have drawn upon in this chapter.

Completion of the Collaborative Research

The feasibility study was successfully completed in 2015, and detailed reports are available elsewhere (Pilkington et al., 2016; Mbai et al., 2017). Here, we summarize the methodology and key findings.

Methodology

A community-based approach was used to obtain the participation of key stakeholders who could assist with achieving the research goal (Pilkington et al., 2016). Before starting the fieldwork, a workshop was held at MU in Eldoret, 18–19 September 2014, which was attended by academic researchers from MU and YU, representatives from three NGOs (Windle International Kenya (WIK), Kenya Red Cross and International Rescue Committee) and Kenya's Ministry of Health (MOH), and three of four refugees from Dadaab trained as CRs. We tried to achieve gender parity in hiring CRs but were only able to recruit one woman who met the position requirements, as follows: Form 4 graduate, resident of the Dadaab camps; relevant work experience; good Somali and English oral and written language skills; willingness to conduct interviews and focus group discussions; and internet and computer skills. All the CRs spoke English and were either enrolled in, or had completed, a teacher education programme. Following the workshop, the CRs conducted fieldwork in Dadaab that consisted of focus group discussions (FGDs) and in-depth individual interviews at each of four sites (Dadaab town, and Hagadera, Dagahaley and Ifo camps). As members of the community, CRs were able to access the targeted groups and gain their trust. Four FGDs were held with BHER students (thrity-one in total), all of whom were untrained refugee teachers enrolled in a BHER related Certificate or Diploma in Education. Participants were asked about their interest in a community health degree programme, their questions/concerns about a community health degree programme, and their suggestions concerning development of such a programme. In addition, four FGDs were conducted with NGO-certified CHWs (thirty-one in total) regarding their job responsibilities, the knowledge and skills required, and gaps in their education and training. These CHWs were refugee incentive workers who had received brief training from the Kenya Red Cross or the International Rescue Committee. Finally, individual interviews were conducted with various MOH and NGO health staff (twelve in total) regarding health issues and priorities in the camps and the training and education needs of CHWs. FGDs and interviews were audio-recorded and transcribed by the CRs in January 2015. The quality of the data gathered by the CRs is very detailed and rich, an indication that those interviewed trusted the CR interviewers. In our view, participants may not have felt as comfortable answering questions posed by academic researchers.

The transcripts of the FGDs and interviews were analysed separately by the Kenyan research team (Mbai, Mangeni and Apaka) and Pilkington (in Canada) using thematic and content analysis approaches. This preliminary analysis was circulated for review and feedback, after which a final, consensus draft was prepared. The findings and their implications for the development of a new community health degree programme were subsequently discussed at a second workshop held in Nairobi in early June 2015 (Pilkington et al., 2016).

Findings

Our findings identified significant health challenges and key health priorities in the refugee camps and Dadaab town, as well as gaps in the education and training of refugee CHWs with respect to addressing these challenges and priorities. Health challenges included the harsh environmental conditions, disease outbreaks, and children who are malnourished and not immunized. In addition, illiteracy, poor help-seeking behaviour for health problems and frequent cross-border migrations among the refugee population also affected mental and physical health. Key health issues included maternal, infant and 'under-five' mortality, female genital mutilation (FGM), and the poor quality of care at health facilities due to a lack of equipment, medicines and trained health workers. In sum, the main health priorities were maternal-child health, preventive and health promotive services including nutrition and water, sanitation, and hygiene (WASH), and clinical care (Mangeni et al., 2016; Mbai et al., 2017).

Health staff and CHW participants in our study identified similar gaps in CHW education and training in areas ranging from general health knowledge, to disease surveillance and control and Kenya's community health strategy. In addition, the CHWs said they would like further knowledge and training specifically around HIV/AIDS, FGM, family planning, drugs and drug abuse, crisis management, strategic management and environmental health. The latter areas were mentioned in answer to the question: 'Are there any areas of your work or responsibilities as a CHW for which you feel you were not very well prepared by your education programme or training? What additional knowledge or training do you think would be helpful?' Moreover, the majority (84 per cent) of CHWs indicated a lack of training on mental health. Overall, health staff and CHW participants thought that CHW education should provide a better theoretical foundation and opportunities to practice newly learned skills (Mangeni et al., 2016; Pilkington et al., 2016).

BHER students (who were currently pursuing teacher education) and CHW participants similarly expressed strong interest in the concept of a degree programme focused on community health (Pilkington et al., 2016). Almost unanimously, CHWs said they would pursue such a programme if they had an opportunity, although some didn't have the necessary educational background. Likewise, twenty-four out of thirty-one BHER students (77 per cent) indicated they would consider this option, if available. Their main reasons were opportunities for career development and to serve their community. These current students raised questions and concerns related to the quality and credibility of the proposed programme, admission criteria and access, location and mode of teaching and learning, relevance/marketability of the programme and cost/availability of sponsorship. They also suggested that those who developed the programme ensure that it would be an accredited university programme with a comprehensive curriculum and a practical focus, and that there should be equitable access, gender balance and sensitivity (Pilkington et al., 2016).

In summary, our 'Researching the Gap' feasibility study was successful in yielding vital information necessary to understand the health context in Dadaab and the education needs of community health education professionals in this context. Moreover, through jointly conducting the study, we (the MU and YU research partners) increased our capacity to collaborate on the CHEd programme development, which happened concurrently.

Development of the BSc CHEd Degree Programme

As indicated above, curriculum development for the new BSc CHEd programme happened concurrently with the 'Researching the Gap' study. This was necessary, because this CHEd project joined the larger BHER project that was well underway, leaving a two-year window within which the new programme would have to be launched in order to ensure that implementation could be funded by BHER. However, research resources were leveraged to support concurrent programme development; for instance, the research coordinator also led programme development. In addition, the concurrent initiatives were possible because we had anticipated the kind of community health education programme that the Dadaab context called for, and the MU School of Nursing had many relevant courses that could be adapted for the new programme, including Behavioural Science and

Ethics, Introduction to Community Health, Basic Skills in Healthcare, and Research Methodology and Project. In addition, several courses from the new BA/BSc Global Health programme at YU (e.g. Social Determinants of Health, Health and Human Rights, Communicable Diseases and Care, Chronic Diseases and Care, Programme Planning and Evaluation) were well aligned with the needs in Dadaab and also provided curriculum ideas for the CHEd programme.

After completion of the study, a knowledge translation workshop was held in Nairobi, 4–5 June 2015, to discuss findings and their implications for programme development. At this workshop, representatives from the School of Nursing at MU shared a draft proposal for the BSc CHEd programme for discussion. In addition, workshop participants discussed insights from the research in relation to the curriculum and the implementation structure for the proposed new programme. Interdisciplinary in its approach, the programme that resulted incorporated curriculum ideas from MU's BSc Nursing programme, MU's Teacher Education Diploma programme and YU's Global Health BA/BSc programme. Based on our research findings, we also developed new courses to fill gaps in the draft curriculum; for example, Disease Surveillance, Drug Substance Abuse and Society; Conflict Management and Resolution; and Risk Reduction during Emergencies/Disasters. A key consideration was the continued use and sustainability of the new programme; thus, it was designed not only for students in Dadaab but for all qualified MU students. The new BSc CHEd programme was approved by the MU Senate on 09 December 2015. Subsequently, the programme had two launches: the first, in July 2016 in Dadaab; and the second, in August 2017 in Eldoret. A total of forty-four students enrolled in the programme, twenty-six in Dadaab (with a retention rate of 81 per cent). An important feature of the programme was the incorporation of online and blended modes of learning (online, face-to-face and practical). This flexibility in online course delivery contributed to education capacity building at MU, where most faculty were relatively new to online forms of distance learning. As of the time of writing, three graduates are reported to have obtained government jobs, but it is still too early to judge the broader impact of improved access to health care on the Dadaab community.

Challenges

The formative evaluation[3] of the project conducted by an external evaluator (Douhaibi, 2016) identified some core challenges faced by the partnership, which included financial, communication and security concerns in the Dadaab region.

We addressed each of these challenges by seeking to mitigate the issue(s) causing difficulty.

Financial Issues

An issue for the BHER collaboration (and perhaps for collaborations or partnerships in general) was having sufficient resources to meet the needs of all partners. Because our collaboration was initiated after the BHER project launched, development of the BSc CHEd programme was not included in BHER's funding envelope. Instead, as mentioned earlier, the development of the partnership was supported by IDRC funds that could only be spent on approved research activities completed within a two-year timeframe (1 August 2014 to 30 September 2016). We leveraged the IDRC grant by proceeding with the curriculum/programme development aspect of our collaboration concurrent with the research. For instance, the research coordinator (Mangeni) also worked with MU faculty on curriculum development and drafted the new programme proposal. Unfortunately, at the outset, due to administrative funding processes at IDRC and YU, MU's access to funds was delayed until after the project had started, and the slow rate of transfer of funds between YU and MU[4] meant that MU could not pay the community researchers until after they had completed three months of work. This delay caused hardship for the CRs (who essentially had to self-fund their research activities) and stress for the MU team responsible for paying them. Unfortunately, the bureaucracies of government funders and academic institutions make them unable to respond with flexibility to situations 'on the ground'. In this case, the situation strained our developing relationship as research partners and required ongoing communication to surmount it.

Another financial issue that resulted in a perception of inequity in the allocation of funds arose, likely due to a lack of communication or miscommunication. Initially, it may not have been clearly communicated that the IDRC funds could not be used for curriculum development expenses. For Mbai, this meant having to convince and motivate faculty colleagues to participate in curriculum development without being able to offer them a monetary incentive to invest their time and effort in this initiative. In addition, the MU research team (coordinator, research assistant, community researchers) incurred out-of-pocket expenses for communication technologies, which had inadvertently not been included in the project budget. However, once this issue came to light, YU sent additional funds from the BHER – Global Affairs Canada project budget to cover the costs of communication, and every effort was made to provide full disclosure around finances going forward. This situation highlights the importance of involving all partners in funding proposal development (which time pressures and busy schedules make difficult) and regular communication throughout the project.

Communication Issues

Conducting a collaborative research project across great distances posed significant communication and logistical issues. The research coordinator and research assistant (RA) at MU managed project logistics and provided oversight for the community researchers (CRs) in Dadaab – mostly, from a distance. In addition, the RA visited Dadaab prior to data gathering to provide additional training to the CRs. Within Kenya, cellular phones were the main mode of communication, so this worked well. However, for communication between Canada and Kenya, we relied mainly on email, since the time difference, technology issues with video conference calls, and busy schedules made it difficult to connect in real-time. Email was not an ideal medium for communication due to the challenge of clearly conveying messages through text. Furthermore, the Kenyan team incurred costs with cellular phones and internet access. As explained above, these costs were not covered by the feasibility study budget but the BHER project stepped in to cover them with other BHER project funds. Thus, we stayed on track, thanks to the vital commitment of all partners, the diligence of the research coordinator and the availability of other funds.

Security Issues

Security in Dadaab was an ongoing challenge to which the community researchers and our NGO partners were accustomed. The second (post-fieldwork) workshop scheduled for June 2015 was nearly derailed due to the April 2015 terrorist attack at Garissa University College (an affiliated college with MU). Yet, because of our strong commitment to completing the project as planned, we decided to go ahead despite the ensuing insecurity. We made this decision because we needed to come together to review the research findings and discuss their incorporation in the new CHEd programme under development. A delay in holding this workshop would have risked delaying the

MU Senate approval process for the new degree programme proposal, which, in turn, would have meant missing the opportunity to implement the new programme within the BHER project funding window, which was essential to offering the programme in Dadaab.

Reflection on Our Success

When asked to identify the reasons for our success, five project team members (Kenyan and Canadian) who were interviewed for the project/partnership evaluation identified several factors. First, the combined knowledge and expertise of the partners, and their diverse backgrounds provided different and complementary perspectives and insights. Mbai's background in community health and health education/promotion and Pilkington's background in maternal-child and women's health, as well as global health, each informed the research project and curriculum development in different and equally important ways. Other project participants, including representatives of WIK and the Kenya Ministry of Health (MoH), similarly contributed their unique perspectives and expertise. As an NGO with extensive expertise in education for refugees and based in Dadaab, WIK was a key partner in our feasibility study, assisting with recruiting and supporting the community researchers. Moreover, the WIK representative (Philemon Misoy), who was also the project manager for the BHER project in Dadaab, contributed valuable knowledge about the Dadaab context and the BHER project in Dadaab at the pre- and post-fieldwork workshops, where development of the CHEd programme was discussed. Likewise, the Kenya MoH representative (Elizabeth Oywer, who was also, a Registered Nurse and Mental Health Nurse) brought knowledge of the training and utilization of CHWs in the Kenyan health system and was an important ally in obtaining the support of government officials for our research project.

Another factor that added to the project success was the passion and understanding that all partners (Kenyan and Canadian academics, NGO representatives and a representative from Kenya's MoH) brought to the project, including goodwill and a desire to make a difference. Motivation came from a sincere desire to participate in an equity-seeking project that brought together North-South partners. This commitment mirrored the principles and underpinning of the 'Partnership Assessment Toolkit' (also funded by IDRC; Afsana et al., 2009) that informed the evaluation of our project. Moreover, everyone expressed a commitment to a health-related higher education programme and was energized by a desire to contribute to skill and capacity development for refugees. As a result, we accomplished a tremendous amount in eighteen months. While the IDRC funding was for two years, we had to obtain MU Senate approval for the CHEd programme proposal and implement the programme within eighteen months to obtain BHER funding support for the first cohort of students. We attribute our successes to the collegial and collaborative nature of the partnership. Those interviewed felt that their input was valued and included throughout the planning and implementation stages of the project (Douhaibi, 2016). Moreover, through engaging in this joint research and education programme development project, we believe that we increased our capacity to engage in such collaborative endeavours in the future.

Key Lessons Learned and Conclusions

We undertook this North-South partnership to develop a health education degree programme that would be responsive to the needs of refugees and the host community in Dadaab. Our reflection on this experience has identified several key lessons. First, when undertaking a North-South academic collaboration, some challenges can be anticipated; and yet, challenges are not always predictable, particularly in complex contexts such as the protracted refugee situation in Dadaab. Partners must be committed to addressing challenges expeditiously and willing to maintain flexibility in executing the project plan, so that the project is adaptable and responsive. It is important to recognize that each partner may offer specific capacities, contacts, or strategies for addressing challenges that arise and that no one partner will have all the solutions. Instead, collaboration is necessary to ensure mitigation of the challenges that arise.

Communication was a significant challenge in our collaboration. Having reflected on this, we learned that prompt and responsive communication between partners is crucial to monitoring progress to ensure timelines are met. As well, communication must be clear to avoid tensions between partners due to potentially different understandings of a message. Moreover, when tensions do surface, for instance, around finances, they can be eased through clear, open and timely communication. To enhance the clarity of messages, we found that multiple forms of communication (written and verbal) were helpful, and at times even necessary, depending on each partner's access to communication technologies.

Success in achieving our goals, especially the development of the BSc CHEd degree programme, has taught us that it is important that partners begin building relationships early and put continual effort into nurturing those relationships throughout the duration of the project to ensure their stability and sustainability. We believe that affirming commitment to a partnership through formal and informal acknowledgement of roles and responsibilities ensures satisfaction with partnership arrangements. The specific skills and expertise that each partner can contribute should be identified and utilized to produce desired outcomes for a project and to ensure equity in the partnership.

Programme development was achieved concurrent with a collaborative, community-based research project that utilized the experience and expertise of the partner institutions. The research provided clear insights into the gaps in healthcare service provision and training of CHWs in Dadaab, the level of interest among potential students in receiving further education and training, and what this education and training should include. Our findings informed the development of the BSc CHEd programme, which launched in 2016, providing access to higher education and practical training to produce well-prepared community health educators in Dadaab and beyond. The success of this project has not only benefited the community in Dadaab by providing access to MU's CHEd programme but also provides a model for similar health education initiatives in the future, and in other low-resource contexts. Now that the BSc Community Health Education degree programme has been implemented, the expertise of MU in delivering the CHEd programme again in Kenya or elsewhere, to support the development of well-educated community health workers, is assured.

Part Two

Students and Teachers: Inside the BHER Supported Classroom

5

Refugees Respond: Using Digital Tools, Networks and 'Production Pedagogies' to Envision Possible Futures

Abdikadir Abikar, Abdullahi Aden, Kurt Thumlert, Negin Dahya and Jennifer Jenson

The relationship between education and technology in the lives of refugees in camps is complex. This landscape includes practical matters of access to higher education under conditions of political change and instability, as well as essential supports like internet connectivity, the varieties of media tools available, and the technological and sociocultural resources in play. In the context of refugees pursuing higher education and engaging in international teaching and learning opportunities, digital technologies have been critical features of programmes offered to those living in and near to the Dadaab refugee camps. These technologies include everything from online learning management systems (e.g. Moodle, through which higher education courses for refugees are in part delivered) to email, discussion boards and emergent forms of pedagogical engagement over mobile devices, including communication using smartphones and cloud-based applications. These educational networks comprise a kind of digital media ecology that is both locally situated, community driven *and* globally connected, and internationally informed.

Social and academic supports for students in courses (often mediated by mobile-phone based communication) are important elements of formal educational enrolment in higher education for refugees in and from Dadaab (Dryden-Peterson, Dahya and Adelman, 2017). At the same time, informal, local and improvised uses of digital tools are also proving to be vital in this landscape – not just for achieving formal educational goals, but for transforming the everyday lives of refugee students, and for enabling local actors and communities to envision possible futures both within and beyond refugee camps. An ecological systems approach considers how individuals and communities interact with(in) the multiple environments in which they are enmeshed, such as the links between settings like home, work and formal education sites (exosystems) or the cultural forms, gender roles and values that influence one's everyday life (mesosystems).

A digital media ecology consists not only of network infrastructure, access to formal educational resources and learning management systems, but also accounts for less conspicuous and emergent sites and practices of learning, where digital media ecologies can, as such, support the emergence of unexpected pathways to participation in academic, cultural and communicative practices (Dryden-Peterson, Dahya and Adelman, 2017; Thumlert, de Castell and Jenson, 2015). As we will discuss below, these ecologies, enabled by networks, mobile devices and new media, go beyond providing mere 'access' to higher education: they inaugurate dynamic and decentralized relations to technology tools, and in ways that can enrich pedagogical opportunities for refugees (e.g. communicating and sharing knowledge with student peers in North America and elsewhere), while also supporting new forms of creative agency using digital tools (e.g. creating video works, websites and other artefacts using new media).

In the introduction to this book, Giles and Miller adopt a similar perspective on technology, challenging what they call the 'MOOC fantasy', that is:

> a pedagogical approach to teaching and learning that contends that making online courses available to refugees and other marginalized people makes higher education accessible. To the contrary, our hard-earned pedagogical success [in the BHER project] is principally due to the creation of a community of scholars or cohorts of students who learn from and support each other in ways that the institution of the university cannot.
>
> p. 12 in this volume

Indeed, Dryden-Peterson, Dahya and Adelman (2017) point out that decentralized and ad hoc media micro-ecologies play a fundamental role in connecting students with one another, and in building organically emergent local/global learning communities. It is here, at the intersection of locally and globally situated technology supports, where refugee students are enabled, with greater local agency, to 'chart pathways' to educational success. Dahya and Dryden-Peterson (2016) also show that media micro-ecologies, including social networks enabled through mobile devices, expand educational opportunities and establish more inclusive pathways to higher education for refugees, particularly for women seeking educational opportunities in refugee contexts. In these same contexts, Giles (2018) states that professors in the BHER programme are thus encouraged to employ technologies in ways that 'keep in mind the interests and needs of the Dadaab refugee and local Kenyan students' (p. 174).

At the same time, how the interests and needs of local actors in refugee camps are defined, and who represents those needs and interests, are determined not only by educational and technological 'exosystems', but also by vast technologies of national and transnational governance that already permeate and define everyday life in Dadaab – from NGOs that mediate the interests of refugees to policies that prevent refugees from leaving the camps. One irony, here, is that while borderless technology resources can be mobilized to connect students with professors and mediate communicative interaction with students worldwide (as well as lead to important symbolic forms of accreditation like advanced degrees and certificates), students in refugee camps like Dadaab are subject to geopolitical constraints, as well as top-down transnational humanitarian efforts that may organize everyday experience on the ground, and even script and coordinate the 'participation' of local actors (Alonso, Thumlert and de Castell, 2016).

Notwithstanding the critical aims and purposes of borderless higher education programmes, Hyndman (2011) points out that we still need to acknowledge the 'contradictions between liberal democratic norms [that inform initiatives like BHER] and the prevailing international, economic, and geopolitical sentiments that favour keeping refugees in camps' (p. 7). This means acknowledging, too, the multiple transnational organizations and state institutions that determine the ambit of local agency, including state educational systems, which themselves may be animated by technocratic (post)colonial forms. Complicating this, we need to also account for the dominant media representations *of* refugees *over which* refugees have no control or sociotechnical position from which to 'speak back'. As Dahya (2017) points out, the dominant media that shape public knowledge about refugees may misrepresent them, and thus 'impact how refugee persons are treated, particularly in host communities. These narratives can also impact how refugee persons perceive themselves as valued (or undervalued) insiders/outsiders throughout their forced migration' (p. 24).

From geopolitical policy to humanitarian governance to the legacy of colonial education forms, in this chapter we argue that technology needs to be theorized not just in terms of digital tools and borderless systems that support access, but also in terms of the complex sociotechnical systems that can scaffold local agency or, conversely, continue to reinforce notions of refugees as 'passive', in 'need of governance by the humanitarian community, rather than as people with opinions about how their lives should be organized' (Duale et al., 2019, p. 56). As these authors also point out, refugee teachers are rarely 'consulted on matters concerning teaching and learning in the school, employment terms and conditions, or curriculum implementation' (p. 58).

A further contradiction, under these conditions, is that the BHER students in Dadaab, many of whom are refugee teachers, affirmatively perceive themselves, fundamentally, as 'change agents' – not just in terms of advancing transformative local change within Dadaab, but also in terms of envisioning reconstruction strategies and taking leadership roles when they return to Somalia or respective countries of origin. As Dryden-Peterson, Dahya and Adelman (2017) signal, 'refugee students' motivation for education is … often tied to a desire to contribute to peace-building and post-conflict reconstruction' (p. 1044). And in their present situations as well, Duale and our Dadaab-based authors (2019) again assert that refugees, and particularly refugee educators, 'must have meaningful participation in the planning and provision of education for refugees since it is refugees, above all others, who have the most to gain from reform' (p. 58), including, we argue, critical and productive uses of networked digital tools and informal media ecologies that are less subject to top-down administration and 'MOOC fantasies'. This ecological view of technology reminds us, too, that our most intuitively given teaching methods and curricular constraints can also be seen as technologies, that is, as subject-forming techniques that might be reconstructed otherwise (Thumlert, de Castell and Jenson, 2015, p. 789).

These considerations bring up new questions regarding technology tools, questions that animate our conversation below: how can technology tools be mobilized by local actors to their own ends, to co-construct their own pathways to educational success, including forms of self-representation in an era where persons experiencing forced migration are subject to dominant narratives that may position refugees as abstract objects of geopolitical policy?

Framing our Conversation: Course Contexts, Tools and Theories

Below, our Dadaab-based authors illustrate how digital tools might be utilized not simply to 'connect' students in refugee camps to higher education but explore how those tools might be mobilized to support the ends and self-defined purposes of local actors and communities.

Our Dadaab-based authors, Abdikadir Abikar and Abdullahi Aden, are currently enrolled as graduate students in York University's BHER cohort. Abdikadir is currently a secondary school maths and computer studies teacher and has been teaching in Dadaab in primary and secondary schools since 2012. Abdullahi is a humanities teacher, school administrator, and has taught religion and history in primary and secondary schools in Dadaab since 2007. Both received teacher education and teacher credentials (2014) through the BHER project and are currently completing their graduate studies through BHER related programmes.

Our Toronto-based authors include Kurt Thumlert (the course instructor, Faculty of Education, York University); Negin Dahya (University of Toronto, who has conducted on-the-ground research in Dadaab and Kakuma refugee camps); and Jennifer Jenson, who, along with Kurt Thumlert, co-developed the pedagogical frameworks mobilized in the course discussed below.

The Course

Cultural Studies of Technology for Education was originally developed as a face-to-face York University course. The autumn 2018 version of the course was modified to include Dadaab-based graduate students. Classroom interactions between Toronto and Dadaab were mediated through tools like the course website, a discussion board, weekly face-to-face Zoom meetings between the instructor and the Dadaab-based authors, communication through email, videos and mobile/smartphone tools like *WhatsApp* (a messaging tool) and *DU Recorder* (a video screen-capture presentation tool for mobile devices), along with one synchronous whole-class meeting using *Zoom*, with a discussion of readings led by the Dadaab-based authors. This class meeting was conducted at 7am (EST) in order to account for time zone differences and connect 'live' with students in Dadaab.

For asynchronous communication, students in Dadaab and Toronto used a discussion board system called DAAGU, which was developed based on complexity theory in education (Mitchell et al., 2015) and, as such, reflexively connected with our course orientations to technology-based learning. Using DAAGU, students co-explored theories from the course readings, shared digital artefacts and engaged in dialogue *about* technology as we *used* technology. As the developers (Mitchell et al., 2015) of DAAGU state (in an article read by the class prior to using the tool), 'our typical educational approaches are still largely informed by assumptions that teachers have knowledge that they dispense to learners in carefully constructed learning activities and sequenced content modules aimed at moving students toward teacher-defined outcomes' (p. 206). By contrast, DAAGU was designed to disrupt conventional epistemologies and e-learning practices and to support open-ended inquiry and collaborative knowledge construction. In the context of working with BHER students, it was not inconsequential that DAAGU was named after the learning practices of the Afar people of Ethiopia, who share knowledge through diverse communicative modes across diverse regions using a 'traditional communication system' that resembles the ad hoc, decentralized and multimodal forms of contemporary media (Menbere and Skjerdal, 2008). The platform developers in fact named the discussion platform DAAGU because it creates a 'networked community that facilitates a collaborative process of exploration of difference and discovery' (Mitchell et al., 2015, p. 206). As these tools mediated class interaction, we begin our conversation below by reflecting on the affordances of the tools used.

Building upon theories/practices explored in the York University Graduate Faculty of Education course, *Cultural Studies of Technology for Education*, the authors in Dadaab enacted a 'production pedagogy' to explore where and how technology-based learning and making with digital tools might be intertwined with local interests and aspirations, leading to the development of *Refugees Respond* (a website/blog and Wikimedia platform), and to the authors' creative use of digital storytelling and video production as vehicles for inquiry, making and sharing. A production pedagogy (one of the course theory frames) is defined as one in which learning actors are enabled to situationally engage practical design challenges through the making of authentic real-world technology artefacts that have social worth, that have use-value to their makers. Production pedagogy links critical inquiry with place-based social action, where design and technological making are informed by the present needs and purposes of learning actors. Further, through cultural production using authentic communicational media, it is argued that learning actors build participative status in cultural practices as they make and share (Thumlert, de Castell and Jenson, 2015; de Castell 2016; Alonso et al., 2019).

We emphasize here that our learning community and the creative artefacts (websites, videos, graphic texts, digital games) produced by our Dadaab-based authors depended upon complex assemblages of other actors and, principally, the foundational efforts of the BHER organization in constructing – from the ground up – an educational centre in Dadaab. Alongside these material supports, our learning together was also scaffolded by a learning culture, a community of scholars, established during the first years of the BHER project.

The following sections were written using a 'conversational' mode of inquiry using Google Docs and Zoom (a video conferencing tool). Dadaab-based authors responded to prompts and questions from the Toronto-based course instructor and co-authors using Google Docs. Preliminary drafts were followed by several recorded video conversations using Zoom; video conversations were then transcribed, merged and revised by all of the authors on Google Docs. The conversation represents the voices and views of the Dadaab-based authors, prompted by the questions and comments (in italics) of the Toronto-based authors.

Outcomes from Our Conversational Inquiry

Questions to the Dadaab-based graduate students co-authoring this chapter are presented *in italics* followed by their responses.

In the first article read by the class, Mitchell et al. (2015) suggest that traditional Learning Management Systems (LMS), such as Moodle and Webct, have not offered sufficient innovation consistent with the new pedagogies required for education in the 21st century. Given that we were all very much improvising as we went, how did tools like DAAGU and Zoom work – or not work – for you? Can you talk about the experience of inclusion as a BHER student, too, and the role of technologies? Were there any things you might change?

Abikar Abdikadir DAAGU was one platform that opened our eyes to what was possible with technology. All the BHER students think that Moodle is the only space for learning, but using DAAGU, it was exciting and we loved working within the new space of learning, the chat rooms with the other [Toronto-based] students. Exchange between graduate students in Dadaab and Toronto is something we would like to see more of, across different systems. From Dadaab, we led a [live] class discussion on course readings using Zoom, meeting early in the morning in Toronto, with students connecting from their homes. It's very hard because of the time differences, but when these meetings happen they are a golden opportunity for both sides, the graduate students in Toronto and the graduate students in Dadaab. Even though it was early for them, it was an eye-opening session and we hope to do more. Moving from the Zoom presentation to the DAAGU discussion board and being able to continue our discussion on DAAGU when the Zoom session was over – that was another way to be connected and answer questions. We hope to build a similar forum for chat on our website, and the course I am enrolled in now [*Digital Games and Learning*] is being run on our own *Refugees Respond* Wikimedia site.

The question I ask myself now is, should I not be doing this in the future? In Somalia? I should be using the Moodle idea, translated, the same idea, but a Somali Moodle for those who can't reach the cities, so they can learn, too. Moodle is something that can be created, or you can make something like Moodle. I have hope to integrate York University's modality of teaching in my homeland, because I see many students in Somalia who are living in rural areas, who need to be reached, so I am of the idea we could use these models of teaching, translated to Somali. For example, we could collaborate with York University in order to serve other marginalized youth who are out there. I am hoping to use technology in my future, making teaching and learning more interesting for teachers in Somalia, and to reach many other teachers who have not had yet the opportunity to use technology in their classroom.

Abdullahi Aden Learning through platforms enabled by the internet holds the future of education, particularly higher education for refugees. Technology promises innovative learning, which shapes education and transforms learner opportunities. Traditional approaches to teaching are challenged, and under transition, as new ways of teaching [have emerged], which are more interactive, meaningful. This is due to the digital materials that complement the intended content or what the teacher has covered in the physical classroom.

Digital platforms have resulted in the growth of knowledge for Dadaab students who are undergoing their higher education, particularly for BHER students. Platforms such as DAAGU, Moodle, Zoom, YouTube and WhatsApp enable students to get connected with their instructors, participate in discussion forums, receive instruction ... post videos ... and even lead class discussions.

At the moment, most universities have adopted a virtual or blended system of learning which offers a collaborative model where student interact freely and discover their own learning through social platforms with less instructor [direction]. Students explore abstract thoughts and justify the results of their thinking. This advancement of technology makes education global, breaks barriers and enhances networking ... And so, we have our website, *Refugees Respond*, which Abdikadir and I developed for the course.

As part of this course on technology and production, you created with technology tools, including building your website/blog and Wikimedia site, and worked with video tools and graphic text-making tools like ComicLife. Right now, as we speak, you are hosting York University students on your Wikimedia platform for our Digital Games and Learning course. In a sense, Toronto-based York students in the course have come to Dadaab. Can you tell us, first, why you picked Refugees Respond as a website domain name?

Abikar The website name suggests that refugees can respond – it shows that refugees are able to act and do some changes in their own lives and share with other people their thinking. It is a site that represents the refugees – and it shows a kind of creativity, that they can also do something. That shows a kind of power and ownership – for education, for teachers and learning – and it may become a learning resource for students and educators around Dadaab. They can add materials into the system so other people can see their thinking or retrieve important materials from the platform. To create awareness among the refugees and communities, to attract people.

How are refugees responding?

Abdullahi This is a significant platform or site because it takes the meaning of being a refugee, [where] refugees are saying something about what they think and feel. Initially, the way Dadaab operates, you find organizations just impose their own things and the refugees normally accept the way it is. Refugees, they don't share in the system or administration in any way. This site [helps] some refugees – particularly [students] – decide for themselves and write about their thinking, and not be subordinate to things imposed on them. They can share their responses and that reaches out all over the world.

And what refugee students in Dadaab now appreciate most is how 'connected learning' allows collaborating with their peers in diverse parts of the world and manipulating the same things, engaging the same challenges. This breaks with the notion that higher education is unattainable in the Dadaab refugee context, and universities like York University have disproved such conceptions, as some students have already accomplished their studies through distance learning programmes, through digital platforms and through onsite visits here [by professors]. It is technology that made the impossible possible.

Abikar This challenged the views of the primary knowledge donors, of individuals and agencies running education programmes in the Dadaab refugee camps. The original expectations, what the UNHCR wanted, was for all the refugees to have a primary education. The basic needs, knowing how to read and write. When we finished the basics, we said we wanted secondary schools, we want secondary education, which is not the mandate of the UNHCR. We [then] wanted higher education, more opportunities, refugees looking for a durable solution for their homeland: an opportunity that UNHCR never imagined. With BHER, the idea was to educate teachers, and to help students, and now we have new opportunities, with different courses, with social and political [themes], and now we are becoming writers and graduate students, looking to the future as change makers and, again, students are still wanting more. We now have a Master's programme and some of us are hoping to get PhDs. We are telling BHER we want more.

Abdullahi   Our website is also a kind of landmark for showing how refugees interact with technology, access education through it, and sometimes post their grievances to concerned stakeholders without any intermediary. The platform, along with smart devices, [is] defining the needs of the refugees, shaping their thinking towards the world; their responses count in the world.

So, now that you have the website/blog and digital storytelling software like ComicLife, how can you use these tools to support learning and self-representation – two themes you explored when you led the class discussion on the readings, 'Voices beyond walls: The Role of digital storytelling for empowering marginalized youth in refugee camps' (Sawhney, 2009) and 'Digital media and forced migration' (Dahya, 2017)? As Sawhney (2009) states, 'Sharing [digital] narratives are important not only for [refugees'] sense of identity, understanding and recognition by others, but as a form of creative expression and advocacy of issues in their lives' (p. 1).

Abikar   This question has been big on my mind a lot lately. Who else can use the site? How? So, I came up with an idea. Last week I saw some students in the school where I teach in Dadaab who are always interested in presenting news at school. They do this on Mondays. International news, local news, sports news. So, I met with them and I said, what if I gave you the website to use and every Monday we can post the news. They were so happy – *where can we get a website*? I plan to meet with them to help them type, and introduce a section called The Writers Club – and release news and information for the school. And then I will tell students, if you want to know more about something, please go this site, please go to this link. This is how I want to start – and expand further once it works. Once it works, we can bring more people. Sunday, they prepare. Every Monday, they release the news. That is the plan. In the meantime, I use my website blog to upload pictures and report on events in Dadaab.

Abdullahi   According to Negin (Dahya, 2017), in her article on digital media and forced migration, she noted that 'digital media can be used in critical ways to promote engagement with content about the refugee crisis among young people' (p. 25). It is true that Dadaab is one of the largest refugee camps in the world, and we are hoping to make use of digital media to promote this engagement.

So, in our course we also used a multimodal graphic narrative making tool, ComicLife, which enables users to create pretty dramatic digital stories where you can integrate your own photographs and images into graphic story forms. How might this tool work for you in these contexts and for those purposes?

Abikar   [ComicLife] was enjoyable – it is a creative way of writing, of presenting your own thoughts and stories. We have the full licences, but we can only use [the software] in the BHER Centre – and, for example, I also showed some students from Kenyatta University how it works. They were interested in using ComicLife, and I gave them a lesson. They enjoyed it and were giving me good feedback – that is what I wanted! To give those opportunities – teachers who can teach other teachers and then work with students. And I asked them to send me their comics so I can post them someday [on Refugees Respond.org].

Yes, the affordances of the software enable people of all ages to create sophisticated graphic narratives.

Abdullahi   Again, the creativity is excellent – [these media] help make things more creative. However, we can't bring local primary and secondary students into the BHER Centre [where the computers are located] and so we can't easily share ComicLife with them.

Abikar   I want to create a computer lab of my own – and my challenge there is that I don't have access to the internet, and I need the internet to install software. But I should have access soon, and when the internet is ready, I can start teaching special needs and deaf students [and] students who cannot write well: these computers can support these students – [the students] are very good with visual representation but do not do a lot of writing [have writing skills] yet. With this programme, *ComicLife*, we can use this tool to teach them. That is one way I am planning to use *ComicLife*, a way for differentiated and multimodal literacy instruction.

I am wondering about the use of smartphones and mobile devices here as well? ComicLife and other graphic text-making software are also compatible with smartphones and tablets. So . . .

Abikar Smartphones are also very important in [the BHER] project – they really help us connect to professors outside the Centre [from home or elsewhere] using data-bundles. If a professor wants to communicate with us, or vice versa, we can communicate using Gmail or through our class WhatsApp page. This was very useful when there was a labour dispute at York University during the winter semester (2018) and courses were suspended for some time. We were grateful to a dedicated professor, Robert Bridi, who was able to guide us while the University and Moodle were shut down. This smartphone alternative helped us during confusing times. First, mobile devices connected us with our professor and, second, we were able to interact amongst ourselves: we started chatting, clarifying ideas and helping each other out on course-related activities.

Abdullahi Students in the camps use smartphones, and they make a lot of videos – funny videos, playful stuff. We need to [in the future] have them use the smartphone to make small projects. But in schools they are not allowed to have mobile phones – that is like a crime and you will be punished, your phone broken into pieces. Some argue that the phone is a destructive agent in the school. And it is concerning that students and teachers don't use the phones well, [don't] use them creatively.

What is the difference between you making video films vs NGOs making films about you?

Abikar The difference is that when NGOs film us, the video speaks for refugees and their interests, but when I make my own films, they represent myself, they speak for my own interests, what I need for others to get to know me. With organisations it is different; they normally guide you on what to say so that they capture what they want. And, lastly, when you are filmed you don't get any compensation, so no one appreciates the time and energy you spend. The difference? I love making my own videos. I am also more confident because they are not cut off, nothing is removed or added. When NGOs make videos, sometimes important messages are trimmed out, and they also moderate. When NGOs film, it is also very hard to be understood when an interpreter translates who may not speak the language, and they do not convey the message you wanted to communicate. If you are serious about videos, you can make your own videos, though we do not have their equipment or editing tools. The difference is, the more you make, the more you work on your own videos, the better it is going to be, and we don't have to depend on somebody who is recording for us. We don't have to rely on somebody else, for example, if they are no longer there.

This issue connects to the idea of student-driven inquiry and media production as pedagogy and as social action. That was a theme in the course. So, how to support students to use tools creatively, to connect inquiry with video production? Or with digital storytelling? In the same way you would like to have a writer's workshop on your website? That seems to me to be a very innovative idea you have there, based on student interest in writing and presenting news within their community.

Abdullahi This kind of production pedagogy would be very good, but the administration does not allow mobile phones in the primary and secondary schools, for the most part. It is a good technology, and the question is, how to make it help the creativity of the students. We just have the tablets for [special education students] right now.

Abikar Another challenge with technology is the curriculum; it does not allow the teacher to manipulate or change content. It's like the content is fixed. What is taught in the farthest ends of Kenya is taught here in Dadaab. It's hard for the teacher to come up with a pedagogy using mobile phones. Once you do that you are 'cheating' the child, you are not helping the child to pass the exams, and there is competition. The system prevents change. The national exams are viewed as a fundamental stage for all students in Kenya. For students to be accepted or be seen as successfully educated, they must do national exams. It is also regarded as a unifying factor, a national interest. All the local universities use the national results to sort their future students; and that is why it is important to the country (see Gitome and Dippo, this volume). Personally, I don't like these kinds of exams, because it cannot be the only way to 'rate' the future of children.

What about out-of-school or after-school media making? If the Kenyan curriculum is fixed – and if the National Exams and the forms of status it confers create a pressure to 'teach to the test' – what are the opportunities of mobilizing these tools outside of the school in Dadaab where you both teach?

Abikar Sure, people are creating things on their own. We can do this through the website, and from home, and from outside of the school, but not in schools. They have to connect outside of school – and that is why I am setting up the writing workshop. But if you are in a developed nation, like Canada, maybe you can come up with your own pedagogy, your own content, the way you want.

To some extent, teachers in North America are constrained by curricular routines, too, as well as by standardized curriculum, content and testing systems. Yet, as explored in our course, some of the most interesting learning spaces are often those outside of schools, as in the article (Sawhney, 2009) about digital storytelling in Palestinian refugee camps. Is there any way you can connect that model to teaching and learning in Dadaab?

Abdullahi In local schools? The problem is that if you [teachers] add something different or creative [to the curriculum], you are taking up time; if you remove anything from the curriculum, you are messing with the child, the student's possibility of passing [the exams]. Again, the same syllabus – what is taught in the farthest end of Kenya – is taught here, and that is what is required to be taught.

It's a problem we have in North America, too: the pressure to 'cover content'. It does not support teacher or student agency and, paradoxically, educators are encouraged – by educational systems – to actually deprive students of potentially richer and more meaningful learning experiences in order to help them 'succeed' in schooling systems. So, that leads us to ask: how does the system of education generate tensions with what you are learning and doing through the BHER project? For example, in our technology course, we explored different approaches to student-directed inquiry, situated learning, and production: specifically, making digital artefacts with technology tools and new media.

Abikar In the Dadaab context, there are four universities that have set up BHER programs: UBC, York, and two local universities within Kenya, Kenyatta and Moi. The only one doing a Master's programme is York. With local BHER programs, students – the students training to become teachers – those students are not transformed through their educational experience as much as the York students are. The students have much less control over the curriculum, their learning. This is different from the York version of the BHER project. The other [teacher education] cohorts don't use the technology as well, and that is a big problem. Their programmes [locally] do not use Skype or Zoom or mobile devices to the extent that they should, and online learning activities that support dialogue, critical thinking and creativity are quite rare, I think.

Yet there is reason for hope. For example, one time – York professor Don [Dippo] was using Zoom and speaking all at once with students in Somalia, in Mogadishu, here in Dadaab, in Nairobi, Garissa and Mombasa – and one BHER professor from a Kenyan university, who was visiting Dadaab, was amazed: 'How do you do that? How have you connected all these students together on the screen? I need to be doing this!' Imagine that: this professor came from Nairobi to Dadaab to teach one student – think of the time and resources that can be saved. But he witnessed the power of technology to connect people, and he wanted to do the same. Technology is important, and in my way of thinking, there should be more ways of connecting students and professors, through online tutorials and by creating networked learning communities. And even when local professors do come to visit, Dadaab is a very complex area, where floods, insecurity and other obstacles may hinder students' access to the BHER Learning Centre.

Can you put this technology discussion within the wider context of pedagogy – and the history of education in post-colonial Africa? Is it just about technology?

Abikar   It could also be about the traditional colonial system of teaching. And changing to new ways, or adapting to new systems, of course takes time. For example, in the York programme, we learn to critically think, criticize, open our eyes, and to see what is beyond the page, and to see what is behind the content on the page. In the traditional university, those students who are taught, they are only reading *this* content [*Abikar holds up a piece of paper*], what's on the page only: they cannot see outside the page. What students do is read line-by-line, cover to cover, just the page, memorizing and repeating facts. This is maybe one effect of colonial education, which is didactic. The students with York – things are different, they are given courses that change them. The creativity is not killed. We are transformed through the educational process.

This leads us to another question: you both sometimes refer to yourselves as 'change-makers'. How do you see yourselves, as change makers, transforming learning and education when you, for example, return to Mogadishu or Somalia?

Abdullahi   [With regards to] production pedagogy, in relation to the current Kenyan curriculum, the educational system is not flexible. You can't apply learning in your daily life. At York, we understand the importance of learning and context and sharing knowledge across the world with others, and the value of student engagement. Here, the system is purely teacher-centred, so innovative pedagogies can't be easily applied. In Somalia, we hope to make change – so students can apply their learning.

Abikar   The problem is that there is very little space to change the system and educational culture here. After decades, the government is now rolling out a new system (the competence-based curriculum, or CBC), but this change is still surrounded by much argumentation and debate. There is still massive cheating on high stakes national exams, which are highly competitive and based on an educational system that force students to memorize content, which leads to widespread cheating. My hope is that the new curriculum will provide new ways of learning and better assessment, and a better teaching and learning culture that is not based on discipline, individualism and competitive exams. The national exam has too much power over students' future possibilities. In my recent Master's research, I have discovered that any system change, including the CBC, should also be accompanied by transformations in educational culture: instead of individualistic and competitive behaviours associated with the old system's teaching and learning culture, my research recommends the creation of local professional learning communities where collaboration and knowledge sharing are central; there needs to be a new sense of community and responsibility to colleagues, students and to students' learning. Finally, we need to question 'individualistic' and competitive dispositions that are learned in schools and become part of the teaching culture, too. We need to understand that no teacher is perfect, and that we need each other, and that we need technology like smartphones to connect these new learning communities.

Abdullahi We hope to bring something else to Mogadishu, with the experience we have from York, and we can work with other universities – any university we like – that can bring new pedagogies to the people of Somalia.

Abikar The students from [other teacher training programmes] say that we, in the BHER graduate cohort, are learning very differently, and even say, 'you, you can rule the world' ... And, so we started engaging them, for example, we gave them the links to courses ... and I showed one student the graphic text making software ... still, even then, the certificate belongs only to the person who is enrolled. But we showed them, this is how we learn. We gave them the links to York so they could do it themselves. And even when they are writing projects, they come to us: they learn how to write, format, not plagiarize, and create a bibliography, and [recently] a York professor was here and helping them as well.

Reflecting on being change agents and leading the way, this brings us to another question: How would you describe the engagement of women compared to men in online and technology-based learning? What do you observe as different among refugee women in Dadaab compared to refugee women outside of Dadaab engaging in this learning, using technology?

Abikar One challenge women have is that many [women and men] believe they need to have families – if they finish secondary school, they marry, and perhaps some have a fear of not having children. And then they [the women] become engaged with [childcare].

One of the things about BHER, they say we need to empower women, but often women come to the BHER Centre with their children, and they need to attend to their children, and that [is a difficulty]. Most men don't have those added responsibilities. Those women who succeed, mostly, are those who wait to get married and finish their courses first.

In the Dadaab camp, women and men are not equal because of the traditional culture. Normally, women have a lot of domestic work at home, and men leave and do tasks outside of the home. For those who may be learning [through the BHER project], it is quite difficult for them as they may have these other domestic tasks and [childcare] – and the online technology helps. I remember women students who were part of the BHER programme who could not make it to the Centre, but they could still connect using their mobile data-bundles. Then they are connected when they are at their homes. The issue of technology can help in terms of men and women, and traditional culture creates different standards between men and women; but technology can help with this, too, as even women who are breastfeeding can Skype or Zoom to attend class. And send their weekly posts from home as well.

And about the women who are waiting to marry and have children, in the programme, how are they regarded for doing that? Do people support that culturally? And, again, how can you, as men, lead the way to support girls and women's full participation?

Abdullahi From the Dadaab level, in the BHER Centre, women, if they are married, normally [they] are assisted: we share our work in groups, we come together and boost others up, so they are not left out. Group work means that no one stands alone.

Those who wait to marry. How are they treated?

Abdullahi They are part of the family in Dadaab, and the BHER family. [Students in the BHER related programmes] don't have any problems, and we don't push them [other women students] to marry – we push them to finish. We advise them to wait and don't marry until they finish the courses and tell them that marriage is another chapter in your life. For example, one student who finished her Bachelor's moved onto the Master's programme with us, and now she has gone to Somalia where she is connected and very hard working. All of the women have graduated with us, and there are two now in the Master's programme, with more women now applying.

Abikar   I want to add that technology and smartphones are very important in helping and confronting gender barriers. It depends first on how the person interacts with the technology. There are many women who are as capable and skilled with technology as the men. [And using *WhatsApp*], they feel they can communicate with one another without men in an online group, too, to protect their privacy. The female students are also role models – with education, they more easily get jobs with local organizations, and NGOs in Dadaab, and elsewhere are also attempting to empower women through increased employment. As role models, female students tell other girls that education is important, and with York's upcoming graduate BHER cohort, 60 per cent of the graduate students will be female. Upcoming Master's students will be role models, the women, the 60 per cent.

When you become professors or educational leaders in Somalia, what do you see as the changes you might bring to the curriculum, for children and young people there.

Abikar   [laughs] We see a lot of hope in the future. We now feel more qualified even than many [local] professors, here, when we compare ourselves, because we can create our courses now, we can create our websites and web pages, we can connect to students with Zoom, or own websites, wikis and discussion boards. And that is how technology changes things, if you know how to use it. This technology helps us connect – and if it were not for this technology, we would not be the people we are today. Yet, we still face internet problems – and that is always an issue. If we don't have the internet, or the cell phone data-bundles, we could not have this conversation now.

Technology is important, and Wifi needs to be powerful wherever we go, in Somalia, [and elsewhere], and so internet connectivity is important. Then we can make changes: some Somali universities have begun operations in cities, so we hope to improve things by adding what we have learned from York University, upgrading the Somalia curriculum with York University methods and technology practices. I think we should be borrowing some of York University's teaching methods and trying to help educate the Somali educators and teacher assistants in order for them to understand better ways to teach and serve the community at large. From Somali universities, we need to use technology to connect students within Somalia. We can have, or create, a BHER-like programme that helps the displaced and marginalized access education within Somalia.

Abdullahi In Somalia, in the future, it will also be possible to apply and introduce the skills we learn [through the BHER project] to where we are teaching. And if it is the case that we become leaders in an educational department or in the educational sector, then we can instruct those who are doing the field work, the real [teaching] work, and how to do that particular work – even as consultants – to bring new skills to the teaching and learning process.

Abikar This also symbolizes the problem of the current curricular system in Kenya, which has been in place since 1985, and is only now being updated to the competence-based curriculum. Learners have been taught within this older system and educational culture for decades, without improvements or adjustments, and this system limits the potential of children, and it also kills creativity. Learning should not be a reformatory, like a predictable situation for the child, but an interactive situation that will allow the learners to learn new things. For example, as a graduate student, last semester, I was struggling with video making, but with some technical help and ideas from the professor, we finally made an impressive video; and, so, the same strategy can be applied to the learners: it can work as it has worked for me, and we learned through trial-and-error and we engaged several video making tools. Sometimes we failed, but we learned through overcoming mistakes, and later we succeeded.

As a game designer [in our *Digital Games and Learning* course], I am hoping to make use of the production method as a starting point for myself and see if I can apply it to a digital game about Mogadishu, one that I am proposing as my final project. Since most kids can get cell phones, I would try to use a mobile-friendly game-making tool, to make a game about rebuilding Mogadishu.

By way of a conclusion, Abikar, can you tell us more about your game?

Abikar My game [using the software, *Twine*] is based on the idea that Somalia's capital, Mogadishu, has been at war for so long, and I think using the game to teach civilians is one way out of war and conflict: this is an important move, and developing a game model to reconstruct the capital city is one idea I hold on to. [With input from BHER students, Ochan Leomoi and Dahabi Ibrahim] my future Somalia game should be about reuniting the Somali people inside and outside the country, and it should also include symbols of unity, peace and reconciliation. And Dahabi also brought the idea that this game should bring hope to the young girls whose rights had been violated, and especially to [today's] women who, during the days of the conflict, had undergone torture and experienced stigma. According to my plan, I want [the player/avatar] to be a university teacher trying to change the system and make lives better through education and building stability. The situation and experience of the game should mitigate the depression, trauma and stress that occurred during the prolonged wars in Somalia ... though the player feels stress while playing the game as they empathize with the [avatar/character] in the game. The game will make them feel they are in other people's stories; and in the game, the player will experience the look of Mogadishu before the civil war, as well as how it currently looks now. And in playing the game, some Somali patriots may feel sorrow. In the game, the future Mogadishu will look different, and this has led us to compare the future Mogadishu in the game with Konza city in Machakos, Kenya, which was designed by the Kenyan government and, as planned, Konza looks promising through the artists' imaginations. This is a good idea and will be a good model for my Mogadishu game, though stability and education will be more important than tall buildings.

My idea is that the player can take the role of a teacher coming home, along with experiencing the story of the past and present and future Mogadishu. The character in the game, the teacher, will return to serve the country after more than two decades away from his or her homeland, who learned outside the country and then came back, trying to see how quickly he or she can bring change and stability to Somalia.

6

Technology and Flexibility: The Online Learning Experience of Teaching Assistants and their Students in the Dadaab Refugee Camps

Hawa Sabriye and Dacia Douhaibi, with contributions from Arte Dagane and Ochan Leomoi

In an effort to provide quality tertiary education in Dadaab, the Borderless Higher Education for Refugees (BHER) Project developed collaborative academic programmes that connect students in Dadaab and Kakuma with instructors from Canadian and Kenyan universities. These programmes began with on-site, intensive courses towards Education Certificates and Diplomas for those teaching at the primary and secondary levels, delivered over a number of three- or four-week periods. A Bachelor of Arts (BA) Human Geography degree was also offered by York University (YU) through an online delivery structure that connected refugee and locally situated Kenyan students in Dadaab and Kakuma with courses delivered at York University to students in Toronto, through the Moodle learning platform. All of these courses, from diploma courses to degree courses, relied heavily on relationships between teaching assistants (TAs) and students. While course directors prepared the content and structure of the courses, it was the TAs who more closely connected with the students in Dadaab and Kakuma, delivering tutorials, grading assignments and maintaining frequent communication with students (the chapter by Youdelis et al. in this volume also speaks to the experiences of TAs in the BHER project).

In Canada, TAs are graduate students employed through a temporary contract by a university or college department and are given teaching-related responsibilities. The TA experience of delivering education in Dadaab is unique – both with regards to the challenges it presents as well as the learning opportunities that it provides. Success requires a deep understanding of the environment, and flexibility when working with students as they navigate a new academic system and ways of learning. In this chapter, we explore the experiences of two students who completed BA degrees and two TAs involved with BHER courses for three and four years, respectively.

We begin by introducing the authors and contributors to the chapter and explain our methodology. This is followed by a description of the experience of providing education in a context of conflict and crisis, both from the perspective of delivery (TAs) and uptake (students). We then focus on the application of innovative pedagogy, through our use of communication platforms such as Moodle and WhatsApp. We examine where rifts in teaching and learning emerged, particularly as external, western pedagogy intersected with local teaching and learning approaches, both embedded in their respective social and cultural contexts. We discuss a flexible learning approach that includes the development of critical thinking skills and a participatory pedagogy.

The Students and Teaching Assistants

The two students who contributed to this chapter completed certificate programmes in primary education and went on to complete four-year BAs in Educational Studies from YU; the two teaching assistants worked with the students over the course of three to four years of study.

Arte arrived in Dadaab in the early 1990s at the age of eight. He grew up in Dagahaley, which is one of the five refugee camps in Dadaab, where he completed his elementary and secondary studies. Following graduation, he worked as a teacher for CARE within the camps and as a community mobilizer[1] for the Norwegian Refugee Council. He joined BHER's Increased Access and Skills for Tertiary Education Program (InSTEP) in 2012, which was a programme designed to prepare prospective students for university education through courses in English language for academic purposes, information and communication technology (ICT) and the development of research skills. Arte then went on to complete his BA degree in Human Geography through YU's Faculty of Liberal Arts & Professional Studies. He is currently a YU Master of Education (MEd) candidate and his research focuses on the high level of female student dropouts in secondary schools in the Dadaab refugee camps. He is also a TA for York University's BA in Educational Studies programme and works with students in Dadaab.

Ochan arrived in Kenya in 1987 from Uganda and settled in the Dadaab refugee camps in July 1995. He began his teaching career in 1998 in Ifo camp, another of the five camps in Dadaab, where he still resides with his family. In 2007, Ochan worked as a psychosocial counsellor with CARE for 6 months. In

2010, he was employed as Deputy Head Teacher for the elementary schools in Ifo camp. In 2011, he became Head Teacher of an Elementary School, a position he held until the end of 2018. Ochan enrolled in YU's Human Geography BA in 2013 and graduated from this programme in 2018. Like Arte, Ochan is currently a YU MEd candidate. His research examines malpractice in secondary schools within the Ifo refugee camp. Ochan also currently works as a TA in Dadaab for the YU BA in Educational Studies programme.

Hawa holds an MEd from YU and during her M.A studies (2015–17) she worked as a TA for the BHER Project. Her graduate research documents the recruitment and retention of Somali female students in higher education in Dadaab. Following the completion of her studies, Hawa continued to support BHER students, providing remedial academic support through visits to Dadaab until the end of 2018. Her work with the BHER project inspired her to move to and work in Mogadishu, Somalia, where she currently resides.

Dacia is a doctoral candidate in the Geography Department of YU and worked with the BHER project from 2013 to 2018. She was a graduate assistant with the BHER project when students were in their first year of the InSTEP programme, and then as a teaching assistant and instructor through the entirety of the first undergraduate student cohort and the first three years of the second cohort.

While Hawa and Dacia are the primary authors of the chapter, Ochan and Arte made significant contributions to its development. They were involved in the initial framing of the structure of the chapter and provided feedback on an early draft. Contributions to the content in the chapter from Ochan and Arte are presented as direct quotes of statements they made through email and verbal conversations regarding their experiences as students of the BHER project. Our objective in sharing these statements verbatim is to provide intimate and unique insight into the learning environment created through the BHER project, drawing attention to the ways that BHER students experienced this unique learning structure. Further, in presenting experiences from the perspective of both students and TAs, we draw attention to our sometimes quite different expectations and experiences of this educational project in order to provide insights that we hope will help others improve on similar education models in the future.

Education in Conflict and Crisis

Refugee education is sparse and underfunded (Nicolai, Hine and Wales, 2016, p. 71). Educational funding is generally provided through humanitarian consolidated appeals, making it difficult to build an education system that is responsive to the protracted nature of refugee experiences (UNICEF, 2016, p. 4). The educational environment in Dadaab is evidence of this, as the educational services are provided at the most basic level and there are no resources in place for long-term development of quality schooling at all levels. Living and studying conditions in the Dadaab refugee camps are quite harsh and produce precarious situations for BHER students who have collectively shared how water and electricity shortages in the camps impede their learning experiences. The provision of education in conflict affected areas has been predominantly focused on primary and secondary education (Dryden-Peterson and Giles, 2010, p. 4), while higher education is perceived as costly, the expense far outweighing the benefits. Some argue that higher education is not valuable to refugees, as most do not have the legal right to participate in the formal economy of their host countries (Bellino and Hure, 2016, p. 47). However, this argument is contested by the aspirations of students in Dadaab who regularly speak about their future lives outside of the camps.

Our research demonstrates that BHER students recognize that a lack of education will hinder their employment possibilities and success outside the camps. Arte writes how he felt when he first heard about the BHER project:

> It was a turning point in my life because I was very desperate for a higher education. After I graduated from secondary school, I stayed seven years without accessing higher education. A friend introduced me to the BHER Project. When I was accepted into a BHER programme, there were some challenges, but everything was worth it because I had waited for so long.

Likewise, Ochan shared his strong desire to complete university:

> Obtaining a bachelor's degree in this BHER project under the stewardship of York University had several ups and downs which I encountered. However, my ambition to wear the gown and attend the degree convocation guided my effort. I never gave up. When I had fled Uganda in 1987, I was a student, and since then I have not been able to complete a degree, until the BHER project came to Dadaab.

Arte and Ochan's determination to pursue higher education paints a different picture than the education models typically delivered in a crisis context. Harber (2014, p. 174) indicates that the main goal of providing education in a crisis environment, through the support of local actors or international aid, is to restore educational services as quickly as possible to children, in accordance with the Sustainable Development Goals (United Nations, 2016).[2] Primary and secondary schools are the main focus of these goals. Arte, who completed both primary and secondary schooling in the camps, writes about his experiences:

> In the middle of the 1990s, classes began under the trees and later changed into classrooms with walls, which did not block the dust and strong wind. The ratio of teachers to students was 1:80 and overcrowding was a big challenge. The primary and secondary schools in Dadaab refugee camps are run by non-governmental organizations. Most of the teachers are untrained, they are just graduates of secondary schools and often depend on their own experiences of schooling for classroom management and pedagogy.

While primary and secondary education is vital, the need for higher education is just as important for the future of youth and adults who complete their studies. Youths are aware that if they are given the chance to gain access to higher education, they will be able to equip themselves with knowledge that can provide them with practical skills and thus hope for the future. Furthermore, educated youth may provide important support towards the stabilization, securitization and peace-building in their countries of origin if they return home (Milton and Barakat, 2016, p. 406). It is commonly accepted that higher education builds skills in critical thinking, problem solving and conflict resolution. Higher education in conflict and crisis situations can be considered as a factor supporting the three durable solutions: voluntary repatriation, local integration and resettlement for refugees (UNHCR Kenya, 2019).

The BHER project demonstrates that higher education can be delivered in refugee camps, thus making educational programmes more accessible for refugees. BHER brought equality of access to academic programmes with no tuition fees for refugee students, local delivery, and an affirmative action programme that encouraged the recruitment and admission of women, persons with disabilities and ethnic/religious minorities. It is vital for the project that the qualifications students receive are recognized locally and also internationally. Nonetheless, due to the nature of the environment, there are a number of factors that positively or negatively impact access to higher education programming. Moser-Mercer, Hayba and Goldsmith note:

> [P]hysical, intellectual, financial and legal factors have hampered this [university] access, including insufficient infrastructure and connectivity, the length and cost of travel to [a] learning center, insecurity, a lack of ICT skills, language barriers, religious and cultural factors, course costs, and a lack of needed legal documentation, particularly education credentials (2016:42).

To address these and other challenges head-on, BHER instructors, TAs and students have implemented various innovative technological approaches, some of which are discussed below.

Experimenting with Innovative Communication Tools

Advances in mobile and communication technology allow learning content to be accessed through mobile devices and social media applications (de Waard, 2014, p. 115). Due to the nature of the delivery of courses in the BHER project, increasingly through online delivery structures, TAs and students gravitated towards effective technological communication tools. York courses utilize Moodle, an open-source learning management programme, to provide course content to students in Toronto, as well as Dadaab and Kakuma. Moodle allows instructors and TAs to provide access to course materials such as readings and videos, pre-recorded video lectures and interactive message boards. Moodle has enabled nearly equal access to post-secondary courses and peer-to-peer discussions linking students in Toronto with refugee students in Kenya. Moodle and other virtual learning platforms have the potential to extend the university classroom across the globe, to anywhere there is internet access, and provide an enabling learning environment that encourages students to develop and build their digital literacy skills. Arte shares how students participating in BHER courses have benefited from the Moodle platform:

> The Moodle is the source for resources because it has the readings. It is a link for interaction or in other words as a form of communication between the students and their professors, TAs and even the students themselves. It helps for posting the assignments whether it is research, forums and wikis. It is the platform that provides all the plan of the course and keeps you updated about assignments, hence making the students to be active.

While there are many benefits to this form of online, shared, classroom experience, there were, however, instances where BHER students felt that the Moodle platform excluded BHER students in Dadaab from the York University community in Toronto, for example, when students in Dadaab were separated into a distinct group with their own Moodle section. Some YU professors choose to separate Dadaab BHER students from YU Toronto students in order to provide more support in the delivery of the course and address the difficulties refugee students faced while navigating online higher education. Ochan writes:

> One issue I had with Moodle was that when we sign into a course, there are two different sections, a page for Dadaab students and one for Toronto students, for the same course. Even if this is a great tool for communication and learning, we are feeling excluded. If we are in the same course with the same instructor, why should there be two pages? Why can't we all be together, so we feel like we are all in the same class working as a team?

Research has shown that online education programmes require learners to have a high degree of self-control, self-management and time management skills, which usually takes time for students to develop (Halkic and Arnold, 2019, p. 347). While the creation of separate groups on Moodle is perhaps intended to provide the Dadaab students with a learning space where they are able to communicate and support each other, as well as give them access to specifically relevant course material, Ochan's experience suggests that this division may lead students to feel marginalized. Though Moodle allows professors, TAs and students to communicate, it does not provide instantaneous support for students in Dadaab and Kakuma, which we learned was critical to the achievement of successful learning outcomes for students. Evidence of insufficient support for students was demonstrated by the frequent use of WhatsApp, Skype and Zoom by TAs, whose students could more easily and frequently communicate with their mobile phones than computers.

Mobile technology and online social networks became the greatest source of support for students in their pursuit of certificate and diploma completion and perhaps particularly, degrees. Most courses employed Skype and Zoom to conduct live tutorials for students, and to discuss readings, assignments and engage with students in the development of their learning and ideas. In order to bring ourselves closer to students and to build a stronger sense of community, we also turned to WhatsApp Messenger, an instant and cross-platform messaging application. WhatsApp quickly became a vital communication tool for both TAs and students, allowing TAs to communicate information about teaching sessions and important due dates, answer questions and also support student learning. TAs and BHER students began actively participating and developing group chats around particular assignments. WhatsApp provided new opportunities for interaction and collaboration between teaching assistants and students in Dadaab – an experience that was more accessible since WhatsApp is free for smartphone users. Our experience was similar to that of Sam (2016), who argues that such messaging platforms allow students to express themselves in an informal environment, and is a more comfortable forum for some, thus increasing participation rates when compared to the classroom setting.

WhatsApp, in particular, helped build a sense of connectedness between TAs and their students in Dadaab and between TAs and BHER field staff throughout each course.

The instantaneous nature of WhatsApp allowed for immediate response to students' questions or concerns relating to the courses and overall programme delivery. This platform helped to ensure that students did not fall through the cracks, but rather strengthened the relationship between TAs/instructors and on-the-ground administrative staff. Students were also able to enhance their technical skills by sharing and discussing course information on WhatsApp. Arte shares his initial challenges with using online applications and platforms for collaboration: 'The system of using a computer and typing words, familiarizing myself with the keyboard, was difficult for me because I didn't even have a smartphone. I was not computer literate and all of the learning activity was dealing through the devices.' The advantages of employing innovative communication tools were multiple: instant feedback, sharing of knowledge and the development of digital literacy skills (see the chapter by Abikar et al. for more information on digital tools). It became clear to us as TAs that access to and the use of mobile technologies and online social networks helped to break down barriers, build confidence and enhance student ICT skills (see also Douhaibi et al., 2020). Further, the inclusion of social and technical tools altered and enhanced how students communicated and collaborated. Our use of these communication tools arose out of necessity, not by programme design. However, the use of these apps could be more purposeful in future courses or programmes and benefit from our and others' prior experience.

Notably, having access to online social networks through the use of mobile phones does not necessarily equate with productivity (Dahya and Dryden-Peterson, 2017, p. 5). Challenges emerge with regards to expectations around the flexibility and availability of TAs. Frequency of communication at all hours of the day through mobile phones made it difficult for a professional line to be drawn between TA personal time and work time and led to far more informal conversations with students than would exist in a more traditional course delivery model. While the use of WhatsApp Messenger provides direct access to TA support, it still fails to give students in Dadaab the sense that their university experience is equal to that of their Canadian classmates. Arte writes:

> The time zone differences [make] it difficult for us to interact live with local Toronto York students. Our professors and TAs sacrifice their sleep to connect with us, which we appreciate, but we would like to feel more connected to the

students in Toronto. We feel like some knowledge, skills and experiences are not being shared properly between us and Toronto students. We believe that through that interaction we could possibly improve our writing, academic reasoning and arguments—different types of communicating that would be helpful for both sides.

The notion of *flexible learning* (Looi and Toh, 2014, p. 163) refers to resources and methods being increasingly shared and personalized in diverse ways, with overwhelmingly positive consequences on both teaching and learning. As we describe below, we began to take advantage of this approach to address the needs of our students, with the main objective being to provide them with as much flexibility as possible in terms of course content, scheduling, accessibility and learning styles.

Flexible Approaches to Learning

Students participating in the BHER related university programmes come from educational backgrounds that differ greatly from those students taught by YU professors and TAs. Early on, it was clear that the learning and teaching structures developed during the delivery of courses were at times in conflict with local learning experiences and expectations. With the implementation of flexible learning, professors and TAs attempted to create courses that were adjustable in design and delivery in order to allow students to adapt to new (to them) pedagogical approaches and to promote both individual and collaborative learning. This teaching method is highly supportive of learners exploring the range and depth of their abilities. Arte expressed his first encounter with this approach:

> In the beginning of the programme, I was challenged and the kind of teaching structures I was introduced to were in conflict with my learning experiences growing up in the camps. My learning experiences [were] similar to Paulo Freire's concept called 'the banking model of education', where I was a passive learner. We were used to teachers coming to the class, reading our textbooks with no personal explanations and then as students we needed to absorb everything in that book. My learning was based on memorization and during evaluations, we were required to mention all concepts we learned, exactly as it was in our textbooks, or else we would fail. We were never given the opportunity to think or share our personal ideas. The notion of critical thinking was new for us and difficult to grasp at first.

It became clear early on that many students found engagement in critical thinking and adherence to academic citation practices challenging; TAs received assignments riddled with plagiarism and lacking in higher-level critical thinking by their students. We quickly realized that we had to introduce, explain and practise new pedagogical approaches with students. Two approaches were particularly important: critical pedagogy and participatory pedagogy.

Critical Pedagogy

We turned to the work of Paulo Freire, whose ideas about critical pedagogy acknowledge that 'human life is conditioned, not determined', and thus the world needs to be read critically, leading to citizens taking responsibility for their actions (Giroux, 2010, p. 716). This approach laid the groundwork for exploring the ways that we could provide new knowledge, skills and social connections to assist students in their explorations into what it means to be critical citizens. The purpose of implementing critical pedagogy, especially in a location like Dadaab, is to encourage students to take responsibility for their own learning, to challenge ideas, and to explore the relationships that they have within their communities and in their classroom. When used appropriately, students will be able to better understand their abilities and positions in society and can develop the necessary tools needed for problem solving and struggling against injustices in their lives. We hoped that this approach would enhance both our teaching and the students' learning experiences. Relatedly, Ochan writes about his personal journey as a university student and teacher in the camps:

> The curriculum I was always used to was very strict and organized in a manner that I could not change, especially as a teacher. There was no flexibility and the planning that I developed for my teaching had to be in line with the curriculum exactly. When we first started in the BHER's teacher training programme, the pedagogy we were taught to use was confusing and the lesson plans that we were told to develop were extremely flexible and included evaluating ourselves and our teaching practices. What worked well was when we were forced to not only see our students improve in their learning, but also us as teachers, and [our] teaching practices. We understood that as learners in the BHER programme, we all learn in different ways. The challenge was for us to break out of our old cycle of teaching and learning, and to see how our traditional learning environment has room for change.

While the introduction of critical thinking skills to our students in Dadaab enhanced their written and verbal communication skills, at first they were not familiar with being asked to share their personal opinions and ideas for fear of being labelled 'wrong'. This resulted in a number of students plagiarizing their academic work. Ochan writes:

> Some of them realized that they could not cope up with the courses and the new approach to learning. On top of that, many of us did not have a firm understanding of what plagiarism was. The transition period was tough on students and as a result many of them used the copy-and-paste method of learning instead of thinking and sharing their own ideas.

It became clear to TAs and instructors that students required encouragement and practice to be able confidently to offer their personal opinions or ideas in their assignments. Participatory pedagogy became important in the encouragement of students' exercise of critical thinking skills.

Participatory Pedagogy

Participatory pedagogy posits that students learn best when a partnership is developed between the professor, TAs and students, leading to students becoming more active in shaping the pedagogy (including technological tools) used for their teaching and learning (DePietro, 2012, p. 37). In this learner-centred education, students are considered active participants in their learning process, as they gain control and responsibility for their own learning. In the case of our courses, a genuine participatory pedagogy was dependent on how students interacted and engaged with each other in person at the BHER Learning Centre and online. A participatory pedagogical approach and the use of new innovative tools helped break down a variety of divisions among the students. Ochan writes:

> When we are using Zoom and Skype, we all sit together and through these discussions we are learning more about each other. In comparison to the schools in the camps, we do not have to separate by gender. We are able to mix freely and engage with each other, regardless of our gender, religion and ethnicity. This learning experience has helped us become closer and broke down barriers and misconceptions we had about each other and our communities.

Similarly, Arte shares how communicating and participating with not only the students, but also the TAs, assisted them in gaining confidence throughout their studies:

> There were certain professors who had not travelled to Dadaab that were stricter in comparison to the professors who had visited and taught us on the ground. This is

when our TAs became our advocates. They were mediators for us, always between us and the professors. They gave us second chances. They were patient with us and our journey in this new education system. They were also mentors for us. They shared their knowledge and experiences with us ... when we did get comments from them, they were very detailed and ensured that we would not make the same mistakes twice and pushed us to improve our writing. This has helped us become more confident in our knowledge and now we have become mentors to the students in the cohorts below us. We have been able to take the skills and experiences we gained with our TAs and use them now with other students.

Critical and participatory pedagogy assisted TAs and BHER students to develop a relationship based on shared trust and understanding. YU's approach to the delivery of higher education, in the context of Dadaab, has been strongly focused on strengthening the quantity and quality of teaching and learning within the camps, bolstering peer-to-peer support for and engagement with TAs and instructors, and building skills that will support students beyond the classrooms and camps. Arte, who experienced online learning through experiences at both YU and other Kenyan universities, shared his personal lessons:

The professors and TAs from York University, who visited and taught us in Dadaab were very flexible for BHER students and extended their help any time we needed their support. Many York professors and TAs have visited us for weeks at a time, and through these on the ground sessions, they have gained a better understanding on how to teach and support us. York University focuses on competencies – the students are taught not only to read the text, but to think beyond the text, hence understand the world. At York University, students are evaluated in writing assignments, this means that students are encouraged to critically think about the concepts of the course, hence the result is a well-rounded education. At other universities in Kenya there is more focus on students reading the content without any critical thinking and their evaluation is based on only exams. Institutions or projects attempting to deliver e-learning, distance education, and build university partnerships will inevitably deal with different challenges, particularly within a context of conflict and crises.

Conclusion

This chapter shares the experiences and relationships of YU students and TAs engaged in innovative learning approaches and technologies to support higher level learning in a complex setting such as the Dadaab refugee camps. The BHER project demonstrates both the power of a borderless, international learning environment across geographical locations to benefit refugees and Kenyan host community students and serves as a lesson for similar future projects. Arte and Ochan explain that for students in refugee contexts, there are critical gains to be had from access to university programmes:

> **Arte**   I have become someone who can compete with other people and it has improved my competence. It has given me a voice, I am speaking for myself, [my] community and my country, Somalia. I have full confidence in myself and my abilities. Education is the best tool for getting people out of their precarious condition. If there is another platform like BHER, providing higher education for the desperate refugees in camps, that would be something so fascinating. Many of these youths will receive knowledge and skills that help them have a way of controlling their lives.
>
> **Ochan**   The way I behave, interact and address myself within my community has completely changed and everyone has noticed it. It has changed the way I teach and interact with my students and their families. Before I used to be the only one speaking and my students were passive learners: they listen, and they do not interact. Now my lessons are interactive; I use student inquiry and want their answers to include their own thoughts, ideas and opinions based off of their experiences. I want my students to also gain the reasoning and the capacity to build arguments and question their surroundings and knowledge. The BHER programme introduced me to practical knowledge, both in my academic and personal life.

Offering this kind of university education programme is challenging and requires strong collaboration between learners and teachers. The provision of access to higher education in protracted refugee situations can lead to the restoration of development after conflict and can serve as the foundation for peaceful reconciliation and conflict resolution within refugee camps and host countries. For projects like BHER to exist, there needs to be collaboration between academics and practitioners, between educators and humanitarian specialists, between institutions in the Global North and the Global South. It is only through such partnerships that higher education for refugees can achieved (Dryden-Peterson and Giles, 2011, p. 7).

Partnership between TAs and students is also vital for the success of projects such as BHER. TAs and instructors, whether online or on the ground, need to manage their expectations when planning courses and pedagogical approaches for students in fragile zones. Students in areas of conflict and crisis will inherently be learning in extremely precarious circumstances. We know that the lack of adequate housing, household latrines and water undoubtedly influence students' learning experiences. Social media tools can ameliorate these difficulties through the provision of connectivity and community; but it is also important to foster supportive relationships among TAs and to seek support from colleagues and faculty members when faced with challenges. Flexible approaches to learning that encompass critical thinking skills and participatory pedagogy are key. Finally, our research supports the conclusion that facilitated online learning along with innovative technological tools can support and create meaningful, collaborative learning and teaching practices when informed by local contexts. Still to be explored and only touched on in this chapter is how the provision of flexible online learning in areas of conflict and crisis can offer students studying in both the local context, as well as in faraway universities, the opportunity to gain cross-cultural awareness and new perspectives relevant to their courses and their own future approaches to teaching.

7

Out of Bounds: The BHER Bones of Teaching Geography Across Borders

Megan Youdelis, Dacia Douhaibi, Devin Holterman,
Kamal Paudel, Valerie Preston, Tarmo K. Remmel,
Elizabeth Lunstrum and Joseph Mensah

Through the Borderless Higher Education for Refugees (BHER) project, students in the Dadaab refugee camp and nearby towns in Kenya completed the course requirements for a Bachelor's degree in Geography. As former BHER professors and teaching assistants, in this chapter we discuss the opportunities, challenges and lessons learned from teaching geography courses required for a degree to students living in the Dadaab refugee camps and environs. The courses vary in terms of their subject matter, required academic background and pedagogy. Their diversity allows a comparative analysis of our experiences that identifies opportunities and challenges for innovation in internationalizing post-secondary education. Teaching in the BHER project from 2014 through 2018 provided invaluable opportunities for both students and instructors, and even in the face of numerous and often unforeseen challenges there were opportunities where best practices evolved in the courses taught.

The professors and teaching assistants (TAs) (four professors and four TAs) who taught the geography courses discussed in this chapter were drawn to the BHER project by a shared conviction that geographical knowledge is crucial for addressing contemporary global challenges such as climate change and forced displacement. We saw BHER as an exciting opportunity to put our professional experience to work by offering a geography degree to Dadaab students who would otherwise not have access to higher education. Teaching Dadaab students also provided opportunities to learn about internationalizing geographical education through online courses. We were especially interested in promoting intercultural learning between students in Dadaab and Toronto, whose everyday lives are ostensibly different and disconnected. Course selection and design were guided by the first-hand knowledge that Mensah and Douhaibi gained during visits to the refugee camps, the expertise of BHER administrators, and advice from professors and TAs who had already taught in Dadaab. We also drew on the geographical expertise of all instructors. The authors include two professors who study development and population issues in Africa, and the research and teaching interests of the other two professors – international migration and the boreal forest – are intimately tied to the uneven impacts of globalization that we examined across the geography curriculum. The lived experiences of the four TAs, who have worked and studied in Africa, Asia and other locations in the Global South, informed all aspects of their teaching and proved invaluable for helping them adapt to unexpected challenges and circumstances.

The courses required for the geography major range from a very large introductory course[1] with hundreds of students that is designed to enhance students' critical reading, writing and analytical skills while familiarizing them with contemporary geographical concepts and thinking, to smaller upper-year courses introducing geoinformatics and examining the geographies of migration, development and gender (Table 7.1). While the introductory course is intended for qualified first-year university students in Ontario, subsequent courses require

Table 7.1 Geography courses in the B.A. Geography degree offered through BHER

Code	Title	Credits	Year	Enrolment Keele	Enrolment BHER	Instructors
GEOG 1000	World Geography	6.00	2016–2017	408	25	**
GEOG 2030	Global Environmental Change	3.00	2014–2015	86	27	E. Lunstrum, D. Douhaibi*
GEOG 2340	Introduction to Geoinformatics	3.00	2017–2018	48	21	T. Remmel, K. Paudel*
GEOG 3370	International Development	3.00	2017–2018	0	21	R. Bridi
GEOG 4380	Urban Social Policy	3.00	2017–2018	0	21	R. Bridi
GEOG 2310	Refugee Migration	6.00	2017-2018	0	25	R. Bridi
GEOG 3070	Gender, Migration, Population	6.00	2017–2018	38	25	J. Mensah, M. Youdelis*

* Teaching Assistant
** GEOG 1000 was team taught by E. Lunstrum, V. Preston, and P. Vandergeest. Teaching Assistants were D. Holterman and D. Douhaibi.

some background in contemporary geography, technical skills including familiarity with software such as Excel and Word, and the critical intellectual skills expected of second and third-year students in the social sciences. All the courses were taught online for Dadaab students with videos of lectures supplemented by tutorials taught over Skype. The same courses were taught in Toronto either in a blended format, where mandatory tutorials supplemented online video recordings of lectures, or in face-to-face lectures and tutorials. The courses were delivered by professors and teaching assistants with professors responsible for the objectives, content and format of each course, recording videos of the lectures, and ensuring each course was delivered successfully and academic standards were maintained across all formats. TAs were responsible for grading assignments, advising individual students, answering student inquiries and teaching online tutorials (see Sabriye and Douhaibi in this volume for more details about TA roles). The division of labour meant that TAs often had more regular and direct contact with Dadaab students than professors did.

Pedagogic innovations to promote intercultural learning through interaction among students from both locations were adopted in some courses while others focused on ensuring students in both locations mastered the same material. Each course included some material relevant to the everyday lives and life chances of Dadaab students, just as the courses taught in Toronto include equivalent material for Toronto students. For example, in *Geoinformatics*, assignments for Dadaab students drew on relevant African information.

Through our varied approaches to addressing common challenges, we have developed suggestions for effective course delivery across borders. We begin with a brief description of the opportunities and challenges that we encountered and demonstrate the importance of adapting to local realities, discuss the pedagogical implications of cross-border course delivery and detail the technological requirements. We conclude with lessons learned from our collective experience and concrete suggestions for future practice. We argue that successfully internationalizing education requires flexible pedagogy, ongoing sensitivity to the dynamic cultural, political and economic context in which courses are delivered, and sustained technical and administrative support. As the number of organizations and institutions supporting refugee education is growing (Dryden-Peterson, 2010; Crea and McFarland, 2015; Sherab and Kirk, 2016). it is timely and necessary to share best practices and lessons learned (Swain, 2018). Our goal is to inform all instructors committed to internationalizing education, especially geographers trying to take advantage of the different environments in which students live and study to enhance post-secondary education.

Geography and the BHER Project: Opportunities and Challenges of Internationalizing Education

Geography as a discipline is well suited for internationalizing education. Geographers, trained to be sensitive to the ways in which political, economic, social and cultural contexts shape local realities, teach about the structural processes such as forced displacement and social marginalization that contributed to the challenges which instructors faced with the BHER courses (Haigh, 2002; Testa and Egan, 2014; Simm and Marvell, 2017; Bellino and Hure, 2018). Our experiences align with observations from other geographical experiments in internationalizing education, which show that sensitivity to the cultural, political and economic context in which courses are being delivered is key to their success and sustainability (Morrice, 2013; Clark and Wilson, 2017; Bellino and Hure, 2018). We also affirm previous findings that opportunities for students to engage in collaborative learning facilitate international geographical education (Solem et al., 2003). The geography courses that we offered also tried to incorporate opportunities for intercultural learning, which is another hallmark of successful international education.

Given the context of the courses we offered, we designed the geography degree programme with sensitivity to UNHCR concerns that postsecondary education initiatives in refugee camps could be seen to encourage permanent settlement in the camps rather than repatriation (Wright and Plasterer, 2010). There were limited employment opportunities in the camp for graduates, especially those obtaining university degrees (Crea and McFarland, 2015). Within the limitations of the geography degree requirements, courses were selected to benefit BHER students and their communities in the camps (Dryden-Peterson, 2012; Sherab and Kirk, 2016) and provide expertise for development, which can facilitate recovery in conflict societies (Wright and Plasterer, 2010; Milton and Barakat, 2016; Kamyab, 2017). The course offerings taught subject matter and skills that students could use as teachers or in other professions that could be pursued both inside and outside of the camps.

Internationalizing education can offer exciting opportunities for students and their communities. When things run smoothly, creating connected, virtual, internationalized spaces and exchanging ideas can be enriching for all involved, exemplifying the worldly university that takes responsibility for its role in combating global injustice (Bender, 1998; Haigh, 2002; Simms and Marvell, 2017; Giles and Dippo, 2019; Shawyer and Giles, 2019). The BHER project provided opportunities for students in Dadaab, who would not otherwise have had access to higher education, to obtain diplomas and degrees such as a Geography degree from York University. We hoped to emulate the results from other pilot projects that used online learning to internationalize geographical education and that demonstrated how students felt empowered through their expanded worldview and new skills (Crea and McFarland, 2015). With their emphasis on intercultural learning, the geography courses attempted to collapse the time and space between students in Dadaab and those in Ontario and facilitate collaborative encounters between the two cohorts. In addition to course material that highlighted the different contexts in which students lived in Toronto and Dadaab, courses examined the economic, political, social and cultural structures and processes that reinforced disparities in students' livelihoods and life chances. For both groups of students, internationalizing education offered exceptional opportunities to learn first-hand about people and places that were otherwise inaccessible. The international learning environment also allowed valuable experiments with course design and form.

Along with a solid background in contemporary geography, the degree provided critical reading and writing skills, policy analysis skills and knowledge of Geographic Information Systems (GIS) and geoinformatics that proved valuable for students' career development and supported BHER's development agenda. Over the duration of the degree programme, the Dadaab students demonstrated tremendous improvements in academic and technical skills. This progress was particularly notable when we consider students' limited capacity to engage in online courses when they began the degree. During the first term, for example, students struggled to log into York University's online learning platform, Moodle, and by the end of the final term, they were using Moodle fluidly – watching lectures online, submitting assignments and participating in discussion forums. Most students' critical thinking, reading and writing skills also improved. Initially, students were flummoxed by the request to contribute a brief opinion justified by examples from the readings or lectures to a discussion forum, but by the end of the degree, the majority were formulating well-justified and clear opinions.

Internationalizing education has far-reaching implications for individual, local and regional well-being. The skills and knowledge gained from their geography degrees improved the life prospects of individual graduates. It also enhanced the quality of education in the camps. Many graduates who had already obtained education diplomas through BHER-related programmes continued to work as teachers, employing their new skills and critical insights to enhance their pedagogy. Additional capacity was created in the camps when several graduates secured jobs with NGOs and GIS companies and others used their new skills to start consulting and work in cartographic businesses. Some students have continued to the Master's level, gaining additional knowledge and skills that will also contribute to local development, conflict resolution and recovery (Wright and Plasterer, 2010; Milton and Barakat, 2016).

While our experiences delivering cross-border education demonstrate the potential benefits of this approach to internationalizing education, we also encountered numerous challenges similar to those reported for other attempts to internationalize geographic education (Wright and Plasterer, 2010; Simm and Marvell, 2017; Bellino and Hure, 2018). These included ensuring course topics and readings were relevant to all students; coordinating class activities across time and space; grappling with issues of language comprehension, vocabulary and knowledge of academic honesty; providing necessary technology; solving technical problems; and dealing with demanding workloads. By comparing the experiences in the various geography courses, we identify four common challenges. After outlining the challenges, we evaluate the effectiveness of different approaches to addressing them and highlight the resources required for success. Throughout this assessment, we note the role of course structure in exacerbating problems or, conversely, facilitating resolutions to these common challenges.

Flexible Pedagogy

The living and working conditions in refugee camps pose challenges for internationalizing education successfully (see Duale, Munene and Njogu in this volume for more details). Dadaab students have demanding lives and little time to study outside their attendance at the BHER Learning Centre one or two days per week. With few financial and material resources, their studies can be derailed easily by unexpected events. Camp administrators also have few resources to ameliorate the impacts of security threats, natural disasters, threats of camp closure, and changes in the policies of international organizations and the Kenyan state on students. Resettlement disrupted students' studies, whether they were moving to Kakuma (another Kenyan refugee camp), or to Australia, the United States, Canada and other countries. The vulnerability of Dadaab students reduced opportunities for intercultural learning and required accommodation so students could complete the degree requirements.

Turning first to the demanding lives of Dadaab students, all students had paid work, family obligations, little access to computers or Wi-Fi at home and poor lighting so they could not study after dark. As a result, students tried to complete almost all their coursework at the Learning Centre, which was only open three days per week. Despite concerted efforts to improve access to the Centre, security concerns meant buses only ran during the day, travel was time-consuming with one-way trips taking thirty to sixty minutes by bus and one to two hours by foot, and travel costs were prohibitive for many students who relied on subsidies that were available only for a specified number of trips to the BHER Learning Centre.

Patriarchal social relations meant the demands of daily life were particularly acute for women. Most of the women participating in the BHER programme were married with children, and they were expected to shoulder childcare and housekeeping in addition to paid work. Family responsibilities sometimes prevented them from going to the Learning Centre, the only place with the technology to complete coursework and the only place where they could focus on their studies. TAs reported that female students struggled with attendance and deadlines even more than male students.

TAs demonstrated sensitivity to a cultural context of gender-based learning inequities by using various strategies to help female students engage in courses. They adjusted deadlines to help female students finish coursework. Instructors and students communicated over WhatsApp,[2] and at the request of women students, a separate WhatsApp group was created to combat men's domination in discussions. The group gave women an opportunity to speak directly and encouraged concise comments that could be read in the short periods of time available to many female students. In tutorials, TAs started calling on students by name, ensuring women had opportunities to speak. TAs recognized that many women were also uncomfortable speaking to an audience of men and women, so the teaching assistants assigned responsibility for summarizing discussions to individual students, always including some women. These pedagogic innovations helped to facilitate the success of many women students who have since gone on to study at the Master's level after completing the BA in Geography.

Although the combined responsibilities of family and paid work curtailed many women's access to the BHER Learning Centre, some men also had limited access for religious reasons. While the majority of students were Muslims who could attend tutorials at the Learning Centre on Saturday following prayers on Friday, four students were Seventh Day Adventists for whom religious observances occur on Saturday. To accommodate these students, some TAs arranged alternate tutorial sessions. In other courses, the TA audio-recorded the Saturday tutorials so that students could listen to them on Monday. Though the recordings were an imperfect substitute for attending the tutorial where students could interact with the TA and other students, they enhanced the availability of course material, and proved unexpectedly helpful for all students, who could thereby catch up and review lessons on their own time.

The refugee experience itself also hampered some students' engagement in courses. Poor living conditions in the camp, threats of closure and resettlement threatened students' academic progress. Significant and regular flooding in Dadaab affected student attendance and engagement. Students lost many of their possessions in the floods and travel became extremely difficult and occasionally impossible. Communicable diseases swept through the camps, a by-product of the standing water and flooded sewage portrayed dramatically in the powerful images and videos of the floods that BHER students sent to Toronto students. Persistent threats of camp closure created significant anxiety for students in Dadaab,[3] which they expressed often in course discussions. Several students were resettled from Dadaab to other camps in Kenya and to other countries including Somalia, Australia, Canada and the United States. While resettlement is a goal for many refugees, building a life in a new place is difficult and time-consuming. To continue their studies, resettled students had to gain access to a computer and the internet in a new environment. Under these circumstances, it is not surprising that students who were enrolled simultaneously in three or four courses expressed being overwhelmed and tried to simply make it through each course as best they could.

Taking into consideration student needs, we found that flexible course requirements and delivery facilitated students' engagement in geography courses. Revising deadlines, working with students one-on-one to help them finish coursework, reweighting assignments, and for resettled students, finding invigilators for exams at different universities around the world enabled a high retention rate for the geography degree programme. Most of all, the retention rate is testament to students' dedication to their studies and their ability to overcome tremendous obstacles.

We created a curriculum sensitive to local circumstances (Simm and Marvel, 2017), thus, providing opportunities for collaborative learning (a hallmark of successful international education (Solem et al., 2003)), as well as for acquiring the concepts and skills required for their geography degree. In each course, professors and TAs tailored course requirements to enable students in Dadaab and Toronto to frame their experiences in relation to broader political, economic and ecological issues, taking account of the interconnections between their locations. Since we had not taught students in a Kenyan refugee camp previously, TAs assessed students' reactions to the curriculum informally and adjusted tutorial content on an ongoing basis. For example, *Global Environmental Change* required students to make observations of climate change in their everyday lives and reflect on how they contribute and are affected by global environmental change processes. The TA encouraged Dadaab students to use the observations to consider how the actions of wealthy, developed states contribute to forced displacement. In another exercise that compared the environmental footprints of Toronto and Dadaab students, both groups of students were surprised by the unequal impacts of global environmental change.

Professors and TAs showed ingenuity in their efforts to incorporate relevant topics in courses. In *Geoinformatics*, which introduces topics including cartography, GIS, photogrammetry and GPS, the course material was modified to be relevant to the daily lives of students in Dadaab. For example, a poll indicated that most students use Android phones, so the tutorial about the use of a smartphone for data collection focused on this type of phone, which would work without the need for a data plan. Students also used local spatial data (e.g. satellite images, air photographs and maps) in tutorials and assignments. Freely available and open source software that would be available after the course at no cost and without licensing challenges was used in tutorials and assignments.

Salient topics had some drawbacks as well as their well-documented advantages (Simm and Marvel, 2017). As we had expected, discussions of forced displacement in several courses including *Introduction to World Geography* and *Gender, Population, and Migration* were especially relevant to Dadaab students. In tutorials and discussion forums, they engaged eagerly with this topic, speaking and writing about their lived experiences of forced migration and gendered inequalities in access to education and certain professions. In Dadaab tutorials, several women shared such harrowing stories about their migration experiences that the TA had to take great care to ensure that class meetings fostered a welcoming, supportive environment where everyone felt they would be heard and respected. Respect and full attention were given to any student that wished to share their experiences, and they were given space to process their emotions and step away from the conversation if need be.

While students' assignments and participation in discussion forums and tutorials indicated that many course topics were relevant to students in Dadaab and Toronto, making material clear and accessible to Dadaab students was an issue in all courses. Although professors and TAs had anticipated difficulties understanding the Dadaab students, we quickly learned that the students also had difficulties understanding our written and spoken language. Students often had questions about expressions and idioms in lecture videos and printed materials. During Skype tutorials, TAs learned to speak slowly and clearly. However, for professors who had already recorded the lecture videos, altering the audio was not possible. To help students, TAs set aside tutorial time to answer questions about the videos and to clarify concepts. TAs also encouraged students to use the WhatsApp group to request video clarification. Experiments with closed captioning for each lecture video and written transcripts of lectures seemed quite effective in resolving students' comprehension issues. However, all of these strategies had drawbacks. Extending tutorials led to scheduling conflicts with other courses and required sustained connectivity that was not always available. Students who had relocated to Kakuma were at a particular disadvantage because they often had little time at functioning computer stations with adequate internet connections. Closed captioning and transcripts also require additional resources and technical support.

Sensitivity to Dynamic Cultural, Political and Economic Context

In all the geography courses, instructors wanted to promote intercultural learning and simultaneously ensure that Dadaab students acquired the equivalent knowledge and skills to their peers in Toronto. These goals were jeopardized by our limited familiarity with Dadaab students' strengths, knowledge and skills, underestimation of the challenges involved in converting courses taught face-to-face to an online format, and scheduling and technology differences between the two locations. Initially, we understood that Dadaab students would have qualifications equivalent to those of students beginning first year at York University. We quickly learned that their enthusiasm and commitment did not compensate fully for unexpected differences in their critical reading, writing and thinking skills. Students also had little experience with the computer hardware and software required for some geography courses and little training in academic citation practices.

Able and eager to express their ideas verbally, students had a wide range of writing abilities, especially in terms of their abilities to formulate a thesis, structure an argument and write in English at the same level as first-year geography students in Toronto. Although these skills improved steadily over time, they required sustained and direct instruction that was only available from the TAs since Dadaab students could not make use of the Academic Writing Centre available in Toronto. Despite their familiarity with keyboarding and basic word processing, Dadaab students were also not well prepared for the technical requirements of advanced geography courses. In these courses, initial tutorials had to focus on building general computer skills such as saving, copying and renaming files before introducing fundamental geoinformatics skills. TAs and professors also spent more time than they had planned teaching about academic honesty.[4] TAs combatted inadvertent and deliberate academic honesty violations in all geography courses by lengthy discussions of academic citation and the principles of academic honesty in tutorials, one-on-one consultations and detailed comments on assignments. They also sought additional pedagogical information about working with ESL students in online courses.[5] TAs and professors could assist each other to a limited extent by sharing ideas about general issues such as how to clarify questions from video lectures. Each TA taught a different course, so each one improvised individually to solve specific problems about topics and assignments in each course.[6]

Professors faced additional challenges dealing with the need to adapt courses in midstream for Dadaab students while converting face-to-face lectures to an online format and teaching a course simultaneously in two formats: online and face-to-face. Only one of the geography courses had been taught online before the degree was offered through BHER. As a result, professors taught two versions of each course simultaneously (one with lectures in class for Toronto students and one online for BHER students). Even with crucial support from staff at the Dadaab Learning Centre and a TA who maintained the course websites, delivering different course requirements for the online and face-to-face formats, recording lectures, and setting up and maintaining multiple course websites proved time-consuming. The ongoing need to revise courses in midstream as we learned more about the strengths and lives of Dadaab students combined with the time and effort required to create online content and teach online and face-to-face formats simultaneously created a demanding, almost unsustainable workload. To manage, professors felt forced to make pedagogical compromises that sapped their enthusiasm for BHER.

Due to scheduling and technology issues, traditional forms of intercultural learning were often curtailed. The seven to eight-hour time difference between Toronto and Kenya made simultaneous Skype and face-to-face tutorials almost impossible. Tutorials were also held on different days for students in Toronto and Dadaab. Differences in software and equipment also limited opportunities for activities to be shared across the two locations. In Dadaab, the software and equipment were often open source and free tools, while Toronto students used proprietary software and equipment. In response to these challenges, some courses did not try to coordinate the online and face-to-face sections. In one case, topics and the accompanying lectures were not scheduled for specific dates, so students in Toronto and Dadaab did not have opportunities to interact with each other or share their experiences.

Sustained Technical and Administrative Support

Facilitating higher education at a distance requires substantial and sustained technical and administrative support. Technical difficulties were by far the most persistent and most pernicious challenges we encountered teaching the geography courses. Lack of internet connectivity was the most pressing concern, as it reduced the already limited time TAs had to both deliver course content and build critical academic skills. Even weather patterns could reduce the availability and strength of the network. While the audio connection usually functioned, Skype calls dropped occasionally, and audio was sometimes difficult to understand. For example, if more than ten desktop computers, combined with mobile phones, laptops and tablets, attempted to access the network simultaneously in the Learning Centre classroom, video could not be used. During concurrent tutorials, the lab with closer proximity to the modems consumed most of the bandwidth leaving the second computer lab too little signal to operate effectively. The poor connection precluded much screen sharing, a common tool in many geography courses, especially technical courses such as *Geoinformatics*.

All TAs developed a variety of strategies to address technical and connectivity challenges. In one course, the TA wrote a course announcement after each tutorial summarizing the discussion and listing links to key documents. To improve online connections, some TAs turned off the video feature for tutorials and used only audio. This strategy, however, created several other problems. The TA could not observe students' body language to assess students' engagement with tutorials and tutorial discussions, so they relied on feedback from the on-site staff and from instructors who observed tutorials during their biannual visits to Dadaab. Some TAs learned to identify students' voices so they could still discern which students were participating in class discussions when video had to be turned off. In many tutorials, students were also asked to identify themselves before speaking, a formality that rarely occurs in face-to-face tutorials.

Connectivity was especially problematic when TAs tried to connect students at multiple locations on the same Skype call. Students in Dadaab and Kakuma were not able consistently to access their computer labs at the same time, and the network in Kakuma was often too weak for reliable participation in the Skype tutorials. After three weeks of failed efforts to connect students in *Global*

Environmental Change at the two locations, we scheduled separate tutorials for students in Dadaab and Kakuma. During class, students not in Dadaab had to mute their microphones while listening, to limit extraneous noise. This muting, however, impeded their participation in the flow of class discussions.

Technology-related accommodations required extensive time from TAs and reduced the time available for critical skill building. Making up lost tutorial time was difficult because of the tight back-to-back scheduling of tutorials and the requirement that students leave the Learning Centre before nightfall for security reasons. The duration of tutorials could not be increased, and disrupted tutorials could not be rescheduled easily. Office hours, an additional source of skill-building support for on-campus students, were impossible to schedule for BHER students due to the time differences between Toronto and Dadaab. As mentioned, one course, *Gender, Population and Migration*, accommodated technical challenges through flexible course design. Lectures were not tied to specific dates, and the TA had a great deal of leeway in terms of assignment due dates. The TA could take additional time for a task in a tutorial and push the remaining undone tasks to the following week. As a result, delays and disruptions associated with connectivity and other technical issues had little impact on students, the TA and the professor.

The impact of technical problems was readily apparent in *Geoinformatics*. To minimize downloading, the professor negotiated free access to a digital copy of the textbook and provided all the videos, data and software to the Learning Centre prior to the start of term. Despite this preparation, the materials were not available when the course began, and the TA had to use the initial tutorials to resolve technical issues. After the initial issues were addressed, students still did not have enough hours in the Learning Centre to complete tutorials, in part because they needed extra time to polish foundational skills.

Lessons Learned

The BHER experience provided instructors with an extraordinary opportunity to learn about effective pedagogy that can be an instrument for social justice. Providing higher education to students in refugee camps can redress global inequalities in access to education and produce educated graduates who may improve living conditions in the camps and catalyse sustainable recovery in their home societies (Wright and Plasterer, 2010; Milton and Barakat, 2016). In this respect, the BHER project has implications for universities in the Global North as they strive to become more worldly (Giles and Dippo, 2019). All of the geography instructors came to admire the determination of students in Dadaab to complete their studies under exceptionally demanding circumstances. We learned three key lessons from teaching the courses required for the geography degree: ensure adequate technical and administrative support for professors and TAs, adopt a flexible pedagogy, and have contingency plans that respond to the shifting cultural, economic and political context of learners.

What turns out to be key for the success of international education initiatives such as BHER is the sustained and substantial support from project administrators and on-site staff in Dadaab and Toronto, along with a passionate commitment from professors and TAs. In terms of technical and administrative support, professors require support for creating and teaching online courses. In addition to support from colleagues who specialize in teaching ESL students and have expertise in teaching foundational skills, such as critical reading and writing, TAs need on-the-ground continuous technical support to facilitate tutorials. Extensive technical support is needed on site in Dadaab to address equipment failure and connectivity problems quickly. Neither professors nor TAs should be bogged down dealing with technical issues, which leaves little time for development of intercultural learning opportunities or even basic course delivery. Each computer lab in the Learning Centre should be equipped with high-grade Wi-Fi systems, webcams/microphones to provide adequate connectivity and reliable Skype video. Although we often focus on the supports needed by students, we came to realize that professors also require ongoing support, especially with video lecture recording and the construction and maintenance of course websites.

Technical and pedagogical issues were most pronounced in classes that had to be converted to an online format. Based on our experience, we recommend that only courses in an online or blended format be considered for international delivery. The creation of an online course should occur well before its delivery to students overseas, with adequate technical support and recognition of the additional work involved for professors and TAs. Subsequently, instructors can customize courses to suit the circumstances of a specific learning community. The successful translation of courses between disparate contexts occurs through practice that is only possible if online courses are available prior to their delivery and are taught repeatedly.

Flexible pedagogy was a critical aspect of the geography courses. In addition to adapting course topics to be relevant to students in both locations, professors and TAs revised course requirements, were flexible about assignment deadlines and developed strategies for dealing with limited tutorial time. We learned that students could better understand lecture and tutorial material when professors and TAs slowed their speech and enunciated clearly. We recommend that additional support be provided to add closed captioning to lecture videos and provide students with transcripts and summaries of lectures and tutorials. Course content that is delivered in multiple media is more accessible to Dadaab students who have demanding living conditions. Again, multiple media are only feasible if a course is already available in an online format.

To overcome technical problems and scheduling challenges that are probably unavoidable in initiatives that aim to internationalize education requires ongoing and sustained coordination and collaboration among professors, TAs, and technical and support staff. Collaboration is crucial to respond to unanticipated events and unexpected differences in students' preparation as they arise during a course. A learning community in which professors and TAs, along with technical and administrative staff, discuss their experiences on a regular basis would allow them to share strategies for dealing with unexpected issues such as students' familiarity with academic honesty, the loss of Skype video capacity during tutorial discussions and the impacts of floods on student attendance. Such a learning community could also undertake formative evaluations with students that would help instructors adapt courses effectively to the shifting circumstances in which students are living and learning.

Alternative models of course delivery may also facilitate international education initiatives. Cross-border education may work better with small courses where instructors have time to work simultaneously with Toronto and BHER students. In Toronto, large courses inhibit the interaction between professors and students and allow few opportunities for professors to bring students together in fruitful ways. Short, condensed courses that allow BHER students to concentrate on one or two courses at a time may also ensure the success of international course delivery. Taking four courses at a time on top of the demanding and precarious conditions of everyday life and resettlement meant that Dadaab students were often in survival mode and they had limited time and energy for their studies. Teaching condensed courses might help students to get more from the material and would cut down on issues relating to tutorial scheduling, especially the challenges of adequate bandwidth. The BHER team could also focus staff resources on ensuring the smooth delivery of one course at a time, which would improve delivery. This approach requires a great deal of initial preparation to ensure that the video lectures, assignments, readings and website content are developed and ready for international delivery prior to the start of each condensed course. Condensed BHER courses are likely to be asynchronous with Toronto-based courses, but intercultural learning is still possible through joint assignments and sharing videos and/or letters. Instructors could consider assignments that involve reflection and sharing local mapping outcomes. These types of assignments can be implemented asynchronously enabling student discussions and ensuring they learn about different perceptions of geographic space. Similar reflective assignments could be used and shared across tutorial sections in all courses to facilitate intercultural exchange despite asynchronous course delivery.

Regular information about the challenging and changing circumstances such as relocation, threats of camp closure and flooding that affected students in Dadaab would have helped TAs and professors adapt course requirements to accommodate the various challenges facing students. Mensah's familiarity with everyday conditions in the camps certainly facilitated the success of *Gender, Population and Migration*, the course that adopted a flexible schedule independent of the course being taught in Toronto. We urge project administrators to consider how to enhance instructors' familiarity with the students and their learning environment by strategies such as a weekly newsletter outlining events in the camps and a required visit to Dadaab by each professor and teaching assistant, ideally prior to teaching a course. Student engagement and success can also be improved by familiarity with their instructors. Project administrators should consider preparing a biography for each student and each instructor to introduce each other before courses begin. Being able to match names with faces and having better knowledge of each other prior to class would benefit students and instructors.

Given the demanding circumstances under which Dadaab students live, work and study, we are truly in awe of their accomplishments. Their tenacity in overcoming setbacks and coming to class regularly is a true testament to their commitment to higher education. Our appreciation of students' accomplishments grew as they taught us more about their daily lives in the camps. The lessons learned provide suggestions to enhance their experiences and success.

Conclusion

Our collective experience teaching some of the courses required for the geography degree in Dadaab demonstrates that flexibility in course design, substantial and sustained technical and administrative support, and courses already in an online format prior to international delivery are essential to internationalize education successfully. As Atkins et al. (2016) suggest, blended e-learning strategies can be particularly productive in facilitating higher education at a distance, however, developing blended/online versions of courses as they are being taught can adversely affect students' abilities to meet learning objectives. We have also illustrated that sensitivity to the cultural and political economic context in which course materials are delivered is key to successful and sustainable internationalization of higher education. As we have shown, students' learning potential is greatly influenced by their lived experiences, which are shaped by cultural and political economic histories and local realities, a point well supported in the literature (e.g. Clark and Wilson, 2017; Simm and Marvell, 2017).

Our training as geographers provided an understanding of the structural processes that shape the learning environment in Dadaab. Appreciating these constraints was crucial to developing the effective strategies for course delivery shared throughout this chapter. Despite the challenges, all authors found the experience to be rewarding. Indeed, many of us try to maintain relationships with BHER students in hopes that their geography degrees will benefit them. We have appreciated the opportunity to experiment with pedagogies and see the difference that they can make in the educational experiences of students in Toronto and in Dadaab. It is our hope that this chapter will be useful for organizations, universities, instructors and administrators alike who attempt to deliver cross-border higher education to globally marginalized communities.

8

Academic Philanthropy and Pedagogies of Resilience

Lorrie Miller, Graham W. Lea, Rita L. Irwin, Samson Nashon, Elizabeth Jordan, Kimberly Baker and Espen Stranger-Johannessen

Although student learning is more often the subject of academic inquiry, in this chapter we foreground the experiences of a programme administrator and four instructors from the University of British Columbia (UBC), a partner institution in the BHER project. We describe our collective effort to build and sustain a Diploma in Teacher Education Secondary,[1] one of the diplomas offered by BHER partner universities (Abdi, 2016), intended to ladder to further credentials, including degrees, and to be recognized internationally, as well as by the Kenyan Ministry of Education. Elsewhere, Boškić et al. (2018), many of whom also taught in this Diploma, describe how we 'had to be "quick studies" as the project progressed and constantly adapted to challenges as they arose. We expected our engagement in this project to be a wonderful learning opportunity for everyone involved...' (p. 289), and while it was, in fact, a rich experience, it was also impactful in ways we had never expected. Most of the students had already been working as 'unqualified' teachers at the elementary level, and a few at the secondary level, despite the fact that most had no formal education beyond high school completion. What seemed at first to be mostly tasks of logistics, arranging and supporting instructors and student teachers, ended up being much more. It is what we learned as teachers and instructors, and the impact of the Dadaab experience on our pedagogical approaches, that is the focus here. Comparisons can be drawn with the Youdelis et al. chapter in this book, which describes the experiences of instructors from York University in a Geography degree programme.

As described in the Introduction, this book responds to the United Nations Educational, Scientific and Cultural Organization (UNESCO)'s 2009 call for the publication of works that capture the experiences of practitioners so that institutional knowledge does not disappear at the conclusion of a programme, or

Figure 8.1 View from within UNHCR compound, Dadaab 2017, courtesy of Lorrie Miller.

the transition of staff from one project to another (Sullivan-Owomoyela and Brannelly, 2009, p. 9). To that end, we have gathered narratives and reflections that provide some insight into the personal and professional experiences of those who developed and delivered a UBC Diploma as part of a transformative education project. Together, these narratives construct a tale of pedagogical resilience, a willingness to adapt rapidly and a commitment to humanity : (Sleeter, 2009).

In addition, the ethic of care is a prevalent theme that shapes this chapter and emerges throughout the coordinator and instructor reflections and in the reports and communications upon which the chapter is also based. During an annual partnership meeting, Marangu Njogu (2018), the director of Windle International Kenya, a BHER NGO partner, noted the importance of instructor attachment to their students, and their willingness not only to accommodate them, but to care, and to get to know them. According to Njogu, there was an emotional bond created between instructors and students and it was not long before professors began to solicit resources to further support the students and their learning: 'The project gave birth to academic philanthropists' (Njogu, Partnership Meeting notes 2018).

The chapter is divided into two main sections: a] administration and coordination, and b] development and delivery of the Diploma in Teacher Education, Secondary. We present the shared challenges faced by the programme coordinator and instructors along with the necessary adaptations they employed, followed by their reflective narratives. The programme was situated in several key sites: in the Learning Centre in Dadaab, at a distance at UBC in Canada, and at Moi University (MU) in Eldoret, Kenya, where 50 per cent of the courses originated.[2]

The authors of this chapter were all involved in some way in the creation of the Diploma. Early in her position as a Programme Coordinator in the Faculty of Education at the University of British Columbia (UBC) in Vancouver, Lorrie Miller – a teacher education programme coordinator/lecturer – was assigned the work of coordinating courses and supporting UBC instructors, who were teaching both at a distance from Canada and on site in Kenya, for the Diploma in Teacher Education – Secondary. Elizabeth Jordan, now a Professor Emerita from UBC, was involved as an instructor in the Dadaab project from its beginning stages in 2013. Kimberly Baker was a UBC PhD candidate in the Faculty of Education from 2014 to 2017 and co-taught as a teaching assistant[3] in Dadaab. Espen Stranger-Johannessen was also a PhD candidate in the Faculty of Education at UBC at the time of his involvement with BHER and co-taught with Kimberley Baker in Dadaab. Both Professor Rita Irwin and Professor Samson Nashon from UBC Faculty of Education oversaw the planning, organization and implementation of the practicum experiences for the secondary teacher candidates/student teachers in Dadaab and were responsible for planning, developing and implementing the entire program. Graham W. Lea was a UBC doctoral candidate and teaching assistant in the Faculty of Education at UBC.

Administrative Assumptions about Dadaab

In August 2014, the first of the on-site academic courses for Diploma students in the Secondary Teacher education programme were offered jointly by MU and UBC through the BHER project. This meant that two UBC teaching assistants travelled to Dadaab and supported the students as they engaged at a distance with their instructors who remained in Canada.

BHER students had spent the previous year in preparatory studies at the BHER Learning Centre in Dadaab. The first step for these students was to obtain student cards in order to be officially registered for their UBC courses. The UBC students also had to establish their own specific login name and passwords in order to obtain library and online course access. Yet, in order to set up their accounts, they were required to navigate arcane 'security' questions, such as identifying *your first vacation place*, the *make of your first car*, or your *first musical instrument*. Even the assumption of knowing a unique *date of birth*, and providing a *last* name proved to be challenging for the students in Dadaab. Such culturally loaded assumptions overwhelmed some of the students as they attempted to navigate the virtual halls of our institution (Boškić et al., 2018; Dahya et al., 2019). In addition, students were simultaneously enrolled in two institutions (MU and UBC) with widely differing platforms and practices.

Despite being somewhat connected by the worldwide web, students in Dadaab faced technical barriers to their access to education, and this was exacerbated by UBC's misplaced assumptions about the technical literacy levels of students who had access to cellular phones and relatively inexpensive data. One of Miller's first communications from a frustrated student was entirely written within the subject line of the email without any punctuation. Little did Miller know at the time that the student was sending the message from her flip-phone using the same protocols she'd typically use with text messaging. By the second year of the programme, UBC had established several technical adaptations. Miller supported students at a distance by connecting directly with the UBC online security office to facilitate the CWL (campus-wide-login) sign-up protocols. This meant that students would not need to phone long distance from Dadaab to do this directly. The time-zone challenge was evident, and students teased that *Madame Lorrie never sleeps*, as she was always working in the middle of their night. Such time challenges were evident across the BHER project, as noted by Sabriye et al. in this volume.

Miller at UBC in Vancouver and the BHER staff in Dadaab constantly reviewed and updated their records with current student emails and alternate contact information (as we found that emails were frequently changed and passwords forgotten), and they established a reliable means of communication for those students who used a single email address. Finally, UBC ordered official student identification cards in Vancouver using photos taken on site at the BHER campus and verified with corroborating identification in Dadaab by BHER staff. In order to get the cards to the students, they were sent to them with the next group of UBC instructors travelling to the campus in Dadaab. The cards provided photo identity for the UBC-MU Diploma students entering the Learning Centre campus and classrooms. These were just a few of the early challenges in the Diploma programme and our various resolutions, but not the only ones that we and our partner institutions faced in this complex programme.

Lorrie Miller Reflecting on Working from Vancouver

The impact from my involvement in this project continues to this day. During the first two years, I was in regular communication with instructors, staff, and students alike. When a student didn't sit an exam, I'd reach out to them via email, and if that failed, I'd connect with local staff to check in to see what the situation was for them. With each communication, I would pull up the student's file on the university's system, check their name, student number, and look at and their individual student photo. This was my deliberate protocol that served as a reminder that while we had never met in person, these were individuals, people, living with challenges beyond my comprehension. When some of the student 'excuses' for late work, absences, or tardiness, at first seemed extreme, I would verify with the local staff or instructors who had more detailed knowledge of the person. Time and time again, their rationale was verified, so we would approve the sitting of a supplementary exam at the end of term.

One day I received an email from an academically strong student without any history of absenteeism or failure, the subject line read: "BLEEDING FOR YOUR HELP". The full-caps subject line was enough to remind me of the terrible attack on Garissa in 2015 as, I knew the student had returned to Somalia to teach and was in a rural area with little internet or cellular connectivity. They had been in Somalia for nearly a year with a goal to help fellow Somalis who hadn't had an opportunity for education. But now international NGO workers in Somalia were fearful for their own safety and could not return to Dadaab to complete the final examination. Through our correspondence, they told me:

> With fears and frustration towards my journey to Dadaab via Al-Shabab ruling regions in Somalia made me to miss my classes ... And to let you know if in case Al-Shabab would have identified me as an international NGO staff they will chopped off my head completely, and for that reason therefore I could not dare to travel the same route. (2016 email communication shared with permission by former student.)

The student was asking for an extension to their courses and an opportunity to write the exam. Of course, we granted the extension, and arranged for exam invigilation that met the time restrictions of their Kenyan visa to travel back to Dadaab. The student has since graduated with a Diploma in Secondary Teacher Education. This message has stayed with me, and reminds me that there are many, to use their words, who are still bleeding for help, and higher education is one important aspect of this help. My engagement during those three years, albeit at a distance, only somewhat prepared me for my ultimate visit to the site in 2017 to celebrate the programme conclusion with those finishing the humanities cohort in teacher education.[4]

Figures 8.2, 8.3 and 8.4 Scenes on the road from Dadaab town, 2017, courtesy of Lorrie Miller.

And from Dadaab

This was my first time to Africa, let alone Kenya and Dadaab. I'd never been to any United Nations compound, anywhere. My only previous work with refugees, before BHER, was as a teacher in Vancouver's adult education programmes, where some of the students had fled their homelands and landed in Vancouver. When I arrived in Dadaab, aboard a designated flight for NGO and other development workers, I realized that despite all the conversations I'd had with instructors and administrators who had visited before, nothing could have fully prepared me for my first visit. I took note of my observations in my journal so that I might be able to recall the sense of the place with my new eyes, not yet accustomed to the sights, smells, sense of it all.

The red parched earth gives way as our driver, Hassan, expertly navigates the road through Dadaab town. Deliberate bumps in the road along with tire and spike strips planted by army to slow a charging vehicle, which we are not. The fact that Kenya has left-sided driving gives me the feeling that we are perpetually heading into oncoming vehicles ... The clapboard and corrugated metal buildings are a patchwork of rusted repurposed roofing material, a desperate quilt. Groups of people sit at each building, children, and women in long bright coloured and dark scarves and robes. Shredded plastic tangle in wire fencing, plastic bottles and debris litter the roadsides amid ash from recent garbage burn. Goats and donkeys wander the road nosing through these piles. The acrid scent of burnt plastic mingles with dust, and ochre iron clay, a warm terracotta of colours indicates nothing hospitable in the soil. The trees around our UNHCR oasis were all planted 25 years ago, when the camps first settled in, and the NGOs established somewhat permanency. These pampered trees that shade us in the heat of the day are watered daily, yet the soil between them remains barren, without a single volunteer weed between them.

Inside my cinder block residence within the UN compound, a friendly blue sign spray-painted on the heavy steel bathroom door reads: 'In case of an attack, close the door and lock yourself in.' Tomorrow I will meet the students I have supported throughout their studies over the past two and three years. I have reviewed and assessed their files, followed-up with them via email, and coordinated their supplemental work all the while referring to their student numbers, names and official photos for their student identification.

So here, amid many similar names and heavy accents, it is their faces that I recognize, and their stories of why they need to write supplementary exams, submit additional work, the hardships that set them apart from one another. They all face tremendous hardships, but some have faced more than I could imagine, until now. May I leave class early ... I am needed to dig a grave for my best friend. This was a true account from an instructor report. Such a request, even when in grief, would be unheard of from our North American university students. Instructors, rightly so, were moved by the struggles, and resilience these students endured, and exhibited.

Pedagogy and Course Delivery

The sixty-credit Diploma in Teacher Education – Secondary Diploma offered in Dadaab from 2014–17 includes familiar foundational courses that all students, including those at UBC in Vancouver take: The Principles of Teaching, Global Education, Teaching Special Needs, Adolescent Years, Language across the Curriculum, Peace Education and Curriculum Development. As is the norm in such a programme, additional courses related to classroom teaching at the secondary level included mathematics, biology, chemistry, English literature, religious studies (Islamic in the Dadaab programme) and history. But that is where familiarity ended for the UBC coordinators and instructors.

Course delivery, content and scheduling had to fit a context impacted by strict security measures. Those UBC instructors who taught in Dadaab arrived in Nairobi and within a day travelled to the UNHCR compound in Dadaab, where they settled in for the week or weeks. They were escorted to and from the Learning Centre in an armoured vehicle and their students arrived in the classroom after a strict security screening. Security protocols meant that there was no opportunity to linger and discuss or help students after class or during the lunch break. Online courses were more akin to email assignments with some pre-readings offered in print format from the BHER Learning Centre. Early in the programme, some students handwrote assignments on paper, took a photo of the page and emailed it to the instructor – a workaround for those who had limited access to internet and computer, once they had left the Learning Centre for their home in the camps or town.

Boškić et al. (2018) tell us that the technical divide between Vancouver and Dadaab was often increased by the gender divide (see Bishop et al. in this volume). Women had less access to technology, or less time for attention to studies due to family obligations when compared with their male counterparts. Internet access was spotty for students in the camps and occasionally in the Learning Centre; however, cellular access was more stable. As many of the instructors adapted their course delivery, developed 'workarounds' and modified their communications to include programmes such as WhatsApp, increased student engagement ensued.

Early on in the programme delivery, the online course delivery through Moodle, which had proven to be very challenging for the students, was abandoned and we ceased to use videos in the courses due to internet bandwidth challenges. Instead, we opted for more direct approaches, including a single UBC programme blog, where all course content resides directly on a UBC WordPress site. This meant that any student could go to the blog page to find current assignments and due dates; there, they would also find links to readings and resources, and could post comments about readings.

In-school teaching practicum experiences are essential for a teacher's initial preparation and development. With this understanding, the UBC Dadaab programme designed two practicum courses that provided a practical teaching experience with local mentor teachers. These mentor teachers held Kenyan teacher certification and were working in the same subject area as the student teachers. Sometimes the mentor teachers also held leadership roles in the school. While incentive teachers[5] had experienced classroom teaching, they lacked opportunities to visit other classrooms, or to discuss teaching with other teachers. The first practicum encouraged student teachers and their mentor teachers to meet regularly to reflect on and discuss their teaching practices. Due to security concerns and financial limitations, diploma students only occasionally received feedback from BHER staff members. Then, near the end of the extended three-month practicum, a Moi University faculty member travelled to the schools and gave supportive feedback to each student teacher. The intent of this practicum was to support the student teachers in growing as teachers and to develop self-reflective skills to carry forward into their professional practice. This meant that by the time the student teachers began their second practicum, where they received final grades, they felt well-prepared and integrated into a learning community of educators. Moreover, a decision by some student teachers to use WhatsApp lead us to adopt that social media platform to encourage the sharing of ideas, resources and planning. It was then that we realized just how important this regular communication and community development were for all of the educators working together. Student teachers quickly and positively shared ideas, despite their vast distance from their instructors.

By the third year of the programme, some of the online courses were offered in a hybrid format with on-site support in Dadaab by UBC teaching assistants and the BHER staff. By the final term of studies for the Teacher Education Diploma in 2017, instructors' teaching practices had become nimble, resilient and patient. Students, in turn, also understood the expectations of the different post-secondary institutions. They realized that though we offer academic courses within their programme, our institutions each have their own practices, protocols and cultures. We asked students to try not to compare the four university institutions and instructors, but to rather learn from each in their own way. Tolerance was requested all around, as we were learning alongside our students every step of the way.

As she describes below, Jordan's experience teaching in Dadaab underscores the need to know and to understand the context ahead of time and to plan with a particular student audience in mind. She was familiar with an African context and had visited the camps in Dadaab prior to designing her courses. Although students were accustomed to rote learning, Jordan felt it was important to persist with a pedagogical practice that involved problem-based learning, even though this was a new way of learning for the students. This resulted in student teachers being fully engaged in their teacher education classes, and further, they then took their problem-based methods into their own high school and elementary classrooms. When interviewed or surveyed about their learning experiences in the programme, student teachers commented that they noticed a positive difference with how UBC instructors were teaching them, when compared to their own learning as children. In other words, *how* they were being taught (not just what they were taught) impacted them in their learning experiences and also their pedagogical approaches to teaching their classes.

Elizabeth Jordan on Teaching Science and Special Needs Courses in Dadaab

One of the greatest insights into working on this project was getting a chance to visit the U.N. Somali Refugee Camp [Dadaab camps] and meeting the students prior to constructing the courses. Since I wrote two courses, the Biology Curriculum course and the Introduction to Special Education course, it was vital to know and understand the background these teachers were bringing to the classes. Generally, their Biology knowledge was fairly traditional. The access to and/or lack of materials and equipment had to be taken into consideration. Their teaching relied upon memorization and talking through many of the laboratory experiments (with demonstrations when materials were available) explaining the outcomes. Within the curriculum course I focused more on the use of Problem-Based Learning (PBL) and using discussion to develop understanding, rather than rote learning all of the time. I have utilized PBL for a number of years in my own teaching. With PBL, teachers are encouraged to become creative in their approach to topics. It took some time to have them feel comfortable with this shift, but by the end of the course they were encouraging each other with a variety of ideas and alternatives for teaching the textbook topics.

The biggest comparison to students in Canada was in the Kenyan and Somali awareness of individuals with special needs. Since people with visible disabilities and handicaps were supported by the Salvation Army within the camp, not one of the teachers (both trained and untrained) admitted to having any students with special needs within their classes. This meant when designing the course, my largest goal was also an unwritten goal. I wanted these teachers to become aware of hidden disabilities, such as a Learning Disability or Hearing Impairment. I focused primarily on disabilities that they would encounter within their classes, the hidden disabilities. The course covered characteristics, identification from a teacher's perspective and sources for possible ideas to help with the pedagogy for those students. I encouraged understanding and creativity for helping their students with special needs. By encouraging flexibility, creativity, collaboration and a deeper understanding of their students, many teachers felt empowered to take more leadership in their schools as evidenced by the student feedback we have received.

For me the biggest challenge was working to change an attitude toward their own students, how they learn and what prevents learning from taking place. I feel my unwritten goal of creating awareness seems to have worked. I have had teachers approach me with questions that showed how they were analyzing some of their students who had obvious Learning Disabilities (primarily reading). I have also heard that these teachers felt the course in Special Education was particularly valuable. I am very pleased with the feedback I have heard from those two courses taught in Dadaab.

As Stranger-Johannessen describes below, what began as a programme to expand education in Dadaab became an opportunity to build learning communities within the refugee camps themselves. Groups of teachers responded with an intention to think, work and experiment together during the programme and beyond. While it was something we had hoped would happen, we never realized the grassroots efforts would be so profound.

Espen Stranger-Johannessen on Collaborative Student Learning in Dadaab

Before going to Dadaab I had worked as a schoolteacher in Norway, taught at a teacher education programme in Canada and conducted literacy research in Uganda. While all these experiences were clearly relevant, they did not readily merge into a sense of preparedness to teach at a secondary school teacher education programme in Dadaab. One of the students commented that she was surprised that I didn't write everything on the whiteboard, just key points in a bullet list and other shorthand notes. The comment may seem innocuous, but it expresses a crucial point about teaching: how we teach is as important as what we teach. In the case of Dadaab, I would argue that how I taught was even more important, since my way of teaching was probably less familiar to them.

While Canadian teacher candidates used to use a range of teaching methods such as group discussions, peer feedback, process writing, emphasis on students' prior knowledge, I thought such ways of teaching were less familiar to the students in Dadaab. The large number of students, both student teachers and in schools, meant challenges for me as an instructor and them as future teachers. In such a context, the challenge of large numbers of student teachers [more than 80 in a single class] should be turned to an advantage, where students learn from each other. A particular strength shared among the Dadaab students was their ability to self-organize, share information and speak as one voice when they raised concerns. In this context of a paucity of materials and physical infrastructure, social cohesion and organization was a crucial resource, and one the students mastered well. This insight gave me a new understanding of drawing on students' prior knowledge, which is much more than just subject matter knowledge. Inside and outside the classroom the students worked together, discussing, sharing notes, reading and commenting on each other's writings. While I tried to stress the social and collaborative aspect of teaching and learning, it became clear to me that the students were already experts at this in their own lives, which made it easy for me to bring this into my teaching.

As a teacher, one often hears about the need to draw on students' interests and strengths. My experience from Dadaab gave new meaning to this, and in my lessons, I now point out to my students that they are each other's best resource. Working together, sharing, discussing, and self-organizing are crucial for learning, and we teachers often initiate it. But reaping the benefits of learning as a social practice is most efficient when students take the initiative.

Baker's reflections above also highlighted the impact that her teaching experience had on her as an educator researcher. Her involvement as a researcher and teaching assistant demonstrates that when given the opportunity to communicate and connect worldwide with others in the same academic interest, we can come to understand one another better, and more, to develop greater appreciation of the challenges faced by those living in fragile zones.

Kimberly Baker on Relationships with and in Dadaab

In 2014, I started a Ph.D. at the University of British Columbia, Curriculum, and Pedagogy, in Art Education. At UBC, I was invited to join a team working on the BHER connected research project Living, Learning and Teaching in Dadaab (LLTD), that centered around the education in the Dadaab Refugee Camps in northeastern Kenya.[6] I was called upon to do this research work due to my background of volunteering and conducting research in Africa since 2008. First with my master's research in culturally responsive museum education practices with the Museums of Malawi; then in 2010, I volunteered at the Garissa Cultural Center in Kenya, which is near the Dadaab Refugee camps. There, I became familiar with working with Somali refugees, their culture and customs. I had the opportunity to teach for UBC at the Borderless Higher Education for Refugees (BHER) Learning Centre in Dadaab on two occasions, the first being in 2015 when I taught Communication for Teachers, and the second in 2017 when I facilitated an art-based research project Cultivating Creative Communities, which was supported by the 2016 UBC Equity Enhancement fund.

In 2015, it was the first time I flew above Dadaab's barren red scrubland, and I saw a city of white tents[7] arranged in endless rows for the people living in the world's largest protracted refugee camp. I had three overall personal aims: firstly, to support the UBC-Moi Student Teachers' goal of achieving their teacher Diploma; secondly, to build relationships with them that would be sustainable during and following project completion; thirdly, to foster an awareness and deeper understanding of the cultural diversity of students in UBC's global community to the UBC students at the Vancouver campus.

The experience revealed that even though the UBC-Moi Student Teachers and UBC Ph.D. candidates are separated by geography, culture, and diverse social worlds, we have more in common than we had initially thought at the beginning of the project. Through sharing our growth experiences about our education programmes, we discovered that we became more confident in our teaching abilities, developed critical thinking skills and were more committed to our teaching practices. The LLTD project[8] encouraged relationships, fostered cultural understanding and generated conversations between the students, which revealed our similar challenges within our education programmes, but also made known the different daily realities. Many of the Dadaab students continue to correspond with UBC doctoral candidates today.

These experiences have provided me with a greater understanding of refugees' barriers to post-secondary education. According to the UN High Commissioner for Refugees (UNHCR), there are 68.5 million people that are displaced worldwide due to persecution, violence, or human rights violations (UNHCR, 2017). Refugee camps are becoming permanent homes for multiple generations of people. The Dadaab Refugee camps are one such example, being established in 1992. Education is a human right, and people in refugee camps need more significant opportunities to fulfill their human potential. The University of British Columbia's project Living, Learning and Teaching in Dadaab is an extraordinary example of how higher learning institutions can support students above and beyond the current offerings within the camps.

Like Kimberly Baker, Rita Irwin describes below how she gravitated to this project based on meaningful prior life experiences that she had working with teachers in a professional development capacity elsewhere in Africa, and decades earlier.

Rita L. Irwin on Learning from Dadaab

In 1986, I spent my summer holidays teaching as a Project Overseas instructor in Cameroon, Africa. Twelve Alberta educators, including myself, were sent there to work with teachers as they were participating in professional development activities we designed with them. That trip was my first overseas journey and marked the beginning of my interest in working with people in developing countries. I learned so much about my profession in that summer. It has since impacted my interest in international education, in helping teachers everywhere embrace creative forms of engagement, and professional learning communities. Now at UBC, I learned about the opportunity to work with Dadaab teachers, I remembered how important that [earlier] experience was for me... and jumped at the chance to be involved. All through this I have learned to be more culturally sensitive, learning from others, and situating learning from the learner's perspective. In doing this, I also learned that cultural groups other than my own also want to learn about my context and what I know from my context. Thus, I have learned to share materials from that context with those who desire this knowledge.

Working with refugees has been new to me... it has certainly opened my eyes to the huge crisis worldwide. As human beings, we cannot ignore the vast waste of human potential occurring, in addition to the enormous injustices happening on so many levels. I believe higher education should be involved in stewardship – that is, offering leadership and assistance in the world on refugee education.

Below, Lea's narrative paints a vivid picture of his teaching experiences, using a poetic inclusion of a common Swahili proverb – *Haraka Haraka Haina Baraka,* which translates as: *haste makes waste*; the direct translation is *hurry hurry has no blessing*. This is a reminder about the challenges of sticking to a timeline that is beyond our control, which may make little sense in the local context of Dadaab.

Graham W. Lea on Teaching and Time in Dadaab

The learners called me to be with them, to learn with them, not to just teach them. As they became my students' teachers, classes became a sharing of experiences, ideas and languages.

Haraka Haraka Haina Baraka

In August 2014, I represented UBC as part of the first teaching term in the BHER programme in what became one of the most challenging, rewarding, and thought-provoking experiences of my career.

I knew I was entering a cultural and pedagogic context very different than those with which I was familiar. Flying across the Atlantic, the reality of where I (thought) I was going and what I (thought) I was doing set in. Somewhere over Egypt I put racing apprehensions to paper asking, 'Who am I to teach these people?'

Haraka Haraka Haina Baraka

Teaching in Dadaab can only be described as chaotic. Even the best-laid plans struggled against unexpected challenges. Navigating the needs of working in Dadaab required flexibility, independence, and a multiplicity of skills. I found myself registering learners in their programmes, wiring computer labs, and navigating the needs of a North American university with the realities of learners in a Kenyan refugee camp.

Haraka Haraka Haina Baraka

One morning I came to class caught up in the whirlwind of activity and the realization that there was much more to be done than I could possibly do. More content to deliver, more administration, more setting up the learning environment. A seemingly endless list of mores. Seeing my harried state, a learner decided to teach me some Swahili: Haraka Haraka Haina Baraka – Hurry Hurry Has No Blessing

Freire (2000/1970) disrupts the binary student/teacher dynamic suggesting the 'teacher-of-the-students and the students-of-the-teacher cease to exist and a new term emerges: teacher-student with students-teachers ... they become jointly responsible for a process in which all grow' (p. 80). That learner saw my humanity, my need. He became my teacher, not just of Swahili but of the importance of slowing down and being in the pedagogic moment.

Other learners also wanted to share, to teach. When I began, I had asked, 'who am I to teach them?' Instead, the learners called me to be with them, to learn with them, not to teach them. As they became students-teachers, classes became a sharing of experiences, ideas, and languages. Education has the opportunity to be a shared gifting, something through which we 'actively acknowledge kinship and coexistence with the world' (Kuokkanen, 2007, p. 38). Such a gifting can only take place as teacher-student and students-teachers take the time to exist in relationship with each other, to be genuinely present in their educational encounters. As I was reminded on a chaotic morning in Dadaab, Haraka Haraka Haina Baraka.

As insider and an instigator in UBC's involvement in the BHER project, Samson Nashon, shares his own inspirations for engaging in this needed work in the region.

Samson Madera Nashon's Concluding Thoughts

Although I did not teach a course per se, I was there from inception of the BHER project and the teacher education programme. My experience having grown and been educated largely in Kenya, and where I worked as a teacher, teacher educator and curriculum developer gave me a deep inside knowledge of the cultural and social life in the region. This enabled me to play roles that ensured togetherness and resilience. The BHER project inspired my passion that had been influenced greatly by Kenya's First President, Jomo Kenyatta and the late former USA President, John F. Kennedy.

In his speech inaugurating the newly independent Kenya, President Jomo Kenyatta made his solemn pledge in 1963 that the new government would tackle the three big challenges of poverty, ignorance and disease. In my humbled view and that of many, this was to be and still should be the role of education. The BHER project evoked this view that I had held for most my teaching life. Further, inspired by the late former USA President, John F. Kennedy's speech about the educated citizen when he addressed graduates at a convocation ceremony at Vanderbilt University, I saw the world awakening to this reality. President Kennedy said: 'If the pursuit of learning is not defended by the educated citizen, it will not be defended at all ... And, therefore, the educated citizen has a special obligation to encourage the pursuit of learning, to promote exploration of the unknown, to preserve the freedom of inquiry, to support the advancement of research, and to assist at every level of government the improvement of education for all ... [Furthermore] ... "knowledge is power", more so today than ever before ... [and] only an educated and informed people will be a free people, that the ignorance of one voter in a democracy impairs the security of all ... [T]herefore, the educated citizen has a special obligation to encourage the pursuit of learning, to promote exploration of the unknown, to preserve the freedom of inquiry, to support the advancement of research, and to assist at every level of government the improvement of education for all...' (Kennedy, 1963)

Guided by the spirit embodied in the above narrative, I often travelled to the refugee camps, and stayed there when our UBC instructors were on site. The reason I did so was to ensure that I shared the same risks as the instructors. It was also a way to offer support to my colleagues from Canada and Kenya and help to educate future world citizens.

Conclusion

At the beginning of this chapter, there is an image of razor wire that rings the perimeter of both the UNHCR compound for workers and the BHER campus. This is a reminder of the fragile nature of this zone; yet, we see a flowering vine winding its way around the sharp wires. The juxtaposition of this living beauty on a constructed barrier is a symbol of resilience, which reminds us that something good can develop in challenging areas. Likewise, the narratives presented in this volume as part of an accumulated institutional memory, tell us about the resilience, flexibility and creativity that emerged from and was necessary for teaching in Dadaab. They affirm our belief that place and time are important factors in higher education and in particular in teacher education (Abdi, 2016). Finally, by collecting and analysing these instructor narratives, a pedagogy is revealed that has care at its core, and that is nimble and responsive to a shifting terrain (the chapter by Alsop and Cohen in this volume also uses a place-based methodology).

In the context of teaching and learning, attention to place is necessary as we build and deliver curriculum that reflects and respectfully responds to the local context and goals (Magee and Pherali, 2017). Place-based and place-conscious curriculum and pedagogies are profoundly important to teaching and learning in sensitive zones. We see this in particular during teaching practice in the teacher education programme described in this chapter, along with the community health education and geography programmes described earlier in this volume. Aslop and Cohen in this book tell us that 'Place-based teaching recognises the fundamental importance of these experiences as basis for (re)conceiving, interrupting and (re)performing quality and relevant education' (p. 171).

Time, as in current events and circumstances along with the allotted amount of time given for a particular task, is likewise a critical factor when building and delivering a curriculum. We have learned that rushing when faced with obstacles can lead simply to further obstacles. So, curricular adaptation and allowing for interruption can lead to a richer and more robust pedagogy. Likewise, other researchers and instructors from BHER connected with the LLTD research project tell us that there is an 'immense urgency for curriculum theorists to rethink emphases and create pedagogical possibilities commensurate with: the exigency of time in long-term displacement situations; the implications of crossing physical, social and cultural borders; the losses endured by marginalized communities; and the problematics of adaptation in lieu of choice in the daily life of displaced people' (Meyer et al., 2018, p. 324). Their call reinforces findings from this chapter and volume overall.

It was a common sentiment of university instructors and student teachers alike in the UBC programme that, ultimately, we teach people not just subjects; and we agreed that it is *how* one teaches that matters as much, if not more, than *what*. The ethic of care wove throughout the practices of our experience in the BHER project. Gichiru and Larking (2009) note that '[t]eachers who enact an ethic of caring with their students, both in regard to their academic work and their socioemotional growth, perform differently than teachers who see their work as simply delivering curriculum' (p. 235). This ethic of care was evident in two major areas in the secondary teacher education diploma: first, in the interest expressed by UBC educators in the lived experiences and challenges of their students, thus modelling a way of being a teacher within this context; and second, in the ways that student teachers taught and supported their own secondary students with care, thus bringing into practice the pedagogical approaches they experienced as learners.

We still hear from students, now graduates, as they start their own schools in Somalia (Miller and Nicol, 2018) or go on to study in York University graduate programmes on site in Dadaab (Miller et al., 2019). The goal of our efforts is not fully met, as the need for tertiary education in fragile zones still persists. It is our hope that other universities will take up this challenge, and benefit from our collective experiences as they move forward with their own endeavours to give higher education access to refugees and other marginalized populations.

9

Refugee Students' Experience of Accessing English Language Learning in Dadaab, Kenya

HaEun Kim, Nombuso Dlamini, Dahabo Ibrahim,
Seraphin Kimonyo and Johanna Reynolds

We begin this chapter by privileging storytelling as an important vehicle for reflecting on English language learning (ELL) in the Dadaab refugee camps and town in north-eastern Kenya. Borderless Higher Education for Refugees (BHER) graduate students Dahabo Ibrahim and Seraphin Kimonyo share their stories as examples of the English language learning trajectory of many refugees in Dadaab. These reflections are the result of observations and conversations co-author Kim undertook with Ibrahim and Kimonyo about their language experiences in the camps. As these conversations unfolded, these three co-authors realized their value as educational data and Kim requested the documentation of what were initially oral conversations, culminating in the vignettes below. We present these vignettes in their fullness to honour storytelling as 'voice' and as an important epistemological tool that grants privilege to unwritten knowledge conveyed in words and sometimes in silence or any other form of gestural communication. Chilisa (2012) states, 'most postcolonial indigenous thought systems have not been documented and are not available in the written literature' (p. 211), which is also a reality in many places in crisis (e.g. Dadaab) because of the challenging circumstances under which forced migrants reside. For Ibrahim and Kimonyo, telling and writing their stories allowed for meaningful self-reflection that helped them understand their experiences (Smith, 2010). This chapter is a documentation of language learning stories and trajectories, which, in turn, have resulted in the collective reflection, analysis and pedagogical possibilities for us, as people who work with and support learners in crisis/refugee spaces (see also Smith, 2010). We present these narratives in their fullness to give a stronger sense of voice to each of the co-authors, as well as a means of privileging orality in our documentation.

Dahabo Ibrahim's Language Journey

My personal language journey of English learning in Dadaab and exposure to other new languages in the Dagahaley refugee camp is a tough one. I was born in Somalia and came to Dadaab when I was two years old. Before I joined school, the only language I spoke was Somali, my mother tongue. Seven years later I enrolled in primary school where the languages of instruction were English and Kiswahili, the languages rarely spoken by refugees in the camp. However, because of the education policy, these were adopted by the Government of Kenya as the two languages to be taught in all the public and private schools. English and Kiswahili were mandatory mediums of communication for both teachers and students while in school.

What I personally experienced in primary school at the time was very painful. My memories of primary school are not good, simply because I could not speak the languages of instruction. Furthermore, the teachers also forced us to speak either English or Kiswahili while in school and any child found speaking his/her home language was punished. Those were also the days when there were very few girls in school compared to boys and people from the neighborhood always questioned my mother. They asked why she allowed me to go to school as they always looked down upon the few school-going girls. I still remember how people in the camp ridiculed and laughed at me for attending school back in the day in the mid to late 1990s. I wondered why the communities were not supportive of girl child education and why teachers punished us for speaking the only language we knew in school.

Regarding challenges with languages of instruction, it was not only me but the teachers themselves who had their own problems with the two official languages, English and Kiswahili. Most of my teachers were untrained teachers from the camps who had never completed high school. Most were standard eight dropouts,[1] who were thus lacking knowledge, skills and experiences for teaching second – and third – languages as a subject. This is why most of us at the time failed to understand concepts in the class during lessons. Teachers at that time also held onto the belief that communicating with students in their home language would be risky. This was because any teacher found speaking with students in their home language would lose their job. Therefore, teachers usually ended up code-switching, mixing English and Kiswahili when teaching the two languages I knew nothing about. I have to admit that it took me more than ten years to master both languages. Most girls dropped out of school along the way and at times I felt like doing the same, but my mother always stood by my side and I managed to complete my primary and secondary school education.

In the camps, there are private schools that are responsible for teaching the community languages other than Somali, but the private schools require monthly tuition fees alongside costs for school uniforms, school materials, exam preparations. The fees amount to around 200 Kenyan Shillings (equivalent to approximately CAN$2.50) per student every month[2] which is difficult for refugee families to pay. Even if a family manages to pay, they prefer boys to attend school to learn and understand other languages so that they may get better jobs in the future. This attitude also contributes to girls dropping out of school where families struggle to see the importance of education for females who also have the potential to change the community.

I have heard that behind every successful person is a woman. This type of support is true because behind all my challenges, hard work, and successes was my mother, my soulmate and life mate who showed me how important life and learning is. Without her I would not have completed my education and graduated with a Bachelor degree in April 2019. She put all her effort to make my education a light that never stops shining until it ends itself. I am thankful to God and to my mother, whom I love dearly.

Seraphin Kimonyo's Language Journey

I was born in Kanzenze village, Masisi Zone in the North Kivu Province of the Democratic Republic of Congo (DRC). In Kanzenze, I grew up speaking my mother tongue with all my age-mates until I started primary school. Kinyarwanda is the language that people living in Masisi speak, even if they are not Rwandese. The national split is the result of colonialism. Languages are taught according to the provinces due to the many dialects existing in Congo. Schools in Kivu province teach Kiswahili, French, and English. Kiswahili is taught from nursery to Class Six (primary school), French from nursery up to university, while English starts from Form One up to Form Six (secondary school) and it is taught just to give small basics to learners. As it is well known, Congo is a country where the population has been displaced due to internal and external conflicts. As a result of conflict and instability, my family and I were forced to leave our homeland and we decided to enter Kenya, hoping our lives would be secured.

In 2010, my family and I reached the Dadaab refugee camps as asylum seekers. As new arrivals, we faced many challenges. Among the challenges communication was major because the Dadaab refugee camps are a multicultural space where different nationalities are found and as such, their ways of expression and communicating are different. As Congolese from a Francophone country, it was not easy for my family and I to survive due to the language barriers. All my neighbors were Somali, Sudanese, Ugandan, or Ethiopians and all of them were unable to speak or hear my language. This situation frustrated us so much because it was not easy for us to access facilities or resources. Usually neighbors were the ones to guide new arrivals to the appropriate places to get the help needed, but this was difficult for us.

The Kiswahili I learned from my country is different from the one that is spoken in Kenya. There are enough differences so that Kenyans cannot understand what someone from DRC wants to say. In this case, we needed to learn the Kiswahili [Kenyan] language first so that we would be able to communicate with our fellow refugees who were familiar with the Kiswahili spoken in Kenya. At the same time, we needed support from the agencies that operate in the refugee camp, but how could we do so without the knowledge of the English language which is considered to be the first language in Dadaab camp? There was no other option than to join classes. My family and I joined beginner classes for English in the camps so that we could communicate with workers of the NGOs and access their support.

This was a hard time that I cannot forget amongst other tough experiences we faced in Dadaab. From the beginner English language classes, we moved to intermediate and finally, we graduated to join the upper classes. During all those years, we could have been working like other communities living in Dadaab. We also could have continued with the higher education we were unable to complete in our homeland, rather than spend years learning another language to receive support from the people who were already assigned to support us and get their salary from this work.

In my view, the English language became a new form of colonialism and weapon to intimidate the refugees living in Dadaab camp. For instance, there are men in the Dadaab refugee camps who fear and feel shy because they do not understand or speak English. For this reason, they refuse to approach agencies because they feel their rights will be neglected. Also, there are many who lack support, jobs, and access to facilities without English. There are also instances where the guards at the gates of agencies are illiterate and they are not able to express themselves in English. Meanwhile, when a refugee that speaks English wants to enter to meet officers and staff, the guards become unpleasant to see refugees who speak English.

The English language is like any other language in the world. Though it must be taught in Dadaab refugee camp or in other parts of the world, no one should be marginalized or harassed because of not knowing it. Everyone must understand the value of his/her own language. Let us have in mind that English can be learned to facilitate communication amongst different communities, but it is not worthy to think that English is a better language than others.

Language literacy and university education lay much of the groundwork for full participation and engagement in the world (see Arendt 2006 (1954)), which includes being able to advocate or represent oneself, as well as access employment opportunities and other critical material resources. However, access to higher education is impacted by language proficiency, and whether a refugee can successfully access and remain engaged in the university level programmes associated with the Borderless Higher Education for Refugees (BHER) project in Dadaab depends on their spoken and written English language fluency. Colonial histories demonstrate how and why certain languages, such as English, have been privileged over others. The impact of having to learn new languages, sometimes more than one, has weighed heavily on many of the refugees living in the Dadaab camps in north-eastern Kenya. Through the vignettes presented above, we delve into the language learning experiences of students in Dadaab, some of whom became university students in Canadian and Kenyan universities associated with the BHER project. Their experiences offer insights into the barriers and facilitators to learning and education. In addition, we explore the relationship between language learning and access to education in Dadaab. In their own voices, the stories of two BHER refugee students currently enrolled in the Master of Education programme and co-authors to the chapter, Dahabo Ibrahim and Seraphin Kimonyo, provide a tangible presence for our collective argument that success in a higher education programme has a lot to do with learning the language of instruction competently. This is especially relevant as we consider the fact that much of the educational programming provided in crisis contexts is delivered in English.

There are two main theoretical underpinnings to this chapter that frame our approach: i) the importance of the context in which a language is learned; and ii) the power of language to impact the lives of learners. It has been claimed that while individuals are born with the ability to learn languages, this learning is thought to be context specific (Duranti, 2009). Related to this, the context in which languages are learned and used, and the extent to which such a site facilitates or hinders the achievement of goals, is culturally mediated. In addition, experiences such as displacement and forced migration, will affect the language learning of individuals (Hou and Beiser, 2006). In the context of forced migration, educational access is influenced by a range of political, socioeconomic and historical factors. Numerous scholars have documented the interconnection of language and power (e.g. wa Ngũgĩ, 1986; Simon 1987; Fairclough, 1989; Cummins, 2000) and how language as capital can be convertible and lead to access to material resources (Bourdieu, 1986). Bourdieu defines three types of capital:

economic capital, which is immediately and directly convertible into money and may be institutionalized in the forms of property rights; *cultural capital*, which is convertible, on certain conditions, into economic capital and may be institutionalized in the forms of educational qualifications; and *social capital*, made up of social obligations ('connections'), which is convertible, in certain conditions, into economic capital and may be institutionalized in the forms of a title of nobility.[3]

p. 242 emphasis in the original

Generally, all three of Bourdieu's forms of capital are, however, inseparable. For instance, to know the language and discourse of an interview (cultural capital) facilitates entry to a job, which converts into earnings that provide the ability to buy property such as a house. The opposite is also true: ignorance or failure to demonstrate knowledge of the language of a job interview would result in unemployment, thus, lack of material resources or, in Bourdieu's terms, economic capital.

As authors, we are located in Toronto and Dadaab; thus, our collaboration aligns with scholars who call for a cross-geopolitical and transborder learning that recognizes the importance of drawing on knowledge from diverse places in order to understand the constraints and catalysts to people's localized socioeconomic and political livelihoods (e.g. Connell, 2007; Manzon, 2011, Robinson 2011, 2016a, 2016b).

HaEun Kim is a first-generation Canadian immigrant, for whom the idea that English language proficiency affords different opportunities and resources is not an unfamiliar one. From a young age, she understood that certain languages are privileged and provide access to different spaces. Beginning in 2016, she has worked with students and partners in Dadaab in various roles, as a teaching support and, more recently, as a BHER Programme Administrator. Her interactions with students participating in the BHER Project have sparked numerous questions about the implications of forced migration – particularly surrounding practices of language use and language choice. It is through her interactions with students that she became aware of the language intricacies operating in the Dadaab camps; ultimately, she engaged in listening to language stories, two of which begin this Chapter.

Nombuso Dlamini's role in crafting this chapter is twofold. First, as an African Canadian York University BHER instructor who spent her early years of schooling on the continent, she experienced first-hand the language challenges that many refugee students describe and undergo. Therefore, in her teaching, she often uses her own language learning experiences to reflect and support those who are now going through a journey that resembles her own. Second, her work with young people in Africa (e.g. Dlamini, 2005) indicates ways that English language is used to demarcate the 'knowledgeable' from the 'ignorant' and those who are seen to embrace western modernity from those who hold on to Afrocentric traditions (considered 'backwardness'). Ultimately such demarcations have implications for the distribution and consumption of resources, all which are linked to English language proficiency.

Dahabo Ibrahim's reflections on her journey with language have contributed importantly to this chapter. As a female Somali refugee growing up in Dadaab, access to schooling and to learning new languages were closely tied. There are painful memories associated with overcoming these challenges. In this chapter, she reflects on her journey. As a graduate student in the York University Education programme, she is researching gendered barriers that young girls continue to face in the camps. The experiences shared in this chapter describe some of the challenges, but also the successes of female refugee students in Dadaab.

Seraphin Kimonyo began his education in the Democratic Republic of Congo (DRC) in 1982. He is also a graduate student in the York Education programme through BHER. Refugee students from the DRC and other non-English speaking countries face serious challenges in Kenya's system of education. His experience of learning English was onerous, and like many other refugees, involved the repetition of classes in order to learn basic English reading and writing.

Johanna Reynolds is a York University doctoral student in Geography. In 2013–14, she was a member of the Facebook BHER Student Group that was created as a network of peer mentoring and support for students in the BHER programme. Through this network, she had virtual interactions with BHER students including co-author Ibrahim. She also began to notice how their learning journeys resemble those of the English language students that she has worked with in Canada.

Context Matters

The language of schooling has been a thorny question for Kenya since colonialism. Bunyi asserts that as early as 1905 in Kenya, 'all those participating in language policy decision-making during the colonial period agreed that education in the indigenous languages should be the norm in the first years of primary school

(Gorman, 1974, in Bunyi, 1998). An important question for policymakers at the time was whether Kiswahili or English should take over as a medium of instruction and, if so, when?' (Bunyi, 1998, p. 34). These questions are still central to the way that different regions and local governments address issues of language and schooling in Kenya. Even international organizations that provide education in crisis areas such as Dadaab shy away from investigating the language realities of the communities they support. The result is an unexamined and ad hoc implementation of what has been mandated by the central government, despite the existence of language-based regional decision-making autonomy. Thus, today in Dadaab, as in Kenya more generally, local government institutions including schools utilize English as the official language. This is despite the fact that the north-eastern region of Kenya is heavily populated by Kenyan ethnic Somalis, and 96 per cent of households in the Dadaab camps report Somali as their first language. Somali is not an official working language of the region and is not officially used in the schools in that area (NRC and Reach, 2017). There are also several minority non-Somali languages spoken in the camps by those from Ethiopia, South Sudan, the DRC, Burundi, Uganda, Sudan and Eritrea (UNHCR, 2019).

As well, in Kenya, there are currently more than 40 indigenous languages belonging to variant tribes and groups in different regions. The official policy mandated by the Kenyan government indicates that after the three early years of schooling in a mother tongue, English is to be used as the medium of instruction (Nabea, 2009), but Kiswahili, regarded as the lingua franca, is also taught as a subject from the early years of schooling onwards (Flemming, 2017; Kim, 2018). Other subjects are taught in English and students learn English while utilizing it as part of their curriculum (Campbell-Roy, 2001).

Opportunities for ELL are closely tied to opportunities for education and schooling in the camps. In Dadaab, 56 per cent of the refugees are children and those who become proficient in English are among those who have a greater opportunity to attend schools and succeed in their studies than those who do not (UNHCR, 2019). However, according to Ibrahim, if the English language teaching in the primary and secondary schools is of poor quality, as it was for her and many of her classmates in Dadaab, their overall educational future was put into question. In addition, the result of learning a language in a context of code-switching,[4] from untrained teachers who themselves were not fluent English speakers, along with prohibitions against using one's mother tongue, resulted in great difficulty in mastering any language. The outcome was an inadequate understanding of the course material, as Dahabo has explained.

The educational stakes are high for refugees who wish to leave the Dadaab camps. Those who attain good linguistic skills can more easily access the knowledge and resources needed to better their situations. It is well documented that proficient language and literacy skills facilitate social and intercultural communication and the social, physical and economic well-being of refugees (UNESCO, 2018). Countries, such as the United States, Canada and Australia place a premium on those with English language proficiency in selecting newcomers (Hou and Beiser, 2006).[5] In addition, well-known programmes like the World University Service of Canada (WUSC), which resettles refugee students to Canada, asks applicants to complete an English or French language assessment with their application. English language ability is important for navigating post-migration contexts in English-speaking countries, especially for education and employment opportunities, and can also be crucial in overcoming information barriers in resettlement contexts (Shakya et al., 2012). It facilitates material life in the camp, but it also has consequences for life beyond the camps. While the BHER project does not offer resettlement, it is a powerful example of an opportunity that opens pathways towards a better future.

Language is Power

The Kenyan author Ngũgĩ writes about the role of language in the construction of identities within the Kenyan context. In *Decolonising the Mind*, he offers a vignette of language learning in his childhood where his mother tongue Kikuyu was at odds with English:

> In Kenya, English became more than a language; it was the language, and all the others had to bow to it in deference ... one of the most humiliating experiences was to be caught speaking Kikuyu in the vicinity of the school ... The attitude to English was the exact opposite: any achievement in English was highly rewarded; prizes, prestige, applause; the ticket to higher realms ... Thus language [was] taking us further and further from ourselves to other selves, from our world to other worlds.
>
> Ngũgĩ, 1986, p. 11–12

The colonial legacies of forced language instruction have caused social, emotional and psychological harm, as documented in case studies throughout the world. During the early twentieth century in Canada, for example, indigenous children were sent by the federal government to residential (boarding) schools to learn

English (or French) and adopt Christian values in an attempt to culturally assimilate them. Like students in Kenya in more recent years, as described by Kimonyo, they were also banned (under threat of punishment)[6] from speaking their mother tongue and forced to speak English (Nabea, 2009, p 126). Kimonyo also described the influence of colonialism on languages spoken and taught in his home country, the DRC. His view of the domination of English as the official language for refugees in Dadaab is a powerful statement that 'the English language became a new form of colonialism and weapon to intimidate the refugees living in Dadaab camp'.

Fluency in the English language either limits or provides entry into spaces or offices where food and other resources are distributed by organizations such as the UNHCR. For example, Kimonyo notes that upon his arrival in Dadaab as an adult, he and his family spoke neither English nor Kiswahili. As ethnic and linguistic minorities in the Dadaab camps, they found themselves at a great disadvantage and had to quickly learn at least some Kenyan Kiswahili in order to communicate and receive support from aid agencies in the camp. He highlights some of the challenges related to communication. On the one hand, negotiations with international agency staff require linguistic expertise, and thus English language learning becomes an additional burden in a crisis situation, in addition to mediations about nationality, culture and socioeconomic conditions. On the other hand, English language fluency becomes a point of tension even among some of the gatekeepers to international agency offices. Resentful of the presence of refugees in Kenya, they deride refugees who speak to them in fluent English. In addition to these ethnic and other forms of discrimination that refugees in Dadaab experience, we found that negative language experiences are also greatly heightened by unequal gender relations (see chapter by Bishop et al. in this volume for further discussion on gender relations).

The Gender Relations of Language Power

While there are highly gendered dimensions to ELL, as there are to overall education in the encampments of Dadaab, we see similar dimensions in other contexts of displacement. For example, in a 10-year study of English acquisition by South-East Asian refugees in Canada, it was found that despite the availability of language training for adult newcomers, female refugees were far less likely than males to learn the language (Hou and Beiser, 2006). Sub-Saharan Africa falls behind most other schooling systems in the world on measures of gender equality, as well as in other areas such as enrolment, educational achievement, and basic literacy and numeracy (Bloom, Canning and Chan, 2006). Overall school completion rates (for both males and females) in the region indicate a 64 per cent completion rate at the primary level, 37 per cent at the lower secondary, and 27 per cent at upper secondary (UNESCO, 2018). Adult literacy rates are below the global average in sub-Saharan Africa and gender-disaggregated data herein reveal a 68 per cent literacy rate for men compared to 51 per cent for women (UNESCO, 2015). In Dadaab, the Gross Enrollment Rate[7] (GER) for schools is 70 per cent at the primary level and 23 per cent at the secondary level (for Kenya nationally, it is 88 per cent and 47 per cent). Less than half of those enrolled at the primary level in Dadaab are female, with the number dropping to a third at the secondary level, attesting to the challenges of gender-inclusivity in education (Flemming, 2017). In a region where access to education is already a challenge, the numbers in Dadaab demonstrate that female students face compounded barriers to opportunities for learning. In other words, when opportunities for ELL are tied to opportunities for schooling, as is the case in Dadaab, and when girls and young women's access to ELL is substantially lower than their male counterparts, they will have less access to schooling. Following on from this circumstance, unequal access for girls and women to schooling in Dadaab reproduces boys' and men's privilege and perpetuates young women's unequal access to higher education. Ibrahim talks about some of the ways that learning a language mediated her school experiences and success from a very young age. She felt that because she could not speak fluent English in primary school, and simply because she was a girl, she was judged to occupy a space not intended for her and 'was ridiculed and laughed at'. She 'wondered why the communities were not supportive of girl child education and why teachers punished us for speaking the only language we knew in school'.

Cognizant of the significant gender disparities in education among refugees in Dadaab, the BHER project aimed to ensure that at least 30 per cent of the students in its programmes were women. Based on the view that higher education has 'a greater potential than other levels of education to ... enhance strategic choices that refugees make' (Dryden-Petersen and Giles, 2010, p. 4) as well as to foster a 'generation of change-makers who can take the lead in identifying sustainable solutions to refugee situations' (UNESCO, 2018), BHER made gender equity a key priority (see chapter by Gitome and Dippo for further discussion of this issue). Yet the project has struggled with engaging and retaining female students in its programmes. During the certificate and diploma programme, recruitment and retention of female students remained below target of 30 per cent (26 per cent enrolled at time of admission and 25 per cent retained). Low enrolment was due to poor performance in high school exit exams (conducted in English), leading to low secondary school graduation rates among women. Combined with factors related to traditional gender norms in Dadaab, which include roles and responsibilities that women and girls have in their households that have an impact on schooling at the primary and secondary levels, the numbers of women who are eligible and admissible to university education is limited.

Reports on the BHER related programme offer a glimpse into the role of English language competency in the success of students in certificate studies. In the 2014-15 and 2015-16 academic years, two BHER cohorts were enrolled in a York University Certificate Program.[8] In their follow-up reports, instructors in this Certificate Program expressed concerns over gaps in English language ability. They noted concern over the quality of writing skills (Douhabi, 2015), suggested extra language support (Robinson, 2015), and upon working with the students, felt the need to '[undertake] modifications to the reader itself, in the form of further abridging readings, simplifying some of the language, and adding improved visuals to increase accessibility to concepts for all students' (Granger, 2015). Students with better language skills more often requested clarification regarding content and advocated for themselves on assignment submissions or absences, as opposed to those with poor English language skills, who struggled simply to express themselves in English at a more basic level. Sometimes, the language gap would appear to be gendered. One instructor noted that:

> significant gaps in literacy skills meant difficulty engaging with course content – even if they were present for class. The majority of course content was communicated through the readings. The lack of good [English] reading/writing skills exacerbated gaps in performance as a number of students (many of them female) were unable to engage critically with key concepts raised in the materials they were given.
>
> Kim and Sabriye, 2016

Out of 189 students enrolled in the YU Certificate Program, 65 did not complete the programme.[9] The BHER project later sought to mitigate these language challenges by offering a writing course in the following years. While we acknowledge that other factors might also have contributed to failed programme completion, we contend that English language competence, or lack thereof, was a significant contributor.

Success in the BHER project hinges on the ability to complete university credits offered in the English language. Lower English language abilities have meant difficulty engaging with the course content. These gendered challenges have seldom been discussed in the BHER project in relation to English language learning. When we consider language as a form of social practice, there is a need to examine the individual language learner situated in the larger social world, as we have shown in the section above on the Dadaab context. We require an 'enhanced awareness of the contextual and interactional dimensions of language use' (Firth and Wagner, 1997, p. 285) and its relationship to power inequities.

Concluding Remarks

While the Dadaab refugee camps offer protection to refugees fleeing violence and environmental and other disasters, shelter comes with a price. Our two co-authors, Ibrahim and Kimonyo, describe how the camps robbed them of their home languages and challenged their sense of worth and belonging. Ibrahim recounts how students and their teachers were punished for speaking any other language than English and Kiswahili in primary and secondary school. In another conversation with Kim, she raised the role that parents play in encouraging their children to learn English and Kiswahili, as well as supporting all levels of education in myriad ways, and how crucial this support is to language learning outcomes and experiences in refugee environments such as Dadaab. Without this family support, many young men and women drop out, unable to face the combined challenges of linguistic, financial and societal pressures. Ibrahim reminds us of the gendered forms of discrimination that lead a family to 'prefer boys to attend school' and 'struggle to see the importance of education for females'.

Both narratives describe the gendered and linguistic negotiations in accessing opportunities in the camp. However, we advise against conflating challenges of language learning and (educational) access. Economic challenges, age, migration journey and time in transit, and colonial history, among other factors, all play a role in accessing particular opportunities, including in the BHER project. While the language barrier proved to be a challenge in his early years in Dadaab, Kimonyo recently reflected on its significance:

> Here I am as an MEd student in the Education programme from the great world university called York. I wonder if my three brothers and myself [all four are students in BHER related university programmes] could [now, in retrospect] disregard the simple English basics we were learning in Ifo, Dadaab refugee

camp. Of course, many wanted to join BHER, but they didn't because of the language barrier. People from [a wide] region were very many, with diplomas from their countries, but because they [never learned English in Dadaab], they lost their chance to be enrolled in this super programme. Remember, all the programmes from certificate level up to Masters (MEd) were conducted in the English language. I came to understand that challenges always carry blessings on their backs.[10]

Kimonyo describes the tension between language, identity and power. Language plays a critical role in how individuals and society reflect, reproduce and reconstitute relations of power. Linked to power, is the way that language mediates and organizes a speaker's social identity and sense of belonging (Norton and Toohey, 2011). In the context of Dadaab, if you are unable to speak English, Kiswahili, or even Somali, you are unable to tap into support networks to access resources, whether they are social (community support from neighbours), material (goods and services provided by NGOs), educational (success in school system), or others. In the case of education, the use of the English language reproduces the colonial legacies of power, yet proficiency in the language is needed in order to participate in in a university programme and indeed the wider world today (Giles and Dippo, 2019).

In Dadaab, where the dominant language of schooling, international aid and resources is at odds with the mother tongues of refugees, the stage is set for an unequal balance of power. As cognitive systems, no language is more complex or superior to another; however, as a form of social practice, 'language is firmly embedded in the world of actors, groups, and communities, with all their attendant biases, prejudices, and interests' (Wee, 2011, p. 13). Generations of refugees lose their mother tongue in favour of the 'dominant' language. The tensions of identity, language and politics overlap as English is often seen as a force threatening the existence of indigeneity. As university educators and learners, we recognize the colonial legacy behind the English language, yet we cannot ignore its 'dominance' and the level of participation and access it allows. Egbo (2000) calls for a 'notion of enhancement' where the need for proficiency in a colonial language does not equate with the abandonment of one's mother tongue. We want to see English as an additive (not a replacement) that will support the pursuits and goals of our students both in and beyond BHER related programmes. High levels of reading, writing and oral communication skills become a practice of representation that allows our students to make themselves present in spaces that may normally exclude them – a 'blessing' amidst the 'challenges' to which Kimonyo alludes.

In order to set students up for success in accredited academic programmes, particularly in contexts of extended displacement like Dadaab, careful sociolinguistic considerations are needed. A strong understanding of the history and context of the learner and the place is critical, as was the case for BHER in Dadaab, where project implementation was prefaced by a year-long feasibility study. A scaffolded approach (i.e. one course, practice, or programme building upon another), regular and repeated assessments, one-on-one mentoring/tutoring, extra writing support, and flexibility on the part of instructors and teaching assistants are all required. A coordinated effort is essential between field staff, course instructors/teaching assistants, students and the managerial team to listen to one another. Finally, ongoing consultation and clear communication among all involved is vital for project implementation as different learning needs arise.

10

A Gallery to Rethink and (Re)place the Anthropocene: Framing from A Place-based Borderless Higher Education

Steve Alsop and Roxanne Cohen

Borderless Higher Education for Refugees (BHER) students[1] gather around a whiteboard in the Dadaab Learning Centre, brainstorming meanings and connections with the concept of Anthropocene. As a culminating course assignment, the students are required to work in groups to curate public

Figure 10.1 BHER students in pursuit of the Anthropocene, December 2018, courtesy of Steve Alsop and Roxanne Cohen.

education exhibits in response to the current geological epoch. This is part of an undergraduate course on place-based learning in the Faculty of Education at York University. In what follows, as teachers of the course, we reflect on the course and give an overview of three student curatorial projects on greenbelts, goats and garbage, and youth and beauty.

In these discussions, we hope to offer less conventional ways of representing refugees and refugee education. Other chapters in this volume speak in considerable detail about refugee experiences in terms of everyday challenges and resilience. Here, in contrast, we explore ways in which BHER students engage with global planetary ideas, critically analysing humans as primary driving forces of earthly changes and decline. Global perspectives of this nature always risk concealing regional disparities and impacts. The explicit and implicit 'we' of 'the global' demands close inspection. As Gabrielle Hecht (2018: para. 2.) writes, 'we' in such instances is often 'the centuries-old conflation of *human* with *white man*'. The immediacy of everydayness and localizing experiences also serve to restrain and restrict ideas and actions to particular people, structures, routines, places and times. In what follows, we seek to explore interacting stories with different global and local scales – globally converging stories of how to grapple with earthly perspectives and humanity's impact on planetary ecologies and geologies, and diverging stories concerning specific local conditions, places and times. Our assumption is that if widely circulating narratives of planetary crisis, such as the Anthropocene, are to retain meaning and credibility they need to foster reflections on the complex relationships between a globally shared planet and increasingly locally inequitable access to planetary resources and mobilities (Nixon, 2018). While the students who we worked with are regionally displaced and locally restrained, facing obstacles and setbacks that we are only starting to understand, they continue to be citizens of the world, and as such they have voices that need greater attention in explorations of global planetary concepts and affairs.

We position our teaching within these complex relationships, simultaneously reflecting on our practices as white, middleclass, wealthy, earthly-mobile, resource-heavy Canadian educators. We openly acknowledge that education even in its fullest, most variegated and vibrant sense is a fraught and freighted endeavour. It can be too easily and too readily tied to wishful dreams of change and transformation. As a result, education is far too easily untethered from critical reflections on its complexities, ambiguities, trade-offs and the irreconcilable tensions that all educational practices almost inevitably entail. In what follows, we describe aspects of our collaborative practices and associated tensions with hopes of being respectful and supportive to those involved, and with desires of being helpful, and perhaps even inspiring to others who are or who might wish to take similar educational journeys. Our story carries full-disclosure that our practices – including this narrative – are best conceived as works-in-progress, as messy, partial, incomplete and imperfect attempts at imagining and representing education (with particular ideas and ideals) within complex, dynamic, changeable, global-local contexts. Our teaching builds on historically established cultural and material structures developed by those who led the BHER project as well as instructors and staff who provide ongoing pedagogical feedback. We taught this course after the first cohort of students had already graduated and many of the practicalities of the program had stabilized. These include electronic communication and equipment and transportation to and from the BHER Learning Centre in the town of Dadaab in north-eastern Kenya. These historical practices provide a welcome platform for the analysis that follows.

The Course: Place and Learning

In autumn 2018, we co-taught an undergraduate course as part of a Bachelor of Arts degree in Education Studies. This is a new degree program at York University, which is now in its third year of operation. The course is an introductory course entitled *Place and Learning*. The BHER cohort of students took this course concurrently with a larger group of mainly first year Toronto-based students. We adapted the course for BHER students, our pedagogy operating within an online Moodle course (an online learning management system) and a weekly real-time online tutorial held for one hour early on Friday mornings in Toronto and late afternoon in Dadaab. In these tutorials, we discussed assignments and course themes, and invited students to introduce a course reading by responding to a series of questions sent in advance. The course also included a WhatsApp[2] discussion forum. Then near the end of the course, in December 2018, we held a week of lectures and tutorials in the Dadaab Learning Centre.

Our course focused on place-based education, joining in with a growing number of educators interested in place as an idea and interdisciplinary organizing framework for theorizing and practising education (Gruenewald, 2003). The course discussions explored various approaches to theorizing and practicing place-based education and then turned to a provocation of the Anthropocene (which we explore in more detail shortly) with an open question of framing locally placed pedagogical responses to this global concept.

Place-based education is both an old and a new concept, emerging out of traditions set by John Dewey (1938), Maria Montessori (Montessori, George and Holmes, 1912), Julius Nyerere (1967) and Paulo Freire (1970), who advocate for education reforms centring learners' engagement in local experiences. Place-based education is a responsive pedagogical approach that situates learning within relationships and explorations of the natural, built and socio-political places with/in which we live. More recently, place-based theorists have related devastating ecological destruction with the uprooting effects of colonization (Greenword, 2009), settler colonialism (Seawright, 2014) and globalization(s) (Gruenewald and Smith, 2008). An influential article by David Greenwood (née Gruenewald) (2003) brings together discussions of critical pedagogy, often with an urban focus, with place-based approaches frequently set in environmental and rural contexts. Greenwood advocates for a critical pedagogy of place in which everyday places (urban, rural and ecological) are conceived as pedagogical. He steers attention toward lived experiences of particular places that foster particular relationships and specific learnings that enable some and disable other actions. Education is offered as one way to shape these places through learning and critique and practicing different relationships that might contribute in some desirable ways, for example, to place-building, place-transforming, place-establishment, place-entrenchment, place-dismantlement and place-leaving.

Conceived in this way, places are not merely passive or static but might more fruitfully be conceived as dynamically shaped by and shaping particular pedagogies, ethics and politics. Place-based critical analysis can empower individuals and communities to recognize, deconstruct and challenge the problematic power relations of places, including social, cultural, economic, technological and environmental hierarchies. Understanding place in this way puts a particular weight on place as a stage-for-change; and, in these times of global connection, makes visible the inseparability of the local and the global – the complexities, ambiguities, competing and noncompeting stories, both local and global, residing in and between particular places and times.

In the case of BHER, place-based educational practices invite refugees and refugee teachers to think deeply about their places, associated stories shaping these places, and agencies and identities as professional practitioners. Conversations and practices of schooling often unproblematically valorize particular stories including those, for example, of universalized technical efficiency and personal progress allied with national market-based economic competitiveness. Such stories can render silent the politics of local cultures, communities and ecologies, as well as their complex, often contested, fraught, violent colonial histories. The Dadaab camps pose important questions concerning pastoral and farming communities and their shifting local practices in response to global changes, including changing weather patterns, deforestation and shifting water tables, ongoing wars and conflicts, forced-displacement, resettlement and returning, and, of course, the ongoing sustaining and adapting of everyday living in these refugee camps. Dadaab is a complex landscape in which to invite and dialogue about place-based education, being both a place of refuge and welcome, yet also a place where residents are actively discouraged from settling or naming the place as home.

Place is curiously central to the BHER project which is a Global North-South collaboration in a particular locale. Through BHER, Dadaab has become a local university town. Most opportunities for higher education for refugees worldwide are based on scholarships and mobility, which presume flexibility to travel and study abroad. In addition to fostering local access to study, BHER distinctively engages cohorts of students in particular local educational contexts, embracing stories, histories, justices and injustices that frame lives. Place-based teaching recognizes the fundamental importance of these experiences as a basis for (re)conceiving, interrupting and (re)performing quality and relevant education.

(Re)placing Anthropocene

The Anthropocene is a widely used and heavily contested term originally coined by the atmospheric chemist Paul Crutzen and the ecologist Eugene Stoermer (Crutzen and Stoermer, 2013). It refers to the contemporary geological period in which humans are affecting the Earth's geology and ecosystems in lasting and significant ways. The Anthropocene is an idea that positions humans as geologic agents, making clear what has been known to many peoples for a long time, that human culture and nature inter-influence each other. In our course, we took up specific questions of education. The course booklet (Alsop and Cohen 2018, p. 1), invited students to consider the following:

> Anthropocene poses particular challenges for those of us in education – how might it best be represented? What might be ways of conceiving, curating, and learning the geological present? What images, stories, and experiences might we create that engage learners with associated visions of the places of humans in the future? What education experiences might provoke us into new ways of learning, thinking and feeling human in particular places?

Thus, we turned to the Anthropocene as an idea, with hopes that it might open up generative and helpful conversations of education for our student teachers. We invited reflections on the associated logic. In particular, the ways Anthropocene resides within our pedagogical work (as teacher educators in Toronto and teachers in Dadaab) albeit in distinctive and contradictory ways. Perhaps the Anthropocene offers ways of experiencing these places in different ways, making some things sensory that were previously dulled and muted? Perhaps, from a different perceptual vantage point some global and local forces become apparent? Giles and Dippo (2019) entangle the global and local in the worldly university, mirroring Hannah Arendt's understanding of worldliness as the 'recognition of our dependency on one another'. We, too, sought a place-based worldliness in the course, evoking the Anthropocene as an interweaving of local place-based education and local land with global-senses of place and interdependence.

A Gallery of Possibilities

The Anthropocene exists as a swirl of undetermined questions and contestations: when did it start? Whose story is it? Who is responsible? What do we do about it? At what scales can it be understood? Is Anthropocene even the right word or helpful in the global phenomena encompassed in the term (Haraway, 2015; Hecht, 2018; Davis and Turpin, 2015)? What is lost and gained by adopting this notion of what it means to be human? As educators, we feel a responsibility to show students the array of possible frames and answers; yet we should also take care not to overwhelm. We are seeking to inspire active engagement not confusion and paralysis by 'over-choice' (Toffler, 1970). We took a three pronged-approach to inspire and prepare students to curate their response to Anthropocene: we (i) read about other examples of exhibits and encounters in Robin et al.'s (2014) *Three Galleries of the Anthropocene*, (ii) held in-class discussions and (iii) set up a gallery of images and quotes.

To start these discussions, we presented a geological definition of the Anthropocene, and watched a video from Deutsches Museum (2013) that gives an overview of the Anthropocene from a scientific-technological lens. Hecht (2018), among others, calls for an inter-scalar analysis of the Anthropocene, a call we aimed to meet as we turned the classroom into a gallery of images, graphics and quotes representing multiple scales and narratives through which to understand the Anthropocene. The gallery is available digitally on Moodle, and Esther Munene and Philomen Misoy (BHER administrative colleagues at the Learning Centre in Dadaab) kindly posted the images in the BHER Learning Centre so students could continue to engage with them over the semester.

Figure 10.2 displays some images from the Anthropocene Gallery that comprised a diversity of representations, including scientific definitions drawn from selected authors (Steffen et al., 2011; Stromberg, 2013), feminist narratives

Figure 10.2 Sample of images from our Anthropocene Gallery. Sources: Green Roofs for Healthy Cities, 2013; Steffen et al., 2011; Belcourt, 2015; Bottom Row: Noyle, n.d.; author's personal photograph, 2018; Woods, n.d.

(Gibson-Graham, 2011), Indigenous approaches (Theriault, 2015; Todd, 2015), art theorists (Davis and Turpin, 2015; Nancy and Ricco, 2015) and critical race analyses (Velez and Young, 2018). In class, we discussed the interconnectedness of the Anthropocene, and the co-existence of beauty and ugliness, creation and destruction. We took our time unpacking the 'complex messiness' of the Anthropocene (Robin et al., 2014), returning to it again when we visited the students at the end of the semester.

In our final in-person session, we storied the Anthropocene in three places, emphasizing that Anthropocene means more than just climate change. Building on a class reading, we first visited 'Svalbard (town of Pyramiden) = the Anthropocene', a coal mining centre in the Arctic transformed into what Robin and colleagues (2014, p. 217) describe as a landscape gallery where tourists emit carbon dioxide to come and observe the disappearing Arctic. We contemplated the histories, actors (human and non) and types of learning that happen in a region so strongly identified with environmental and social changes. We then took a virtual class trip to 'Toronto = the Anthropocene' via Google Maps Street View, visiting our homes and offices, and narrating a landscape changed by local and global human activity: buried river tributaries, migration and colonization.

We travelled to 'Dadaab = Anthropocene' on Google Maps too, but met a less precise virtual place, as there are no street-views of Dadaab. We paused to notice the politics of mapping that persist even in the age of satellites, and the narratives of enclosure and disclosure of the Anthropocene in Dadaab. Students shared stories of refugee arrivals, cultures and ethnic communities becoming neighbours, and soil eroding as trees become shelter. Our Anthropocene became more nuanced as we noticed the differences between lush greenery in the UNHCR compound in the town of Dadaab, and the mostly treeless refugee camps. Dadaab was recognized and framed as a site created and strongly affected by climate change and strongly representational of the Anthropocene, very much implicated in, but not responsible for, the large-scale human disruptions to natural cycles. We then asked groups of students to contemplate a small local curation of Anthropocene: if you could put a sign on a tree in Dadaab, what would it say? The groups discussed variations of 'stop cutting down trees' as a response to the rapid felling they have witnessed. Tensions between agencies, state and refugees in Dadaab = Anthropocene, such as how far can local food-production and afforestation efforts go in a place where residents are told to be impermanent, were left unsaid.

The Projects

So, what emerged? In total there were eight group projects from twenty-nine students. The majority of groups wrote about the changed landscape of Dadaab, of pre and post-refugee camp (un)settlement. As we had discussed during our visit, they explored the history of camp landscapes. One student commented, 'In Dadaab, forests are shrinking at a startling pace with an ever-growing refugee population which has more than doubled in the last twenty years.'[3] Due to the rapid and 'traumatic urbanization' of Dadaab (Jelacic 2014:191) and the newly formed borders isolating refugees from the rest of Kenya/the world, the noncitizens of the camps cut down a vast majority of the trees in the area for shelter, protection and heat. Like many of the places from which students originally fled, the land is desertifying. Another student group highlighted the double displacement many refugees experience when, for example, floods hit the area after long periods of drought, and refugees have to move, again, to higher ground. Garbage, pollution and natural resource use in the Dadaab camps was another strong theme across projects. The justifications provided in student narratives for the current situation included lack of knowledge, carelessness, lack of a culture of planting trees, and human needs. Unlike our in-class discussion, none of the curations or reflection papers engaged with the global geopolitics of blame and impacts of climate change, nor the policies and laws that impact the possibility and scale of local response. Rather, students interacted with immediate community problematics and focused advocacy efforts on passers-by to increase their awareness and to change their behaviours. Turning to the assignments, we offer three submissions telling different stories of Anthropocene as Greenbelt, Youth and Beauty, and Goats and Garbage.

Project One: The Greenbelt

Abdi Abdirahman Mohamed, Deko Gaiye Shahow and Arfon Bishar Hassan curated an activity for a group of classmates from both in and outside the BHER program. They took a walking tour of two locations, inviting classmates first to the greenbelt (intentionally forested area around the camps), and second to an arid area where the only 'trees' were branches fashioned into fences.

In Figure 10.3, you can see the size and form of the Greenbelt designed around the Dagahaley camp. The students share that their, 'inspiration to pick this topic was that decades earlier Dadaab was green surrounded by woodlands of different

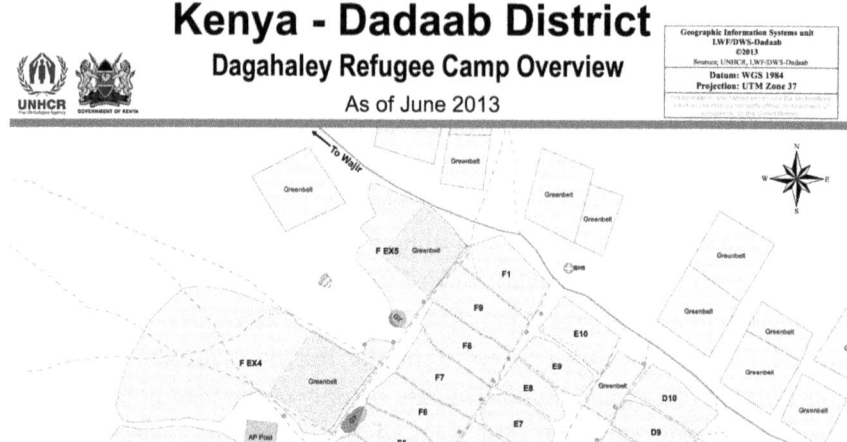

Figure 10.3 Greenbelt in Dadaab: Dagahaley Refugee Camp, 2015, Govt. Kenya & UNHCR. 2015.

sorts of trees ... we want to show off the clear difference between how the land was before human influence occurred'.[4] While standing among the trees, they shared a story from an Anna Tsing (2013) article we had read in class in which a Japanese American immigrant in Oregon, USA, forages for matsutake mushrooms with his family, detailing the health benefits and appreciation for the mushrooms and forest. This narrative of finding a sense of home faraway resonated with many students and BHER staff, some of whom have lived the pleasures and struggles of foraging. Following the slow pace set by Tsing, the group engaged their peers in a sensorial and feelings-based reflection with each place: 'We asked questions related to their visit: What do you see? How do you feel staying here?'[5] In their reflection paper, they detailed the positive feelings associated with the tree-filled landscape, and the lack of those feelings on the treeless patch of land. They argued both places are Anthropocene. The arid land is Anthropocene, telling the overlapping stories of human migration, borders and subsequent overharvesting impacting land and community. 'The greenbelt is [also] the Anthropocene because', as the students wrote, 'trees are presented and planted well' (ibid.). They named this 'natural space' as human designed and manicured, and as another human attempt to manage nature, and balance out ecosystems lost by human activity.

This curated learning encounter invited participants to step into a curious awareness in place. Staying away from academic discussion, this group oriented their encounter to felt relationships with place in the moment, curating a place-based experience. The purpose was to help 'the people accustomed to destroy [sic.] the bushes [to] see the beautifulness of trees', raise awareness of the benefits of trees to human health, and inspire behavioural change in their participants, specifically spending more time in the Greenbelt. They drew attention to the interconnectedness of human health and nature; the health of the ecosystem, and the health of individuals and ultimately the community. While this curation did not engage directly in the global interconnectedness of the Anthropocene, they successfully engaged in course themes and emphasized the personal within this global story.

Project Two: Youth and Beauty

Grace Nshimiyumukiza led a workshop at a youth centre in the Kakuma camp. Grace explains, 'during my workshop, we discussed the uniqueness of the earth and also photos of global warming in relation to changes in the climate'.[6] The first half of their discussion, she reported, centred on the perfect balance that makes life on Earth possible including its distance from the sun, gravitational pull and atmospheric density. Following this, she showed participants three photographs of industrial pollution and asked how they could curb emissions, seeking to open space for emotional responses to 'our changing Earth' through aesthetics (Robin et al., 2014, p. 208). In juxtaposing the beauty of Earth with the ugliness of pollution, she offered a particular answer to the question posed in the Art Musuem, Hasu de Kulturen de Welt (HKW) poster series: 'is the Anthropocene beautiful?' (ibid.) This workshop centres a stark and contradictory characteristic

Figure 10.4 Youth workshop, 2018, courtesy of Grace Nshimiyumukiza.

of the Anthropocene: the ability of our species to revere the sacredness of the planet and simultaneously disrupt its cycles in careless ways. We wonder what critical conversations could have happened or did happen in that workshop on who needs to be held responsible for the emissions they sought to curb; or how the workshop would have changed if participants searched the aesthetics of their immediate surroundings for beauty and pollution rather than photographs of far-away places. In this workshop, the Anthropocene was seen at the scale of Earth in space, and general human activity on it.

Project Three: Goats and Garbage

Five students, Kassahun Tekalign Hiticha, Dahabo Abdi Ibrahim, Kiin Ahmed Mohamed, Salah Mohamud Maalin and Jeylani Hajji Abdullahi, created a public gallery consisting of three photographs they took, displayed in Figure 10.5: a pile of waste along the side of the road, goats drinking from a muddy puddle, and a wider angle of the puddle showing the surrounding plastic waste. This gallery highlights two themes: the issue of waste management in the camps; and human waste reshaping landscapes and animals. In conversation about the project, one student described the goats in Dadaab, who seem to survive eating plastic, something he had never seen before. When buying goat meat in the market, it is common for residents to inquire into the meat's origin: did the goats live in the mountains or in town? Goats in town are not desirable because they eat the plastic and as a result have stringier and less tender meat. The goats of Dadaab are embodiments of the Anthropocene – with every plastic bit their digestive systems absorb, their bodies are absorbing a human-made material, embodying a core lesson of the Anthropocene that natural and cultural are indistinguishable. The goats also express changing relationships in and with place in the Anthropocene: while plastic is a global human object, *this* plastic and *these* goats become particular in their entwinement with each other and with the place of Dadaab.

The students placed their gallery in public and stood next to it engaging passers-by in dialogue. However, unlike the other two exhibits described here, these students sought to engage their public in the academic language that inspired their exhibit. In reflection, they recalled the challenges of engaging passers-by. They argued the word 'Anthropocene' is an exclusive academic word whose meaning is not intuitive, and thus 'will be a very difficult concept for many people to accept'.[7] They connected the unwelcoming nature of the word to human-caused climate change denial, writing that 'many people we asked about

Figure 10.5 Goats and Garbage, courtesy of Kassahun Tekalign Hiticha, Dahabo Abdi Ibrahim, Kiin Ahmed Mohamed, Salah Mohamud Maalin and Jeylani Hajji Abdullahi.

climate change and its effects locally deny the contemporary climate change and its human causes and strongly linked it to God's response to our disobedience and immorality' (ibid.). This interaction again points to the political nature of Anthropogenic change, and the ways in which the stories we tell shape our understanding of change. In these reflections, we are again called to question who is the 'we' of the Anthropocene. Who gets to tell the story of planetary change? What histories are held to account for this change? This gallery also opens questions of where is God in the Anthropocene, and whose God? Can we work across differing narratives to engage ethically in adapting to and mitigating planetary changes? As the educators who provoked the exhibit, this reflection opens several lines of inquiry including: could we have made more space for students to think about their audience and the types of languages that may or may not resonate, to anticipate potential reactions, and use these anticipations to further refine the aims and approaches of student exhibits? Second, we wonder if God was present within our own gallery, and how religious and spiritual stories of current happenings might be positioned alongside academic verbiage. Perhaps in the Anthropocene, academia and God can provide complementary stories, each naming human behaviours such as greed/over-extraction and lack of care that are the root causes of the Anthropocene, and also name complementary ways forward that open better practices of care for the Earth/God's creation. Dadaab is a place that can be storied as the Anthropocene, and yet it is also a place where that name does not resonate with the people whose lived experiences are exemplary of the changing epoch. The framing of and reactions to this exhibit call on us as place-based educators engaged in the Anthropocene to be more attuned to this tension; and to open an even wider plethora of worldviews and associated narratives about human-place relationships that can define the Anthropocene. Perhaps rooting even deeper into place-based pedagogy, future iterations of this course might seek to start with local explanations of locally felt atmospheric and landscape changes and expand outward to the global narratives of the Anthropocene from there, rather than seeking to fit a global narrative into a local place.

Place-based Borderless Higher Education: A Gallery to Rethink and (Re)place the Anthropocene

As teacher educators on the other side of the globe, we hem and haw over the awkward political and historical scales and places that form the landscape of our BHER teacher-student relationships. In reflecting on this course, we wonder on the ethicality of a prescribed community-engaged assignment such as we have outlined. Were student engagements driven by compliance or genuine interest? To what degree were the messages students advocated in their communities influenced by what they thought we, as grade-deciders, as Western educators, wanted to see? In what ways are we imbricated with the UN mass education campaigns that are a part of what education is in Dadaab and that advocate for human rights and health, but through largely Western lenses and assumptions? These are some of the irreconcilable tensions that North-South collaborative partnerships seek to tentatively navigate.

Scalar tensions were a central theme of our pedagogy. As we highlight, increasing global disparities in the Anthropocene are alarming. We continue to grapple with the scalar disparities (financial and material) of our mobility as BHER teachers. In flying to Dadaab (despite carbon offsetting), we produced more carbon emissions than most Dadaab residents produce annually. Most of our teaching was online, and yet we felt that visiting the Learning Centre was important. We were greeted by students with a welcoming enthusiasm, and so we reassured ourselves that this was a necessary part of the program, and that there is only so much that is possible online. Indeed, during our visit, personal relationships between students and teachers, one-on-one support, cross-cultural understandings and political discussions flourished in a way that felt impossible through the computer screen and limited internet access.

Our course is mandatory for students in the Bachelor of Educational Studies, and this raises questions of whether an assignment such as this imposes values/beliefs/or judgements that may or may not be appropriate in the students' contexts; or, if it really does open pathways for students to shape meaning and act on and in their world? It is likely it did both, and as we prepare the course for the next cohort of Dadaab students, we continue to debate these important questions of praxis. We took place-based education to a cosmopolitan whole Earth scale within a program that itself reaches across borders in solidarity. We can view our time together in this course as a cosmopolis of sorts, a temporary virtual assemblage of people and ideas seeking to reshape and re-place citizenship in this globalized epoch (Conley, 2012).

As we commented in the early stages of this chapter, Dadaab is a complex landscape in which to invite and dialogue place-based education. In our temporary community of learning, we asked students to join us in imagining the Earth as place, engaging with us in the 'cosmopolitan imperative' described by Ulrich Beck (2011), as the global need to 'cooperate or die' evolves in this new epoch of climatic change induced by human activity. Both in what they wrote and what they didn't, students engaged in the complexities of the Anthropocene in their local place, navigating human need with resource scarcity, beauty with destruction, animal resilience with human health. It is our hope that this chapter offers more lenses through which to understand the Anthropocene, particularly

African Anthropocenes and specifically, the Dadaab Anthropocene. As with cosmopolitanisms, there is no single scale or narrative that adequately captures the Anthropocene (Vertovec and Cohen, 2002; Hecht, 2018).

We believe in the importance of questions set forth by BHER students: how can we engage communities with the Anthropocene when the word itself disengages? How can we hold onto both the beauty of the Earth and human pollution of it? How can we ethically engage youth in imagining their future in the Anthropocene? Where is God in the Anthropocene? Who has the authority to determine the story of the cause and ways through global climatic changes? How can we slow down, and heal our bodies and spirits by spending time among trees? How can we respond locally to this epochal shift that does not recognize borders, while being deeply constrained by borders? How does the Anthropocene remake our relationships with place and learning? Certainly, there are important temporal distinctions rumbling beneath the surface here of Anthropocene as a spectacular apocalyptic collapse and Anthropocene as 'slow violence' (Nixon, 2013). We have read so many articles exploring Anthropocene as loss that a turn to beauty in contexts of forced displacement and settlement strikes us as extremely profound.

We join with so many others reflecting on the Anthropocene concept. In our opening discussions we argue that if this concept is going to be helpful it needs to invite critical reflection of scale, explorations of complex relationships between a shared planet, an Earthly home, and increasingly inequitable localized access to planetary resources and mobilities. Can Anthropocene-inspired pedagogy bring about necessary social, ecological and educational transformation of this nature? Can it respond to the social, ecological and geological inequalities that it seeks to make visible? These are such vast questions; but nevertheless, they are important ones. For those of us who are working in BHER and the associated promotion of borderless higher education for refugees, such evaluative questions warrant extended reflection and form the basis of this edited collection. What might we hope for borderless higher education?

The Anthropocene has received extensive attention. As Nixon (2018) laments, 'It took a while, but by the millennium's second decade those enthralled and appalled by the Anthropocene were being sucked, in their interdisciplinary masses, into its cavernous maw.' Our BHER Anthropocene pedagogy served as a way of inviting curatorial expressions of global within local. We have little doubt that confronting Anthropocene requires fresh perspectives and contexts. If it is to have real meaning other than a bookmark of global decline, it requires thinking from and with marginalized groups. Hecht (2018) writes of the African

Anthropocene in recognition of the fundamental importance of Africa in our global futures and pasts:

> Africa is the continent where population growth is projected to be the highest. It contains 60 per cent of the world's uncultivated arable land. Some pockets of Africa lie at the forefront of decentralised energy systems (such as solar power) that promise to mitigate climate change. And that's only for starters.

In this respect, Dadaab is a provocative place to rethink and replace the Anthropocene. We reflect on our teaching as inviting colleagues into conversations with global circulation and impact.

When we do this course again, there are ways in which we will modify our approach. When exploring the concept of the Anthropocene, we intend to invite a slower and, invariably, deeper dialogue in which we ask students to pay attention to and note down the ways in which they witness the Anthropocene in their everyday life. Perhaps a collective map of impacts and possibilities of the Anthropocene could be created before asking them to curate it. We may also spend more class time engaging in the ethical questions of curation such as advocating for behaviour change, or the tensions of intentionally presenting a narrative of the Anthropocene through images. Next time, we will present more curatorial examples, and spend more time unpacking what story these examples represent. We also wonder how we can invite further dissent into the classroom, encouraging students to form their own narratives of the Anthropocene (or non-Anthropocene).

The student projects had a future orientation. They didn't take-up the invitation we had offered of exploring the past, and exposing the brutal, debilitating effects of white colonialism and global capitalism. In the course, we sought to ask what happens when we begin thinking about Anthropocene in Dadaab? We sought to unsettle a concept with naturalized origins of industrialization in Europe, and the so-called great acceleration. Dadaab is a settlement with a long history, more recently marked by several waves of migration from civil war in the early 1990s and drought and famine in 2007 and 2011. Local histories matter a great deal for the ways that the Anthropocene might be conceived and discussed. These histories, however, can become erased within scales of geological time and levels and origins of industrialization. The African resources and imperial violence that fuelled the Anthropocene are too easily and too often overlooked. Indeed, so much discussion of the Anthropocene loses sight of human displacement and forced migration. Instead, it fixates on statistics of the magnitude of geological changes, comparing, for instance, the amount of rock that humans move per day, which now exceeds all-natural processes, including rivers and oceans. Such comparisons, although alarming, fail to consider who moves this rock and for what benefits and costs (ibid.). Dadaab offers an illuminating place to reflect on the Anthropocene, as it makes demonstrably clear that the great acceleration (so innocently associated with technological innovation) is simultaneously a crisis of increasing resource disparities and accelerating numbers of refugees, asylum seekers, and displaced people. We remain committed to the importance of the voices and perspectives of students that we had a privilege to work with in this BHER course.

Afterword

Lorrie Miller and Wenona Giles with Fouzia Warsame, the Dean of Education, Somali National University, Mogadishu

In early May 2020, Lorrie Miller and Wenona Giles interviewed Fouzia Warsame, when she was still the Dean of Education and Social Sciences at the Somali National University (SNU) in Mogadishu, Somalia. As a senior faculty member at a major university in Somalia, we were interested in her views on the significance of the Borderless Higher Education for Refugees (BHER) project for Somalia, the home country of so many refugees located in Dadaab and Kakuma.

We would like to begin by asking you to describe a little about your own background, which spans Somalia and Canada.

Yes, I was born in Somalia but left the country as a young child. Thus, I never went to school in Somalia. When the civil war broke out, my whole family emigrated to Canada and my formative years in middle and secondary school and then university were spent in Canada; I have spent more than half my life in Canada thus far. It was in graduate school in the Ontario Institute of Education at the University of Toronto that I began to expand my life skills and experiences and to explore issues of identity. There is a lot of discussion in Canada about notions of identity, and mine, at the time, was a hyphenated identity: Somali-Canadian. As a young adult, it seemed impossible for me to bring the two sides of the hyphen together, nor to blend them or choose one or the other. So, it is not surprising to me that during my PhD studies, nostalgia drew me back to Somalia where I thought I could do my doctoral fieldwork.

Immediately upon arriving here in 2012, I felt that I was home. Then the enormity of the devastation and the vast social and political problems called me to stay. I felt a sense of obligation and duty to try to contribute in some way. Even before I came to Somalia, I knew that teacher education would be a prominent issue coming out of civil war, unrest and insurgency. I thought that if the next generation had access to a better education, this could lead to a better Somalia. As Dean of an Education faculty, my work brings me close to the Ministry of Education, and thus, I am able to have some influence on improving the quality of education in the country. And I do feel that I am making a difference. The job certainly isn't done yet, but I am glad to be here. While I am still stuck with a hyphenated identity, it has changed to Canadian-Somali now, as that is the way I am viewed here.

How did you become involved in BHER?

I was introduced to the BHER program by Don Dippo,[1] who I had originally met when I was a graduate student in Toronto. We collaborated about how I could assist from SNU. It was very good timing as Somalia was beginning to think about mobile populations like IDPs (Internally Displaced Populations), many of whom see themselves as refugees in their own country. A lot of the international organizations were interested in talking about education for refugees and IDPs. At that time, there was interest in establishing a Commission for refugees, IDPs and returnees in Somalia; the Commission is now in place. My involvement in the BHER project has connected me with many other networks concerning access to higher education for refugees. And I now speak in many venues about refugees and access to education. I am still hoping to achieve a partnership with the Faculty of Education at York University, especially because in Somalia there are many Somali-Canadians returning to contribute to the rebuilding in many different sectors. They are keen on alliances with Canada. I am also appealing to Global Affairs Canada[2] to support such a partnership. We have a partnership, for example, with the University of Helsinki in Finland, and they have collaborated with us to develop and update our national teacher curriculum.

What are your thoughts about the impact that BHER has had for refugees, especially those from Somalia?

I know BHER has had a great impact in Dadaab. I think this project has given hope to many young people and has given them possible routes out of encampment. I have met some of the Dadaab BHER students at BHER Annual meetings in Nairobi, as well as in conferences in Europe. They display a real confidence; they do not see themselves as 'refugees' anymore, but have become part of humanity. Their ambition to contribute is so inspiring. At a conference in Berlin, I sat with some of the students, along with policy-makers, NGOs and government people from around the world. The conference attendees were enthralled with the ideas and personal histories of these Dadaab students, including how they ended up at the Berlin conference.

The impacts of such a project are never measurable; the outcomes are not tangible and are not about the numbers who graduate. They are about giving hope and the ripple effect of that hope. To see these young men and women and their confidence and their progressive ways of thinking, their willingness and ambition to make a difference – this inspires the next generation, and the next, and the next. They will be among the ones to make a difference in this region of Africa in the long run.

Is there a current and future need for such programs, beyond Dadaab?

I believe there is going to be a huge need for these kinds of university programs, as I don't see the world becoming more stable. We will likely see an increasing mobility of people who are not in their home countries/state, and who are outside the realm of life opportunities. The numbers of these people are increasing around the globe. The notion that borders and nation-states can contain populations is diminishing. In such a situation, access to education is of first and foremost importance, no matter who you are or where you have come from. We need programs like BHER to push the dialogue towards accessibility, openness and inclusivity.

Within nation-states, like Somalia, there are still struggles for inclusivity, due to regional and ethnic politics. People are moving from ethnic group locations and regions and trying to blend in elsewhere, but many still feel like outsiders and are treated as such. For example, some have flocked to opportunities in Mogadishu, one of the more urbanized regions in Somalia and a place where political power and affluence are located. Currently, there is a debate, a rhetoric emerging about who Mogadishu belongs to, even though we are all Somalis. The regions that IDPs are coming from are maybe two hours away from Mogadishu! That kind of ideology challenges public and free access to education, healthcare and housing. During the current pandemic we are witnessing questions about who should have access to healthcare. Not only does BHER challenge traditional ideas about who should have access to higher education, but it offers the global polity knowledge that challenges traditional ideologies about inclusion and exclusion.

Most of the BHER students were Somali refugees living in Dadaab, and some have now repatriated to Somalia – what is your hope for them and the communities they return to?

My hope is that they are more highly skilled, not only in an academic way, but also in terms of worldly experience, about how things can be done from ethical and professional perspectives. We are missing those experiences among many youths here. Interestingly, employers in Somalia are keen to hire those who have returned. But not enough are returning yet. It is still a risk for them, as often they don't have a host family to come back to, who will help them settle. But the opportunity is great. I have high hopes because returnees can make a difference in terms of relating to those who are still holding onto old ideologies of instability and conflict. Their success professionally also encourages those who remained to do better. And the stories and life experiences of returnees could make a difference for students and youth who remained, to rethink stability and belonging. The youth in Dadaab have asked me several times, 'How is it that the young people who grew up in Somalia and haven't left, do not care for their country? Do they understand what it means to belong somewhere?' Those from Dadaab don't understand why the people in Somalia take for granted their country's existence

What would your message be to those who wish to pursue a project like BHER?

I would encourage them first and foremost, because these kinds of programs provide access to higher education to those who would not otherwise have access. Also, in regards to where we are heading in the world, partnerships, like BHER support the building of future skills, qualities and mindsets that we need. Traditional forms of higher education have not worked in the twenty-first century. People worldwide are not prepared for the current world with our natural disasters, our climate and now with COVID19. We don't yet have the collective mindset to mitigate and solve these global problems. I believe that higher education can help to solve global issues. I think that this kind of education program can bring about a new mindset in the Global South and North.

Notes

Introduction

1 According to the UNHCR, 'The 1% estimate was compiled in consideration of the following: 1) estimated tertiary enrolment rates of Syrian refugees in the five main hosting countries in the Middle East and North Africa region (Lebanon, Iraq, Turkey, Egypt and Jordan); 2) global DAFI enrolment; 3) global Connected Learning enrolment; and 4) a grouping of other known enrolment' (UNHCR, 2001–2019; Bhabha, Giles and Mahomed, 2020, p. 6).

2 Global Affairs Canada (GAC), the aid and development arm of the Canadian government, took an international lead in supporting the implementation of the BHER project in 2013–19. Open Society Foundations (OSF) began to support the BHER project in 2017 and continues to do so as we write this chapter. We thank both GAC and OSF for their financial support, and their strong encouragement over the long-term. MasterCard Foundation funded the initial Feasibility Study (Dippo, Orgocka and Giles, 2013) and the first of two videos (Murphy, 2012). The Social Sciences and Humanities Research Council of Canada funded early research and the development of a partnership between two Kenyan and two Canadian universities, as well as Windle International Kenya and the UNHCR. The Centre for Refugee Studies, and the Faculties of Education, Liberal and Professional Studies, and Health at York University, and the Faculty of Education at the University of British Columbia have provided generous financial and in-kind support to the BHER project from its earliest days. UNHCR has also been supportive, especially with the funding of student transport to the BHER Learning Centre and midday meals for students.

3 We acknowledge the shortcomings of the language 'Global North' and 'Global South', but opt for it over 'Third World', a term associated with a Cold War context. It was recently estimated that at least 86 per cent of refugees live in the Global South (Hyndman and Giles, 2017, p. 25).

4 A protracted refugee camp or situation in the policy discourse of the office of the United Nations High Commissioner for Refugees is defined as a situation in which 25,000 or more refugees originating from the same country have sought asylum in another country (or countries) for at least five consecutive years. This definition does not refer to individuals but to a specific national group of people (Hyndman and Giles, 2017, p. 24).

5 See Bender's [1998] work on New York University and how important it is to him that the university serve its neighbourhood.

6 Thanks to Don Dippo for his interpretative insights on Arendt.
7 The Agenda for Humanity Core Responsibility 3 – 'Leave No One Behind' – focuses on migration and education: https://www.agendaforhumanity.org/cr/3.
8 The detailed BHER Commons or Portal Tool is available at http://bher.eecs.yorku.ca/. The development of this tool was led by Professor Melanie Baljko (Lassonde School of Engineering, York University) in collaboration with Wenona Giles, Michele Millard, Mirco Stella and Theresa Zeng. This tool provides a pathway for the development of academic programs such as those developed for the BHER project. The Commons or Portal Tool was developed in response to the numerous requests from people who asked those of us involved in BHER 'how to' build such a project.
9 This phase of the BHER project has been generously funded by Open Society Foundations.
10 MOOC is an acronym for 'Massive Open Online Course', and such courses are mainly higher education courses. They were first developed in 2008 and touted as the answer to the dearth of HE courses for disadvantaged and other populations, but they are not. They are aimed at unlimited participation and open access via the web and students generally work alone. One of the main issues with MOOCs is that recognized credentials are not generally associated with the courses, unless they are connected with a recognized academic institution and led by an accredited instructor of the institution, and most MOOCs do not meet either requirement. The Dadaab and Kakuma refugees wanted university courses that bestowed officially accepted credentials.

Chapter 1

1 The term *shifta* (or *shufto* in Somali) means outlaw or bandit in Kiswahili. The term was used to describe some of the purported insurgent tactics undertaken by Somali fighters who allegedly conducted roadside robberies during the 1963–7 war to secede from Kenya. It was also a convenient way for the government to delegitimize the separatist movement by reframing the conflict through the lens of law and order. Thus, in Kenyan national historiography, the conflict is remembered as the 'Shifta War'.
2 Garissa University College is now known as Garissa University.
3 All the names of people/participant in this chapter who were interviewed are pseudonyms.
4 Ksh 750 is little more than $9.00 CDN; the current incentive worker monthly wage is higher – around Ksh 7,500 (about $100 CDN)/month, but this is still a tenth of the wage that a Kenyan citizen doing the same job would earn.
5 We believe Fatuma is referring to how restrictions on mobility can complicate emergency transport to a hospital as one can be detained without carrying the right

documents. In addition, there are procedures that cannot be done in camp hospitals and for which one must wait for permission for treatment in Nairobi hospitals.

Chapter 2

1. Although BHER does not have a formal programme or learning centre in Kakuma, the project expanded into Kakuma and its township due to the relocation of some BHER students from Dadaab to Kakuma in 2017, when the Kenyan government threatened to close the Dadaab camps due to terrorist attacks in the country (Mwangi, 2018). During this time, the government began to demand the repatriation of Somali refugees back to their country (ibid.). Refugees from Ethiopia, Burundi and South Sudan were relocated to Kakuma's Kalobeyei camp, which is coordinated by the UNHCR as part of its refugee programme.
2. JWL, formerly known as Jesuit Commons-Higher Education at the Margins (JC-HEM), is a programme that provides education for students from Kenya, Malawi and Jordan. In 2011, JWL partnered with Regis University in Denver Colorado offering a diploma in liberal arts (Lawrence, 2012). JWL also partnered with SNHU's Global Education Movement to offer a Bachelor of Arts in the field of business to refugees and members of the host community. InZone, formerly known as the Centre for Interpreting in Zones of Crisis and War, is a project based at the University of Geneva in Switzerland, which offered interpretation training with UNHCR interpreters in Kakuma. In 2016, InZone pioneered an innovative approach to multilingual communication and higher education in Kakuma using learner-centred pedagogies and human-centred design (Moser-Mercer et al., 2016).
3. All identifiable information has been removed to keep participants anonymous. Any names used are pseudonyms (unless consent was given to use real name) to protect the identity of all respondents.
4. As per data provided by Finnish Church Aid, Kenya, on 30 July 2020.
5. The JWL has eighty-eight current students in total, thirty-two women and fifty-six male students. SNHU current students are fifty-six in total, with eight female and forty-eight male students. UNIGE-Inzone Kakuma has a total of seventy-six students, which includes seventeen females and fifty-nine male students.
6. Kinyarwanda is an official language of Rwanda and specifically a dialect of the Rwanda-Rundi language.

Chapter 3

1. This is as per article 4.5 of Kenyatta University fee guideline for all students, which states that 'students shall pay the following statutory fee per academic year as

approved by Senate from time to time: Tuition; Registration; Examination; Activity; Identification Card; Caution Money (payable once); Library fees and KUSA subscription. The total fees payable will be indicated in the letter of admission' (Kenyatta University, 2018, p. 30).

2   Access to learning content and instructions from the lecturer are governed by article 4.4.C, which states that 'registration for each trimester must be completed within the deadlines set by the Registrar (Academic)' (Kenyatta University, 2018, p. 31).

3   In Canada, the term 'credit transfer' is used to describe a situation where credits earned in one place (another department or another university, for example) are used to satisfy requirements in another place. In Kenya, this situation is described as 'credit waiver'.

4   For example, the Quality Secondary Teacher Education in Emergencies (QTEE) Diploma programme is offered in Kakuma by Utrecht University of Applied Science, Kenyatta University and Windle International Kenya.

Chapter 4

1   We use the terms 'North' and 'South' to refer, respectively, to high-income regions and low to middle-income regions.

2   'Incentive workers' are refugees paid an amount less than a wage by UNHCR to provide certain services to the displaced community (UNHCR Policy Development and Evaluation Service, 2014).

3   A formative evaluation is conducted while a project or programme is in process and is intended to show strengths, weaknesses and areas for improvement.

4   Once a tranche of funds is advanced, it is a standard Canadian accounting practice that 80 per cent of that funding must be cleared before the next tranche of funds (based on a forecast) can be forwarded. York University adheres to this practice.

Chapter 6

1   A community mobilizer is responsible for community engagement and empowerment in an assigned area, in this case Dagahaley, one of the Dadaab refugee camps. They work on awareness, monitoring and outreach activities.

2   Sustainable Development Goal number four points to the importance of inclusive and equitable quality education and the promotion of lifelong learning opportunities for all.

Chapter 7

1. Although courses may have been large in Toronto, the BHER versions taught to students abroad were much smaller and were taught independently and concurrently with local courses in Toronto.
2. WhatsApp is a widely used communications app that facilitates group conversations.
3. At the time that many geography courses were being taught, the Kenyan government was threatening to close the refugee camps at Dadaab (BBC, 2017).
4. For ESL students, fear of failure and time management problems often exacerbate academic honesty problems that originate in ignorance and inexperience (Hayes and Introna, 2005).
5. TAs consulted the Teaching Commons at York University as well as the Academic Writing Centre in the faculty of Liberal Arts and Professional Studies.
6. Such individual isolation is unusual in the Geography Department where TAs often work in pairs or large teams so they can discuss teaching challenges.

Chapter 8

1. The goal of the UBC Teacher Education Secondary Programme was to prepare university students to teach at the secondary (high school) level in the Dadaab camps. The average age of secondary school students in Canada is 13–18 years.
2. The focus of this chapter is about the UBC experience. Although all instructors across the programme were invited to share their experiences, just a small group of instructors did so.
3. A UBC teaching assistant supports the principal instructor and teaches under the guidance of that lead instructor.
4. Two distinctive cohorts, one focused on humanities, the other on sciences, each with differing start dates made up the secondary teacher education diploma programme. A few humanities students began with the majority of the science students in the first intake in 2014, whereas the remainder of the students began in 2015. That last group graduated with their diploma in 2017.
5. An incentive teacher is one that is paid a nominal amount and has no formal training as a teacher, but works as a teacher nonetheless.
6. Led by Dr. Cynthia Nicol, Dr. Karen Meyer, Dr. Samson Nashon, Dr. George Belliveau and Dr. Rita L. Irwin LLTD is a research project connected to BHER, and was funded by Social Science and Humanities Research Council SSHRC: https://lltd.educ.ubc.ca. Nicol and Meyer (Meyer, K. et al., 2019) taught in Dadaab for UBC and visited the site several times. Nashon is the UBC lead for this project.

7   White UNHCR tents were common in the newer camps, but in the more established camps, residents lived in various brick and mud structures.
8   The LLTD project hired several research assistants who were UBC students in Vancouver, BC, but were originally from Dadaab, having come to UBC previously, not a part of the BHER project. However, through the LLTD project, they supported and connected with the students on site in Dadaab.

Chapter 9

1   Standard 8 is the final year of primary education in Kenya. If students begin primary schooling at the age of 6, standard 8 students should be around 14 years of age; however, there are many older students who are enrolled into lower grades as a result of years of missed schooling due to displacement.
2   The monthly rate for private schools in Dadaab is not uniform. The rates vary depending on the school, ranging between 200 to 1500 Ksh from the primary level. These rates increase as students progress from primary to secondary.
3   In referring to the convertibility of economic capital into 'a title of nobility', Bourdieu means the potential use of money to achieve society's valued category such as marrying into royalty. In the case of Dadaab, where refugee status is simultaneous with poverty/lack of money, it is not money per se that is convertible; rather, to have an education, or to be a teacher, may lead to networks/connections (social capital), that give one a status of respect/'nobility'. In this sense, in crisis situations, the conversion of Bourdieu's forms of capital vary: cultural capital and economic capital converge in complex ways.
4   Code-switching is a linguistic phenomenon where, during one given conversational encounter, speakers move between two or more languages/dialects.
5   French language fluency is also important for Canada.
6   While corporal punishment was abolished in Kenya in 2001, the practice continues in many parts of Kenya today.
7   The Gross Enrolment Rate is the total enrolment in a specific level of education, regardless of age, expressed as a percentage of the eligible official school-age population corresponding to the same level of education in a given school year.
8   The York University Certificate Program is indicative of entry-level English fluency skills of Dadaab students, as it was the equivalent of a first-year university program.
9   Numbers from the York University Certificate Program are used here as the instructor reports cited above pertain to these students.
10 Personal email communication between HaEun Kim and Seraphin Kimonyo on April 8, 2020.

Chapter 10

1. We would like to thank all members of the *Place and Learning course*, particularly Jeylani Hajji Abdullahi, Arfon Bishar, Kassahun Tekalign Hiticha, Dahabo Abdi Ibrahim, Salah Mohamud, Maalin Abdi Mohamed, Kiin Ahmed Mohamed, Grace Nshimiyumukiza and Deko Shahow, who kindly gave consent for their course projects to be featured in this chapter.
2. An instant messaging application that allows users to exchange text, image, video and audio messages for free.
3. Quotation taken from students' curatorial project reflections: Kassahun Tekalign Hiticha, Dahabo Abdi Ibrahim, Kiin Ahmed Mohamed, Salah Mohamud Maalin and Jeylan Hajji Abdullahi.
4. Quotation taken from students' curatorial project reflections: Abdi Abdirahman Mohamed, Deko Gaiye Shahow and Arfon Bishar Hassan.
5. Quotation taken from students' curatorial project reflections: Abdi Abdirahman Mohamed, Deko Gaiye Shahow and Arfon Bishar Hassan.
6. Quotation taken from students' curatorial project reflections: Grace Nshimiyumukiza.
7. Quotation taken from students' curatorial project reflections: Kassahun Tekalign Hiticha, Dahabo Abdi Ibrahim, Kiin Ahmed Mohamed, Salah Mohamud Maalin and Jeylan Hajji Abdullahi.

Afterword

1. Don Dippo co-led the BHER project.
2. Global Affairs Canada (GAC) is the development and international aid department of the Canadian Government.

References

Introduction

Agier, Michel (2011), 'From Refuge the Ghetto is Born: Contemporary Figures of Heterotopias', in Ray Hutchinson and D. Bruce (eds), *The Ghetto: Contemporary Global Issues and Controversies*, Chapter 11, Haynes, Boulder: Westview Press.

Baud, I. S. A. (2002), 'North-South Partnerships in Development Research: An Institutional Approach', *International Journal of Technology Management & Sustainable Development*, 1 (3): 153–70.

Bhabha, Jacqueline, Wenona Giles and Faraaz Mahomed (2020), 'Introduction', in Jacqueline Bhabha, Wenona Giles and Faraaz Mahomed (eds), *A Better Future: The Role of Higher Education for Displaced and Marginalised People*, 1–18, Cambridge: Cambridge University Press.

Bishop, Danielle E. (2019), 'Kakuma's Shadows: Everyday Violence in the Lives and Livelihoods of Young People Living In and Around the Turkana-Kakuma Refugee Camp Nexus', PhD diss., Toronto: York University.

Black, C. (2010), 'Schooling the World: The White Man's Last Burden' Producers: N. Hurst, J. Grossan, M. Marlens, 6 February, 2019. Available online: https://schoolingtheworld.org/film/.

Chernikova, E. (2011), *Shoulder to Shoulder or Face to Face? Canada's University-Civil Society Collaborations on Research and Knowledge for International Development*, Ottawa: International Development Research Centre.

Clark-Kazak, Christina (2019), 'Partnering on Research Methodologies in Forced Migration: Challenges, Opportunities, and Lessons Learned', in Susan McGrath and Julie Young, *Mobilizing Global Knowledge: Refugee Research in an Age of Displacement*, 273–87, Vancouver: University of British Columbia Press.

Crisp, Jeff (2000), 'Forms and Sources of Violence in Kenya's Refugee Camps', *Refugee Studies Quarterly*, 19 (1): 54–70.

Dippo, Don, Aida Orgocka and Wenona Giles (2013), 'Feasibility Study Report: Reaching Higher: The Provision of Higher Education for LongTerm Refugees in the Dadaab Camps, Kenya', 20 April, 2020. Available online: http://refugeeresearch.net/ms/bher/workshops/feasibility-study-report/.

Freire, Paulo (1993), *Pedagogy of the Opressed*, New York: Continuum Publishing Company.

Giles, Wenona and Aida Orgocka (2018), 'Adolescents in Protracted Refugee Situations: The Case of Dadaab', in Jacqueline Bhabha, Daniel Senovilla Hernandez and Jyothi

Kanics (eds), *Research Handbook on Migration and Childhood*, Cheltenham: Edward Elgar Publishing.

Giles, Wenona and Don Dippo (2019), 'Transitions from Knowledge Networked to Knowledge Engaged: Ethical Tensions and Dilemmas from the Global to the Local', in Susan McGrath and Julie Young (eds), *Ethical Networking for Research and Practice: Reflections on the Refugee Research Network*, Calgary, ON: University of Calgary.

Goodman, Paul (1962), *The Community of Scholars*, New York: Random House.

Grabska, Katarzyna (2011), 'Constructing "Modern Gendered Civilised" Women and Men: Gender-Mainstreaming in Refugee Camps', *Development*, 81–93.

Gregory, Derek (2004), *The Colonial Present*, Oxford: Blackwell Publishing.

Hall, Stuart (1996), 'When was the Post-Colonial?: Thinking at the Limit', in I. Chambers and L. Curti (eds), *The Post-Colonial Question: Common Skies, Divided Horizons*, 242–59. London: Routledge.

Horst, Cindy (2008 [2006]), *Transnational Nomads: How Somalis Cope with Refugee Life in the Dadaab Camps of Kenya*, New York and Oxford: Berghahn Books.

Hyndman, Jennifer (2000), *Managing Displacement: Refugees and the Politics of Humanitarianism*, Minneapolis: University of Minnesota Press.

Hyndman, Jennifer and Wenona Giles (2017), *Refugees in Extended Exile: Living on the Edge*, Abingdon-on-Thames: Routledge.

Hynie, Michaela, Susan McGrath, Julie E. E. Young and Paula Banerjee (2014), 'Negotiations of Engaged Scholarship and Equity Through a Global Network of Refugee Scholars', *Scholarly and Research Communications*, 5 (3): 1–18.

Jayawardena, K. (1986), *Feminism and Nationalism in the Third World*, London: Zed Books.

Jazeel, Tariq and Colin McFarlane (2007), 'Responsible Learning: Cultures of Knowledge Production and the North-South Divide', *Antipode*, 39 (5): 781–9.

Kimari, Wangui and Wenona Giles (2020), 'Building Ethical Relationships Through the Borderless Higher Education Project in Dadaab, Kenya', in Jacqueline Bhabha, Wenona Giles and Faraaz Mohamed, *A Better Future: The Role of Higher Education for Displaced and Marginalized People*, 407–26, Cambridge: Cambridge University Press.

Landau, Loren B. (2019), 'Capacity, Complicity, and Subversion: Revisiting Collaborative Refugee Research in an Era of Containment', in Susan McGrath and Julie Young, *Mobilizing Global Knowledge: Refugee Research in an Age of Displacement*, 25–43, Vancouver: University of British Columbia Press.

Mabokela, Obakeng Reitumetse and Kaluke Felicity Mawila (2004), 'The Impact of Race, Gender, and Culture in South African Higher Education', *Comparative Education Review*, 396–416.

Mama, Amina (2003), 'Restore, Reform but do not Transform: The Gender Politics of Higher Education in Africa', *Journal of Higher Education in Africa*, 101–25.

Murphy, Peter (2012), 'Hunger for Education on the Edge of the Planet', Toronto. video: http://www.bher.org/bher-videos.

Ogden, Jessica A. and John D. H. Porter (2000), 'The Politics of Partnership in Tropical Public Health: Researching Tuberculosis Control in India', *Social Policy & Administration* 34 (4): 377–91.

Pittaway, Eileen and Linda Bartolomei (2001), 'Refugees, Race and Gender: The Multiple Discrimination against Refugee Women', *Refuge: Canada's Journal on Refugees*, 21–32.

Rizvi, Fazal, Bob Lingard and Jennifer Lavia (2006), 'Post Colonialism and Education: Negotiating a Contested Terrain', *Pedagogy, Culture and Society* 14 (3): 249–62.

Said, Edward (1993), *Culture and Imperialism*, New York: Vintage Books.

Spivak, G. (1988), 'Can the Subaltern Speak?', in C. Nelson and L. Grossberg (eds), *Marxism and the Interpretation of Culture*. Urbana: University of Illinois Press.

Sullivan-Owomoyela, Joan and Laura Brannelly (2009), *Promoting Participation: Community Contribution to Education in Conflict Zones*, Paris, France: International Institute for Education Planning & CfBT Education Trust.

UNDP (2019), 'Sustainable Development Goals: Quality Education', 06 February 2019. Available online: https://www.undp.org/content/undp/en/home/sustainable-development-goals/goal-4-quality-education.html.

UNHCR November (2011), 'Joint Strategy for Education in Dadaab', 18 August 2015. Available online: http://data.unhcr.org/horn-of-africa/region.php?id=3&country=110.

UNHCR (2001–19), 'Tertiary Education', 04 July 2019. Available online: https://www.unhcr.org/tertiary-education.html.

UNHCR (2020), 'Monthly Operational Update Dadaab, Kenya, March 2020'. Available online: https://www.unhcr.org/ke/wp-content/uploads/sites/2/2020/04/Dadaab-March-2020-operational-Update-.pdf.

UNOCHA (2016), 'Agenda for Humanity', 28 May 2020. Available online: https://agendaforhumanity.org/.

WIK (Windle International Kenya) Scholarship Program Office (2019), Report on BHER Project Enrolment numbers for 2019', Nairobi: unpublished report.

Chapter 1

Agamben, Giorgio (1998), *Homo Sacer: Sovereign Power and Bare Life*, Stanford, CA: Stanford University Press.

Agier, Michel (2010). *Managing the Undesirables: Refugee Camps and Humanitarian Government*, Cambridge, UK: Polity.

Allison, Simon (2015), 'World's Largest Refugee Camp Scapegoated in Wake of Garissa Attack', *The Guardian*, 14 April 2015. Available online: https://www.theguardian.com/world/2015/apr/14/kenya-garissa-dadaab-scapegoat-al-shabaab.

Bannon, Brendan and Eveline Wolfcarius (2009), 'Somali Bantus Gain Tanzanian Citizenship in Their Ancestral Land', *UNHCR (The UN Refugee Agency)*, 3 June.

Available online: https://www.unhcr.org/news/latest/2009/6/4a28cd886/somali-bantus-gain-tanzanian-citizenship-ancestral-land.html.

Blanchard, Lauren Ploch (2013), 'In Brief: The September 2013 Terrorist Attack in Kenya', *Congressional Research Service*, 27 September. Available online: https://digital.library.unt.edu/ark:/67531/metadc227943.

Callanan, Anne (2006), 'WFP/UNHCR/GOK/Donors: Joint Assessment Mission, Kenya', *World Food Programme*, 6 October. Available online: https://documents.wfp.org/stellent/groups/public/documents/ena/wfp121116.pdf?iframe.

Government of Kenya (2018), 'Social Assessment Report Kenya Development Response to Displacement Impacts Project (KDRDIP) Additional Financing (P166266)', *Executive Office of the President*, 01 May. Available online: http://documents.worldbank.org/curated/en/534001531467006900/pdf/KDRDIP-Social-Assessment-Report.pdf.

Hyndman, Jennifer (1997), 'Border Crossings', *Antipode*, 29 (2): 149–76. Available online: https://onlinelibrary.wiley.com/doi/abs/10.1111/1467-8330.00040.

Jensen, Bram (2015), '"Digging Aid": The Camp as an Option in East and the Horn of Africa', *Journal of Refugee Studies*, 29 (2): 149–65.

Kamau, Christine and John Fox (2013), 'The Dadaab Dilemma: A Study on Livelihood Activities and Opportunities for Dadaab Refugees', *Danish Refugee Council and UNHCR (The UN Refugee Agency)*, 01 August 2013. Available online: https://www.alnap.org/help-library/the-dadaab-dilemma-a-study-on-livelihood-activities-and-opportunities-for-dadaab.

Kuch, Amelia (2018), 'Lessons from Tanzania's Historic Bid to Turn Refugees to Citizens', *Refugees Deeply*, 22 February 2018. Available online: https://www.newsdeeply.com/refugees/community/2018/02/22/lessons-from-tanzanias-historic-bid-to-turn-refugees-to-citizens.

Mamdani, Mahmood (2012), *Define and Rule: Native as Political Identity*, Cambridge, Mass.: Harvard University Press.

Milner, James (2009), *Refugees, the State and the Politics of Asylum in Africa*, London: Palgrave Macmillan.

Milner, James (2019), 'Understanding the Everyday Politics of the Global Refugee Regime: Collective Action in a Time of Populism?' *Presentation at Carleton University*, 06 February 2019. Available online: https://carleton.ca/polisci/2019/james-milner-understanding-the-everyday-politics-of-the-global-refugee-regime-collective-action-in-a-time-of-populism.

New Humanitarian, The (2015), 'Somali Refugees Feel Remittance Pain after Kenya Attack', *The New Humanitarian*, 10 April 10 2015. Available online: http://www.thenewhumanitarian.org/news/2015/04/10/somali-refugees-feel-remittance-pain-after-kenya-attack.

Sperber, Amanda, (2015), 'Little Mogadishu', *Foreign Policy*, 14 April. Available online: https://foreignpolicy.com/2015/04/14/kenya-shabab-somalia-garissa-kenyatta.

Sweeney, Damien Mc. (2012), 'Conflict and Deteriorating Security in Dadaab', *Humanitarian Practice Network*, March. Available online: https://odihpn.org/magazine/conflict-and-deteriorating-security-in-dadaab.

Turner, Simon (2015), 'What Is a Refugee Camp? Explorations of the Limits and Effects of the Camp', *Journal of Refugee Studies*, 29 (2): 139–48. Available online: https://academic.oup.com/jrs/article-abstract/29/2/139/2362940.

UNHCR (2015), 'Voluntary Repatriation of Somali Refugees from Kenya: Operations Strategy 2015–2019', *UNHCR (The UN Refugee Agency)*, 29 July. Available online: https://www.unhcr.org/protection/conferences/5616280b9/voluntary-repatriation-somali-refugees-kenya-operations-strategy-2015-2019.html.

UNHCR (2018), 'Operational Update: Dadaab, Kenya 01–15 June 2018', *UNHCR (The UN Refugee Agency)*, 15 June. Available online: https://www.unhcr.org/ke/wp-content/uploads/sites/2/2019/01/15-June-Dadaab-Bi-weekly-Operational-Update.pdf.

Whittaker, Hannah Alice (2012), 'The Socioeconomic Dynamics of the Shifta Conflict in Kenya, C. 1963–8', *The Journal of African History*, 53 (3): 391–408. doi: https://doi.org/10.1017/S0021853712000448.

Chapter 2

Andrade, Filomena, Paulo de Carvalho and Gabriela Cohen (2001), A Life of Improvization: Displaced People in Malanje and Benguela, In Paul Robson (Ed) *Communities and Reconstruction in Angola Guelph Canada Development Workshop* (pg. 120–161).

Abdi, Awa M. (2004), 'In Limbo: Dependency, Insecurity and Identity in Dadaab Camps', *Refuge: Canadian Periodical on Refugee Issues*, 22 (2): 2–31.

Abdi, Farhia (2016), 'Behind Barbed Wire Fences: Higher Education and Twenty-first Century Teaching in Dadaab, Kenya', *Bildhaan: An International Journal of Somali Studies*, 16 (8): 21–35.

Bellino, Michelle J. and Mohamud Hure (2018), 'Pursuing Higher Education in Exile: A Pilot Partnership in Kakuma Refugee Camp', *Childhood Education: Innovations*, 94 (5): 46–51.

Bellino, Michelle J. (2018), 'Youth Aspirations in Kakuma Refugee Camp: Education as a Means for Social, Spatial and Economic (Im)mobility', *Globalisation, Societies and Education*, 16 (4): 541–56.

Bishop, Danielle E. (2019), 'Kakuma's Shadows: Everyday Violence in the Lives and Livelihoods of Young People Living In and Around the Turkana-Kakuma Refugee Camp Nexus.' PhD diss., York University, Toronto.

Boateng, Alice (2010), 'Survival Voices: Social Capital and the Well-Being of Liberian Refugee Women in Ghana', *Journal of Immigrant & Refugee Studies*, 8 (4): 386–408.

Carlson, Sharon (2005), *Contesting and Reinforcing Patriarchy: An Analysis of Domestic Violence in the Dzaleka Refugee Camp (Working Paper 23)*, Oxford: Refugee Studies Centre, University of Oxford.

Chatty, Dawn and Gillian Lewando Hundt (2005), 'Introduction: Children of Palestine Nar-rate Forced Migration', in Dawn Chatty and Gillian Lewando Hundt (eds), *Children of 212 – Children of the Camp Palestine: Experiencing Forced Migration in the Middle East*. New York: Berghahn Books, pp. 1–34.

Chege, Fatuma and Daniel N. Sifuna (2006), 'Girls' and Women's Education in Kenya', in *Gender Perspectives and Trends* (February), UNESCO.

Clark-Kazak, Christina (2010), 'The Politics of Formal Schooling in Refugee Contexts: Education, Class and Decision Making among Congolese in Uganda', *Refuge: Canada's Journal on Refugees*, 27, (2): 57–64.

Darling-Hammond, Linda (2000), 'Teacher Equality and Student Achievement', *Education Policy Analysis Archives*, 8 (1).

Douhaibi, Dacia, Negin Dahya, Olivier Arvisais and Sarah Dryden-Peterson (2020), 'Culture, Gender and Technology: Mediating Teacher Training Using Text Messaging in Refugee Camps', in Bhabha, J., W. Giles and F. Mahomed (Eds) *A Better Future: The Role of Higher Education for Displaced and Marginalised People*, UK: Cambridge University Press.

Dryden-Peterson, Sarah and Negin Dahya (2017), 'Tracing Pathways to Higher Education for Refugees: The Role of Virtual Support Networks and Mobile Phones for Women in Refugee Camps', *Comparative Education*, 53 (2): 284–301.

Dryden-Peterson, Sarah and Wenona Giles (2010), 'Higher Education For Refugees', *Refuge: Canada's Journal on Refugees*, 27 (2): 3–9.

El Jack, Amani (2010), '"Education Is My Mother and Father": The "Invisible" Women of Sudan', *Refuge: Canada's Journal on Refugees*, 27 (2): 19–29.

Fawole, Olufunmilayo I. (2008), 'Economic Violence To Women and Girls: Is It Receiving the Necessary Attention?' *Trauma, Violence, & Abuse*, 9 (3) (July): 167–77.

Grayson, Catherine-Lune (2017), *Children of the Camp: The Lives of Somali Youth Raised in Kakuma Refugee Camp, Kenya*, Oxford: Berghahn Books.

Giles, Wenona (2013). "Women Forced to Flee: Refugees and Internally Displaced Persons" In Carol Cohn (Ed), *Women and Wars*. Cambridge UK: Polity Press.

Harrell-Bond, Barbara E. (1986), *Imposing Aid: Emergency Assistance to Refugees*, Oxford: Oxford University Press.

Hill, M. Anne and Elizabeth M. King (1993), 'Women's Education in Developing Countries: An Overview', in *Women's Education in Developing Countries: Barriers, Benefits and Policies*, The World Bank.

Horn, Rebecca (2010), 'Exploring the Impact of Displacement and Encampment on Domestic Violence in Kakuma Refugee Camp', *Journal of Refugee Studies*, 23 (3): 356–76.

Hyndman, Jennifer (2000), *Managing Displacement: Refugees and the Politics of Humanitarianism*, University of Minneapolis: Minneapolis.

Jacobs, Jerry A. (1996), 'Gender Inequality and Higher Education', *Annual Review of Sociology*, 22: 153–85.

Kabeer, Naila (1999), 'Resources, Agency, Achievements: Reflections on the Measurement of Women's Empowerment', *Development and Change*, 30: 435–64.

Kirk, Jackie (2006), *Education in Emergencies: The Gender Implications. Advocacy Brief*, UNESCO Bangkok.

Kirk, Jackie (2010), 'Gender, Forced Migration and Education: Identities, and Experiences of Refugee Women Teachers', in *Gender and Education*, 22 (2): 161–76.

Lawrence, Mary (2012), 'Education at the Margins: Ubuntu at our Core', *Education* 1 (1).

Loescher, Gil and James Milner (2008), 'Understanding the problem of protracted refugee situations', in *Protracted Refugee Situations: Political, Human Rights and Security Implications*, New York: United Nations University Press.

Lowe, Sophia (2019), 'A Bridge to The Future: From Higher Education to Employment for Displaced Youth in Africa', *World University Service of Canada for Mastercard Foundation* (October).

Lutheran World Federation (2015), *Rapid Assessment of Barriers to Education in Kakuma Refugee Camp: Access and Quality in Primary Education*, Kenya-Djibouti.

Mendenhall, Mary, Sarah Dryden-Peterson, Lesley Bartlett, Caroline Ndirangu, Rosemary Imonje, Daniel Gakunga, Loise Gichuhu, Grace Nyagah, Ursulla Okoth and Mary Tangelder (2015), 'Quality Education for Refugees in Kenya: Pedagogy in Urban Nairobi and Kakuma Refugee Camp Settings', *Journal on Education in Emergencies*, 1 (1) (October): 92–130.

Moletsane, Relebohile (2005), 'Gender Equality in Education in the Context of the Millennium Development Goals: Challenges and Opportunities for Women', *Convergence* 38 (3): 59–68. Toronto: International Council for Adult Education.

Moret, Joëlle, Simone Baglioni and Denise Efionayi-Mäder (2006), *The Path of Somali Refugees into Exile: A Comparative Analysis of Secondary Movements and Policy Responses*, Neuchâtel: Swiss Forum for Migration and Population Studies.

Moser-Mercer, Barbara, Erin Haybe and Joshua Goldsmith (2016), 'Higher Education Spaces and Protracted Displacement: How Learner-Centered Pedagogies and Human-Centered Design Can Unleash Refugee Innovation', in the UNESCO *Chair Conference on Technologies for Development* (pp. 41–52). Springer, Cham.

Mwangi, Pius Muiru (2018), 'The impact of security policies on refugee repatriation of Somali Refugees from Dadaab refugee camp, Kenya', Doctoral diss., Moi University, Kenya.

Olson-Strom, Solveig and Nirmala Rao (2020), 'Higher Education for Women in Asia', in *Diversity and Inclusion in Global Higher Education, Lessons From Across Asia*, Singapore: Palgrave Macmillan.

Organization for Economic Co-operation and Development (OECD) (2005), 'Teachers Matter: Attracting, Developing, and Retaining Effective Teachers'.

Plasterer, Robyn and Laura-Ashley Wright (2010), 'Beyond Basic Education: Exploring Opportunities for Higher Learning in Kenyan Refugee Camps', *Refuge: Canada's Journal on Refugees*, 27 (2): 42–56.

Putnam, Robert (1993), 'The Prosperous Community', *The American Prospect*, 4 (13): 35–42.

Putnam, Robert (2000), *Bowling Alone: The Collapse and Revival of American Community*, New York: Simon & Schuster.

Schwille, J., M. Dembélé and J. Schubert (2007), *Global Perspectives on Teacher Learning: Improving Policy and Practice*, International Institute for Educational Planning (IIEP) UNESCO.

Sengupta, Enakshi and Patrick Blessinger (2018), 'Refugee Education: Integration and Acceptance of Refugees in Mainstream Society', in *Innovations in Higher Education Teaching and Learning*, Volume 11. UK: Emerald Publishing.

Stromquist, Nelly P. (1989), 'Determinants of Educational Participation and Achievement of Women in The Third World: A Review of The Evidence and a Theoretical Critique', *Review of Educational Research*, 59 (2) (Summer): 143–83.

United Nations High Commission for Refugees (2017), 'Education Strategy Kakuma Refugee Camp Kenya.'

United Nations High Commission for Refugees (2019), 'Kakuma and Kalobeyei Settlement.' Briefing Kit (May).

Verdirame, G. and B. Harrell-Bond (2005), 'Rights in Exile: Janus-Faced Humanitarianism', *Studies in Refugee Migration*, Volume 17. Oxford: New York.

Wessells, M. and C. Monteiro (2004), 'Internally Displaced Angolans: A Child-focused, Community-based Intervention'. In Miller, K. E and Rasco, L. M. *The Mental Health of Refugees: Ecological Approaches to Healing and Adaptation*. Mahwah, New Jersey (pg. 67–94).

Yick, A. G. (2001). 'Feminist Theory and Status Inconsistency Theory: Application to Domestic Violence in a Chinese American Community', *Violence Against Women*, 7: 545–62.

Zeus, Barbara (2010), 'Exploring Barriers to Higher Education in Protracted Refugees Situations: The Case of Burmese Refugees in Thailand', *Journal of Refugee Studies*, 24 (2): 256–76.

Zeus, Barbara and Josh Chaffin (2011), 'Education for Crisis-Affected Youth: A Literature Review. INEE Adolescent and Youth Task Team (AYTT)', in *Inter-Agency Network for Education in Education*.

Chapter 3

Bailey, F. and A. Dolan (2011), 'The meaning of Partnership in Development: Lessons in Development Education', *Policy & Practice: A Development Education Review*, 13 (Autumn): 30–48.

Bellino, M. J. and M. Hure (2018), 'Pursuing Higher Education in Exile: A pilot partnership in Kakuma Refugee Camp', *Childhood Education*, 94 (5), 46–51. Available online: https://doi.org/10.1080/00094056.2018.1516472

Bergan, S. and I. Harkavy (2019), 'Academic Freedom, Institutional Autonomy and Democracy', *University World News*, 31 August 2019. Available online: https://www.universityworldnews.com/post.php?story=20190827130223856

Blessinger, P. and B. Cozza (2016), *University Partnerships for Academic Programming and Professional Development*, Bingley, UK: Emerald Group Publishing Ltd.

Chernikova, E. (2011), *Shoulder to Shoulder or Face to Face? Canada's University – Civil Society Collaborations on Research and Knowledge for International Development*, Ottawa: International Development Research Centre.

Connected Learning in Crisis Consortium (n.d.), Available online: https://connectedlearning4refugees.org.

Dippo, D., A. Orgocka and W. Giles (2012), 'Feasibility Study Report: The Provision of Higher Education for Long-Term Refugees in the Dadaab Camps, Kenya', *MasterCard Foundation*. Available online: http://crs.yorku.ca/bher-dadaab-feasibility-study-report.

Downes, G. (2013), 'A critical Analysis of North-South Education Partnerships in Development Contexts, Policy & Practice', *A Development Education Review*, 16 (Spring): 1–12, retrieved from www.developmenteducationreview.com/issue/issue.

Eastman, J., G.A. Jones, O. Begin-Caouette, S. Li, C. Noumi and C. Trottier (2018), 'Provincial Oversight and University Autonomy in Canada: Findings of a Comparative Study of Canadian University Governance', *Canadian Journal of Higher Education* 48 (3): 65–81.

Giles, W. and D. Dippo (2019), 'Transitions from Knowledge Networked to Knowledge Engaged: Ethical Tensions and Dilemmas from the Global to the Local', in S. McGrath and J. Young (Eds), *Mobilizing Global Knowledge: Refugee Research in an Age of Displacement*, Calgary: University of Calgary Press. Available online: https://press.ucalgary.ca/books/9781773850856.

Global Affairs Canada (2019), *Official Development Assistance Accountability Act – Contributing to Poverty Reduction*, Ottawa: Government of Canada. Available online: https://www.international.gc.ca/gac-amc/publications/odaaa-lrmado/odaaa-pov_red.aspx?lang=eng&_ga=2.92866398.278701851.1578863471-30765039.1571676469

Gutman, A. (1983), 'Is Freedom Academic? The Relative Autonomy of Universities in Liberal Democracy', *Nomos*, 25 (1983): 257–86.

Halvorsen, T. and J. Nossum, eds (2017), *North/South Knowledge networks: Towards Equitable Collaboration Between Academics, Donors and Universities*, Somerset West, South Africa: African Minds.

Ishengoma, J. M. (2016), 'Strengthening Higher Education Space in Tanzania through North- South Partnerships and links: Experiences from the University of Dar Es

Salaam', in *Comparative and International Education*, 45 (1). Available online: https://www.questia.com/library/journal/1P3-4308106061/strengthening-higher-education-space-in-tanzania.

Karim-Haji, F., P. Roy and R. Gough (2016), 'Building Ethical Global Engagement with Host Communities: North-South Collaborations for Mutual Learning and Benefit', Resource Guide presented at the 10th Annual Global Internship Conference, Boston, MA.

Kimari, W. and W. Giles (2020), 'Building Ethical Relationships through the Borderless Higher Education for Refugees Project in Dadaab, Kenya', in J. Bhabha, W. Giles and F. Mohamed (eds), *A Better Future: The Role of Higher Education for Displaced and Marginalized People*, Cambridge: Cambridge University Press.

Landau, L. (2015), 'Communities of Knowledge or Tyrannies of Partnership: Reflections on North-South Research Networks and the Dual Imperative', *Journal of Refugee Studies*, 25: 555–70.

Local Engagement Refugee Research Network (LERRN) (n.d.). Available online: https://carleton.ca/lerrn.

Nakabugo, M. G., E. Barrett, P. McEvoy and R. Munck (2010), 'Best Practices in North-South Research Relationships in Higher Education', *The Irish African Partnership Model* (10). Retrieved from www.developmenteducationreview.com/sites/default.

Nkrumah-Young, K. K. and P. Powell (2011), 'Exploring Higher Education Financing Options', *European Journal of Higher Education*, 1 (1): 3–21. Available online: https://doi.org/10.1080/21568235.2011.577181.

ODEL (n.d.), Kenyatta University Students' Orientation Guide to Open Distance and E-Learning (ODEL) system handbook for students 2018–2020, retrieved from http://www.ku.ac.ke/dsvol/images/Updated%20DIGITAL%20PLATFORM%20STUDENTS%20HANDBOOK_new2018.pdf, pp. 30–1.

Ontario Human Rights Commission (1962), *Ontario Human Rights Code*. Available online: http://www.ohrc.on.ca/en/ontario-human-rights-code.

Shore, C. and M. Taitz (2012), 'Who Owns the University? Institutional Autonomy and Academic Freedom in an Age of Knowledge Capitalism', *Globalization, Societies and Education*, 10: 1–19.

Umoren, R. A., J. E. James and D. K. Litzelman (2012), 'Evidence of Reciprocity in Reports on International Partnerships', *Education Research International*. Available online: https://doi.org/10.1155/2012/603270.

Woldegiorgis, E. T. and C. Scherer (eds) (2019), *Partnerships in Higher Education: Trends Between African and European Institutions*, Boston: Brill Sense Publishers.

Yarmoshuk, A. N., D. C. Cole and M. Mwangu. (2019), 'Reciprocity in International Inter-University Global Health Partnerships', *Higher Education*, doi: 10.1007/s10734-019-00416-1.

Chapter 4

Afsana, K., D. Habte, J. Hatfield, J. Murphy and V. Neufeld (2009), *Partnership Assessment Toolkit*, Wakefield, QC: Canadian Coalition for Global Health Research. Available online: https://www.ccghr.ca/resources/partnerships-and-networking/partnership-assessment-tool.

Agee, J., F. Breuer, K. Mruck, W-M. Roth, C. Ellis, K. Etherington, F. L. Finlay C. Gerstl-Pepin, K. Patrizio, M. Guillemin, L. Gilliam, D. Macbeth, C. Ratner, E. Said and D. Watt (2011), 'Reflexivity', in M. Lichtman (ed.), *Understanding and Evaluating Qualitative Educational Research*, 287–98. Thousand Oaks, CA: SAGE Publications. DOI: 10.4135/9781483349435.

Bhutta, Z. A., Z. S. Lassi, G. Pariyo, and L. Huicho (2010), Global Experience of Community Health Workers for Delivery of Health Related Millennium Development Goals: A Systematic Review, Country Case Studies, and Recommendations for Integration into National Health Systems. Geneva: World Health Organization & Global Health Workforce Alliance. Accessed August 7 2012, http://www.who.int/workforcealliance/knowledge/resources/chwreport/en/

Coghlan, D. and M. Brydon-Miller, eds (2014), 'Positionality', *The Sage Encyclopedia of Action Research*. DOI: https://dx.doi.org/10.4135/9781446294406.n277.

Dippo, D., A. Orgocka and W. Giles (2012), *Feasibility Study. Reaching Higher: The Provision of Higher Education for Long-term Refugees in the Dadaab Camps, Kenya*, Toronto: York University.

Douhaibi, D. (2016), 'Researching the Gap between the Existing and Potential Community Health Worker Education and Training in the Refugee Context: An Intersectoral Approach.' Formative Evaluation Report, February. Toronto, York University.

Ehiri, J., J. Gunn, K. Center, Y. Li, M. Rouhani and E. Ezeanolue (2014), 'Training and Deployment of Lay Refugee/Internally Displaced Persons to Provide Basic Health Services in Camps: A Systematic Review', *Global Health Action*, 7 (1): 23902. DOI:10.3402/gha.v7.23902.

Ingram, Maia, Kerstin M. Reinschmidt, Ken A. Schachter, Chris L. Davidson, Samantha J. Sabo, Jill Guernsey De Zapien, Scott C. Carvajal (2012), 'Establishing a Professional Profile of Community Health Workers: Results from a National Study of Roles, Activities and Training', *Journal of Community Health*, 37 (2): 529–37. DOI:10.1007/s10900-011-9475-2.

Mangeni, J., F. B. Pilkington, I. Mbai and I. Abuelaish (August 2016), *Training and Utilization of Refugees as Community Health Workers in a Protracted Displacement Situations*. Policy Brief, IDRC Grant No. 107467-00020799-030. Available online: http://hdl.handle.net/10625/55840.

Mbai, I., J. Mangeni, I. Abuelaish and F. B. Pilkington (2017), 'Community health worker training and education in a refugee context', in A L. Fymat and J. Kapalanga (eds),

Science Research and Education in Africa, 163–86, Newcastle Upon Tyne, UK: Cambridge Scholars Publishing.

Pilkington, F. B., I. Mbai and I. Abuelaish (July 31, 2016), *Researching the Gap between the Existing and Potential Community Health Worker Education and Training in the Refugee Context: An Intersectoral Approach*. Final Technical Report, IDRC Grant No. 107467-00020799-030. Available online: http://hdl.handle.net/10625/55849.

Pilkington, F. B., I. Mbai, J. Mangeni and I. Abuelaish (August 2016), *An Education Model for Building Health Care Capacity in Protracted Refugee Contexts*. Policy Brief, IDRC Grant No. 107467-00020799-030. Available online: http://hdl.handle.net/10625/55850.

UNHCR Policy Development and Evaluation Service (2014), 'Which Side are You On?' Discussion paper on UNHCR's policy and practice of incentive payments to refugees. Available online: https://www.unhcr.org/research/evalreports/5491577c9/whos-side-discussion-paper-unhcrs-policy-practice-incentive-payments-refugees.html.

Chapter 5

Alonso-Yáñez, G., K. Thumlert, S. de Castell and J. Jenson (2019), 'Pathways to Sustainable Futures: A "Production Pedagogy" Model for STEM Education', *Futures*, 108 (April): 27–36.

Alonso-Yáñez, G., K. Thumlert and S. de Castell (2016), 'Re-Mapping Integrative Conservation: (Dis)Coordinate Participation in a Biosphere Reserve in Mexico', *Conservation and Society*, 14 (2): 134–45.

Dahya, N. (2017), 'Digital Media and Forced Migration: Critical Media Education for and about Refugees', *TELEVIZION*, 30: 24–5.

Dahya, N. and S. Dryden-Peterson (2016), 'Tracing Pathways to Higher Education for Refugees: The Role of Virtual Support Networks and Mobile Phones for Women in Refugee Camps', *Comparative Education*, December: 1–18.

de Castell, S. (2016), 'A Pedagogy of Production: An Introduction to New Media Modules', (video file). Available online: https://vimeo.com/181978126.

Dryden-Peterson, S., N. Dahya and E. Adelman (2017), 'Pathways to Educational Success among Refugees: Connecting Locally and Globally Situated Resources', *American Educational Research Journal*, 54 (6): 1011–47.

Duale, M., O. Leomoi, A. Aden, O. Okello, D. Arte and A. Abikar (2019), 'Teachers in Displacement: Learning from Dadaab', in Couldrey, M. and J. Peebles (eds), *Forced Migration in Review: Education: Needs, Rights and Access in Displacement*, 60 February: 56–9.

Giles, W. (2018), 'The Borderless Higher Education for Refugees Project: Enabling Refugee and Local Kenyan Students in Dadaab to Transition to University Education', *Journal on Education in Emergencies*, 4 (1): 164–84.

Hyndman, J. (2011), 'A Refugee Camp Conundrum: Geopolitics, Liberal Democracy, and Protracted Refugee Situations', *Refuge*, 28 (2): 7–15.

Menbere, G. and T. S. Skjerdal (2008), 'The Potential of Dagu Communication in North-Eastern Ethiopia', *Media Development*, 1 2008: 19–21.

Mitchell, G. J., N. Cross, O. George, M. Hynie, K. L. Kuman, R. Owston, D. Sinclair and R. Wickens (2015), 'Complexity Pedagogy and E-Learning: Emergence in Relational Networks', *International Research in Higher Education*, 1 (1): 206–15.

Sawhney, N. (2009), 'Voices Beyond Walls: The Role of Digital Storytelling for Empowering Marginalized Youth in Refugee Camps', *Interaction Design and Children: IDC 2009*, 3–5 June.

Thumlert, K., S. de Castell and J. Jenson (2015), 'Short Cuts and Extended Techniques: Rethinking Relations between Technology and Educational Theory', *Educational Philosophy and Theory*, 47 (8): 786–803.

Chapter 6

Abdi, Farhia A. (2016), 'Behind Barbed Wire Fences: Higher Education and Twenty-first Century Teaching in Dadaab, Kenya', *Bildhaan: An International Journal of Somali Studies*, 16 (1): 8.

Bellino, Michelle J. and Mohamud Hure (2018), 'Pursuing Higher Education in Exile: A Pilot Partnership in Kakuma Refugee Camp', *Childhood Education*, 9(4) 5: 46–51.

Dahya, Negin and Sarah Dryden-Peterson (2017), 'Tracing Pathways to Higher Education for Refugees: the Role of Virtual Support Networks and Mobile Phones for Women in Refugee Camps', *Comparative Education*, 53 (2): 284–301.

DePietro, Peter (2012), 'Transforming Education with New Media: Participatory Pedagogy, Interactive Learning and Web 2.0', *International Journal of Technology, Knowledge & Society*, 8 (5).

de Waard, Inge Ignatia (2014), 'Using BYOD, Mobile Social Media, Apps, and Sensors for Meaningful Mobile Learning', *Increasing Access*, 113–24.

Douhaibi, Dacia, Negin Dahya, Olivier Arvisais and Sarah Dryden-Peterson (2020), 'Culture, Gender, and Technology: Mediating Teacher Training Using Text Messaging in Refugee Camps', in Jacqueline Bhabha, Wenona Giles and Faraaz Mahomed, *A Better Future: The Role of Higher Education for Displaced and Marginalized People*, Cambridge: Cambridge University Press.

Dryden-Peterson, Sarah and Wenona Giles (2010), 'Higher Education for Refugees', *Refuge: Canada's Journal on Refugees*, 27 (2): 3–9.

Giroux, Henry A. (2010), 'Rethinking Education as the Practice of Freedom: Paulo Freire and the Promise of Critical Pedagogy', *Policy Futures in Education*, 8 (6): 715–21.

Harber, Clive (2014), *Education and International Development: Theory, Practice and Issues*, Oxford: Symposium Books Ltd.

Halkic, B. and P. Arnold (2019), 'Refugees and Online Education: Student Perspectives on Need and Support in the Context of (Online) Higher Education', *Learning, Media and Technology*, 44 (3): 345–64.

Looi, Chee-Kit and Yancy Toh (2014), 'Orchestrating the Flexible Mobile Learning Classroom', *Increasing Access*, 161–74.

Milton, Sansom and Sultan Barakat (2016), 'Higher Education as the Catalyst of Recovery in Conflict-Affected Societies', *Globalization, Societies and Education*, 14 (3): 403–21.

Moser-Mercer, Barbara, Erin Hayba and Joshua Goldsmith (2016), 'Higher Education Spaces and Protracted Displacement: How Learner-Centered Pedagogies and Human-Centered Design can Unleash Refugee Innovation', in *UNESCO Chair Conference on Technologies for Development*, 41–52, Cham, Switzerland: Springer.

Nicolai, S., S. Hine and J. Wales (2016), *A Common Platform for Education in Emergencies and Protracted Crises: Evidence Paper*, London: Overseas Development Institute.

Sam, D. Praveen (2016), 'Learning Beyond the Classroom through WhatsApp: An Informal Channel to Motivate Learners to Stay Connected', *Asian Journal of Research in Social Sciences and Humanities*, 6 (9): 1826–33.

United Nations (2016), 'Education – United Nations Sustainable Development', 22 August 2019. Available online: https://www.un.org/sustainabledevelopment/education.

UNHCR Kenya (2019), 'Durable Solutions – UNHCR Kenya', *UNHCR*. Available online: www.unhcr.org/ke/durable-solutions.

UNICEF (2016), 'Education Cannot Wait: a Fund for Education in Emergencies', UNICEF Briefing (2016).

Chapter 7

Atkins, Salla, Sophie Marsden, Vishal Diwan and Merrick Zwarenstein (2016), 'North-South Collaboration and Capacity Development in Global Health Research in Low- and Middle-Income Countries – The ARCADE Projects', *Global Health Action* 9 (1). Available online: https://doi.org/10.3402/GHA.V9.30524.

BBC News (2017), 'Kenyan Closure of Dadaab Refugee Camp Blocked by High Court', *BBC News*, 9 February. Available online: https://www.bbc.com/news/world-africa-38917681.

Bellino, Michelle J. and Mohamud Hure (2018), 'Pursuing Higher Education in Exile: A Pilot Partnership in Kakuma Refugee Camp', *Childhood Education*, 94 (5): 46–51. Available online: https://doi.org/10.1080/00094056.2018.1516472.

Bender, Thomas (1998), 'Scholarship, Local Life, and the Necessity of Worldliness', in H. van der Wusten (ed.), *The Urban University and Its Identity*, 17–28, Netherlands: Kluwer Academic Publishers..

Clark, Charlotte H. and Benjamin P. Wilson (2017), 'The Potential for University Collaboration and Online Learning to Internationalise Geography Education', *Journal of Geography in Higher Education*, 41(4): 488–505. Available online: https://doi.org/10.1080/03098265.2017.1337087.

Crea, Thomas M. and Mary McFarland (2015), 'Higher Education for Refugees: Lessons from a 4-Year Pilot Project', *International Review of Education*, 61 (2): 235–45. Available online: https://doi.org/10.1007/s11159-015-9484-y.

Dryden-Peterson, Sarah (2010), 'The Politics of Higher Education for Refugees in a Global Movement for Primary Education', *Refuge: Canada's Journal on Refugees*, 27 (2): 10–18. Available online: https://refuge.journals.yorku.ca/index.php/refuge/article/view/34718.

Giles, Wenona and Don Dippo (2019), 'Transitions from Knowledge Networked to Knowledge Engaged: Ethical Tensions and Dilemmas from the Global to the Local', in Susan McGrath and Julie Young (eds), *Ethical Networking for Research and Practice: Reflections on the Refugee Research Network*, Calgary, ON: University of Calgary.

Haigh, Martin J. (2002) 'Internationalisation of the Curriculum: Designing Inclusive Education for a Small World', *Journal of Geography in Higher Education*, 26 (1): 49–66. Available online: https://doi.org/10.1080/03098260120110368.

Hayes, Niall and Lucas D. Introna (2005), 'Cultural Values, Plagiarism, and Fairness: When Plagiarism Gets in the Way of Learning', *Ethics and Behavior*, 15 (3): 213–31. Available online: https://doi.org/10.1207/s15327019eb1503_2.

Kamyab, Shahrzad (2017), 'Syrian Refugees Higher Education Crisis', *Journal of Comparative & International Higher Education*, 9: 10–14.

Milton, Sansom and Sultan Barakat (2016), 'Higher Education as the Catalyst of Recovery in Conflict-Affected Societies', *Globalisation, Societies and Education*, 14 (3): 403–21. Available online: https://doi.org/10.1080/14767724.2015.1127749.

Morrice, Linda (2013), 'Refugees in Higher Education: Boundaries of Belonging and Recognition, Stigma and Exclusion', *International Journal of Lifelong Education*, 32 (5): 652–68. Available online: https://doi.org/10.1080/02601370.2012.761288.

Remmel, Tarmo (2020), Table 7.1. Geography courses in the B.A. Geography degree offered through BHER. Prepared for Youdelis, Megan, Dacia Douhaibi, Devin Holterman, Kamal Paudel, Valerie Preston, Tarmo K. Remmel, Elizabeth Lunstrum and Joseph Mensah (2020), 'Out of Bounds: The BHER Bones of Teaching Geography Across Borders', in Giles, Wenona and Lorrie Miller (eds.), *Borderless Higher Education for Refugees: Lessons from the Dadaab Refugee Camps*.

Shawyer, R. and W. Giles (2019), 'Different Funding Structures: Scholarship and Tuition-free Models in the Worldly University', paper presented at York University, May.

Sherab, Domenique and Kelly Kirk (2016), 'Access to Higher Education for Refugees in Jordan', Arab Renaissance for Democracy and Development (ARDD)-Legal Aid Report.

Simms, David and Alan Marvell (2017), 'Creating Global Students: Opportunities, Challenges and Experiences of Internationalizing the Geography Curriculum in Higher Education. Introduction', *Journal of Geography in Higher Education*, 41 (4): 467–74. Available online: https://doi.org/10.1080/03098265.2017.1373332.

Solem, Michael N., Scott Bell, Eric Fournier, Carol Gillespie, Miranda Lewitsky and Harwood Lockton (2003), 'Using the Internet to Support International Collaborations for Global Geography Education', *Journal of Geography in Higher Education*, 27 (3): 239–53. Available online: https://doi.org/10.1080/0309826032000145034.

Swain, Harriet (2018), 'Refugees Lose Friends, Money, Home – "Only Knowledge Lasts"', *The Guardian*, 26 June 2018. Available online: https://www.theguardian.com/education/2018/jun/26/refugees-lose-friends-money-home-only-knowledge-lasts-universities-courses.

Testa, Doris and Ronnie Egan (2014), 'Finding Voice: The Higher Education Experiences of Students from Diverse Backgrounds', *Teaching in Higher Education*, 19 (3): 229–41. Available online: https://doi.org/10.1080/13562517.2013.860102.

Wright, Laura-Ashley and Robyn Plasterer (2010), 'Beyond Basic Education: Exploring Opportunities for Higher Learning in Kenyan Refugee Camps', *Refuge: Canada's Journal on Refugees*, 27 (2): 42–56. Available online: https://refuge.journals.yorku.ca/index.php/refuge/article/view/34721.

Chapter 8

Abdi, Farhia A. (2016), 'Behind Barbed Wire Fences: Higher Education and Twenty-first Century Teaching in Dadaab, Kenya', *Bildhaan: An International Journal of Somali Studies*, 16 (8). Available online: https://digitalcommons.macalester.edu/bildhaan/vol16/iss1/8.

Boškić, N., T. Sork, R. Irwin, S. Nashon, C. Nicol, K. Meyer and S. Hu (2018), 'Using Technology to Provide Higher Education for Refugees', in E. Francois (ed.), *Transnational Perspectives on Innovation in Teaching and Learning Technologies*, 285–90, Boston: Brill Sense.

Dahya, N., S. Dryden-Peterson, D. Douhaibi and O. Arvais (2019), 'Social Support Networks, Instant Messaging, and Gender Equity in Refugee Education', *Information, Communication & Society*, DOI: 10.1080/1369118X.2019.1575447.

Freire, P. (2000/1970), *Pedagogy of the Oppressed*, trans. M. B. Ramos, New York, NY: Bloomsbury.

Gichiru, W. P. and D. B. Larkin (2009), 'Reframing Refugee Education in Kenya as an Inclusionary Practice of Pedagogy', in S. Mitakidou, E. Tressou, B. B. Swadener and C. A. Grant (eds), *Beyond Pedagogies of Exclusion in Diverse Childhood Contexts. Critical Cultural Studies of Childhood*, 225–40, New York: Palgrave Macmillan.

Kennedy, J. (1963). *Remarks at Vanderbilt University, Nashville, Tennessee*, 18 May. Retrieved 27 July 2020, from John F. Kennedy: Presidential Library and Museum: https://www.jfklibrary.org/asset-viewer/archives/JFKPOF/044/JFKPOF-044-020.

Kuokkanen, R. (2007), *Reshaping the University: Responsibility, Indigenous Epistemes, and the Logic of the Gift*, Vancouver, Canada: UBC Press.

Magee, A. and Pherali, T. (2017), 'Freirean Critical Consciousness in a Refugee Context: a Case Study of Syrian Refugees in Jordan', *Compare: A Journal of Comparative and International Education*, 1–17. Available online: https://doi.org/10.1080/03057925.2017.1403312.

Meyer, K., C. Nicol, S. Maalim, M. Olow, A. Ali, S. Nashon, M. Bulle, Ahmed Hussein, Ali Hussein and M. Hassan Said (2019), 'Crossing Borders: A Story of Refugee Education', in C. Hébert, N. Ng-A-Fook, A. Ibrahim and B. Smith (eds), *Internationalizing Curriculum Studies*, 290–329, New York: Palgrave Macmillan.

Meyer, K., C. Nicol, S. Maalim, M. Olow, A. Ali Hirsi, S. Nashon, M. Bulle, A. Hussein, A. Imaan, H. Hassan (2018), 'Dadaab Refugee Camp and the Story of School', in C. Leggo and E. Hasabe-Ludt (eds), *Provoking Curriculum Studies: A Manifesto of Inspiration/Imagination/Interconnection*, 257–75, Toronto: Canadian Scholars Press.

Miller, L., A. O. Aden, J. A. Mohamed, Z. Bishar and A. O. Okello (2019), 'The Ripple Effects When a Refugee Camp Becomes a University Town: University Teacher Education in Dadaab, Kenya', *Journal for Education Research and Innovation*, 7 (1). Available online: http://digscholarship.unco.edu/jeri.

Miller, L. and C. Nicol (2018), 'Teacher Education in Refuge Environments', *Journal of the World Federation of Associations of Teacher Education*, 2 (3a): 121–34.

Njogu, M. (2018), 'Lessons Learnt from the Implementation of BHER Project 2013–2018.' BHER Annual Partnership meeting (April 30).

Sleeter, C. E. (2009), 'Pedagogies of Inclusion in Teacher Education: Global Perspectives', in C. Mitakidou and S. Mitakidou (eds.), *Beyond Pedagogies of Exclusion in Diverse Childhood Contexts: Transnational Challenges*, 49–165, New York: Palgrave Macmillan.

Sullivan-Owomoyela, Joan and Laura Brannelly (2009), *Promoting Participation: Community Contribution to Education in Conflict Zones*, Paris, France: International Institute for Education Planning and CfBT Education Trust.

UNHCR (2017). Global Trends: Forced Displacement in 2017. Available online: https://www.unhcr.org/globaltrends2017/#:~:text=In%202017%2016.2%20million%20people,new%20high%20of%2068.5%20million.

Chapter 9

Arendt, H. ([1954]2006), 'The Crisis in Education', in *Between Past and Future: Eight Exercises in Political Thought*, 170–93, London: Penguin Books Ltd.

Bloom, D. E., D. Canning and K. Chan (2006), *Higher Education and Economic Development in Africa*, Boston, MA: Harvard University. Available online: https://www.edu-links.org/sites/default/files/media/file/BloomAndCanning.pdf

Bourdieu, P. (1986), 'The Forms of Capital', in J. G. Richardson (ed.) *Handbook of Theory and Research for the Sociology of Education*, 241–58. New York: Greenwood Press.

Bunyi G. (1998), 'The Language of Instruction and the Development of Full Literacy in Post-colonial Africa', *Transforms*, 3 and 4, 56–72.

Campbell-Roy, Z. M. (2001), 'Globalisation, Language and Education: A Comparative Study of the United States and Tanzania', *International Review of Education*, 47 (3–4): 267–82.

Chilisa, B. (2012), 'Decolonizing the Interview Method', in *Indigenous Research Methodologies*, 203–24, LA: Sage.

Connell, R. W. (2007), *Southern Theory: The Global Dynamics of Knowledge in Social Sciences*, Malden, MA: Polity.

Cummins, J. (2000), *Language, Power and Pedagogy: Bilingual Children in the Crossfire*, UK and Canada: Multilingual Matters.

Dlamini, S. N. (2005), *Youth and Identity Politics in South Africa, 1990–94*, Toronto: University of Toronto Press.

Douhabi, D. (2015), *Borderless Higher Education for Refugees Term Report*, unpublished report.

Duranti, A. (2009), 'Linguistic Anthropology: History, Ideas and Issues', in Alessandro Duranti (ed.), *Linguistic Anthropology: A Reader*, 1–59. Oxford: Willey-Blackwell.

Dryden-Peterson, S. and W. Giles (2010), 'Introduction: Higher Education for Refugees', *Refuge: Canada's Journal on Refugees*, 27 (2): 3–10.

Egbo, B. (2000), *Gender, Literacy and Life Chances in Sub-Saharan Africa*, Clevedon (UK): Multilingual Matters.

Fairclough, N. (1989), *Language and Power*, London and New York: Longman.

Firth, A. and J. Wagner (1997), 'On Discourse, Communication, and (Some) Fundamental Concepts in SLA Research', *Modern Language Journal*, 81: 286–300.

Flemming, J. (2017), 'Case Study Report: Norwegian Refugee Council, Dadaab, Kenya', *Education in Crisis and Conflict Network* 3. Available online: https://scholarworks.umass.edu/cie_eccn/3.

Giles, W. and D. Dippo (2019), 'Transitions from Knowledge Networked to Knowledge Engaged: Ethical Tensions and Dilemmas from the Global to the Local', in S. McGrath and J. Young (eds), *Ethical Networking for Research and Practice: Reflections on the Refugee Research Network*, 87–106. Calgary, ON: University of Calgary.

Granger, C. (2015), *Sessional Report*, unpublished report.

Hou, F. and M. Beiser (2006), 'Learning the Language of a New Country: A Ten-Year Study of English Acquisition by South-East Asian Refugees in Canada', *International Migration*, 44 (1): 135–65.

Kim, H. (2018), *Women, Literacy, and Opportunity: A Gendered and Generational Analysis of Female Refugees in Dadaab, Kenya*, MRP, York University.

Kim, H. and H. Sabriye (2016), *Sessional Report*, unpublished report, April.

Manzon, M. (2011), *Comparative Education: The Construction of a Field*, Hong Kong: Springer/University of Hong Kong.

Nabea, W. (2009), 'Language Policy in Kenya: Negotiation with Hegemony', *The Journal of Pan African Studies*, 3 (1): 121–38.

Ngũgĩ, Thiong'o wa (1986), *Decolonising the Mind: The Politics of Language in African Literature*, London: J. Currey.

Norwegian Refugee Council and Reach Initiative (2017), 'Dadaab Movement and Intentions Monitoring: Dadaab Refugee Camps, Garissa County, Kenya', 30 November. Available online: https://reliefweb.int/report/kenya/dadaab-movement-and-intentions-monitoring-dadaab-refugee-camps-garissa-county-kenya.

Norton, B. and K. Toohey (2011), 'Identity, Language Learning, and Social Change', *Language Teaching*, 44 (4): 412–46. DOI: 10.1017/S0261444811000309.

Robinson, J. (2015), *Report for BHER*, unpublished report.

Robinson, J. (2011), 'Cities in a World of Cities: The Comparative Gesture', *International Journal of Urban and Regional Research*, 35 (1): 1–23.

Robinson, J. (2016a), 'Thinking Cities through Elsewhere: Comparative Tactics for a More Global Urban Studies', *Progress in Human Geography*, 40 (1): 3–29.

Robinson, J. (2016b), 'Comparative Urbanism: New Geographies and Cultures of Theorising the Urban', in J. Robinson and A. Roy (eds), *International Journal of Urban and Regional Research Debates and Developments Symposium, Global Urbanisms and the Nature of Urban Theory*, 40 (1): 187–99.

Shakya, Y. B., S. Guruge, M. Hynie, A. Akbari, M. Malik, S. Htoo, A. Khogali, S. A. Mona, R. Murtaza and S. Alley (2012), 'Aspirations for Higher Education among Newcomer Refugee Youth in Toronto: Expectations, Challenges, and Strategies', *Refuge: Canada's Journal on Refugees*, 27(2): 65–78. Available online: https://refuge.journals.yorku.ca/index.php/refuge/article/view/34723.

Simon, R. I. (1987), 'Empowerment as a Pedagogy of Possibility', *Language Arts*, 64 (4): 370–82.

Smith, B. (2010), 'Narrative Inquiry: Ongoing Conversations and Questions for Sport and Exercise Psychology Research', *International Review of Sports and Exercise Psychology*, 3 (1): 87–107.

UNESCO Institute for Statistics (2015), 'Adult and Youth Literacy'. Available online: http://www.uis.unesco.org/literacy/Documents/fs32-2015-literacy.pdf.

UNESCO (2018), 'Global Education Monitoring Report 2019: Migration, Displacement and Education – Building Bridges, not Walls', *Paris, UNESCO Digital Library*, 2018. Available online: https://unesdoc.unesco.org/ark:/48223/pf0000266274

UNHCR (2019), 'Operational Update: Dadaab, Kenya', March. Available online: https://reliefweb.int/sites/reliefweb.int/files/resources/March%202019%20-%20Dadaab%20Monthly%20Operational%20Updates.pdf.

Wee, L. (2011), *Language Without Rights*, New York: Oxford University Press.

Chapter 10

Alsop, Steve and Roxanne Cohen (2018), *Place and Learning Course Booklet*, York University: Faculty of Education.

Belcourt, Christi (2015), 'Aabaakawad Anishinaabewin (Reviving Everything Anishinaabe)', *Christi Belcourt: Recent Works*. Available online: http://christibelcourt.com/ancestry.

Beck, Ulrich (2011), 'Cosmopolitanism as Imagined Communities of Global Risk', *American Behavioral Scientist*, 55 (10): 1346–61. Available online: https://doi-org.ezproxy.library.yorku.ca/10.1177/0002764211409739.

Conley, Verena Andermatt (2012), 'Chaosmopolis', *Theory, Culture, & Society*, 19 (1–2): 127–38. Available online: https://doi-org.ezproxy.library.yorku.ca/10.1177/0263276402019900106.

Crutzen, Paul J. and Eugene F. Stoermer, (2013), 'The 'Anthropocene' in L. Robin, S. Sörlin and P. Warde (eds), *The Future of Nature: Documents of Global Change*. New Haven: Yale University Press.

Davis, Heather and Étienne Turpin (2015), *Art in the Anthropocene: Encounters among Aesthetics, Politics, Environments and Epistemologies*, London: Open Humanities Press.

Deutsches Museum (2013), 'Welcome to the Anthropocene', *YouTube*, September 21. Available online: https://www.youtube.com/watch?v=h8S4nrTzCwE.

Dewey, John (1938), *Experience and Education*, United States: Kappa Delta Pi.

Freire, Paulo (1970), *Pedagogy of the Oppressed*, New York: Herder and Herder.

Gibson-Graham, J. K. (2011), 'A Feminist Project of Belonging for the Anthropocene', *Gender, Place & Culture*, 18 (1): 1–21. Available online: https://www-tandfonline-com./doi/abs/10.1080/0966369X.2011.535295.

Giles, Wenona and Don Dippo (2019), 'Transitions from Knowledge Networked to Knowledge Engaged: Ethical Tensions and Dilemmas from the Global to the Local', in *Mobilizing Global Knowledge: Refugee Research in an Age of Displacement*, Calgary: University of Calgary Press (2019): 86–106.

Govt. Kenya and UNHCR (2015), 'Kenya: Dadaab District, Dagahaley Refugee Camp Overview as of June 2013 – Kenya.' *ReliefWeb. OCHA Services*, 24 August: https://reliefweb.int/map/kenya/kenya-dadaab-district-dagahaley-refugee-camp-overview-june-2013.

Greenwood, David (2009), 'Place, Survivance, and White Remembrance: A Decolonizing Challenge to Rural Education in Mobile Modernity', *Journal of Research in Rural*

Education, 24 (10): 1–6. Available online: https://www.tandfonline.com/doi/abs/10.1080/13504620903132701.

Green Roofs for Healthy Cities (2013), 'The Consorcio-Santiago Building', in *Living Architecture and Sustainable Energy Resource Manual*.

Gruenewald, David and Gregory Smith (2008), *Place-Based Education in the Global Age*, New York: Lawrence Erlbaum Associates, pp. xiii–xxiii.

Gruenewald, David (2003), 'The Best of Both Worlds: A Critical Pedagogy of Place'. *Education Researcher*, 32 (4): 3–12. Available online: https://doi-org.ezproxy.library.yorku.ca/10.3102/0013189X032004003.

Haraway, Donna (2015), 'Anthropocene, Capitalocene, Plantationocene, Chthulucene: Making Kin', *Environmental Humanities*, 6: 159–65. Available online: https://doi.org/10.1215/22011919-3615934.

Hecht, Gabrielle (2018), 'The African Anthropocene', *AEON*. Available online: https://aeon.co/essays/if-we-talk-about-hurting-our-planet-who-exactly-is-the-we.

Jelacic, Matthew (2014), 'From Polybius to Dadaab: Traumatic Urbanization in the Anthropocene', *Procedia Engineering*, 78: 191. Available online: https://doi.org/10.1016/j.proeng.2014.07.056.

Montessori, Maria, Anne E. George and Henry Wyman Holmes (1912), *The Montessori Method; Scientific Pedagogy as Applied to Child Education in 'The Children's Houses' with Additions and Revisions by the Author*, New York: Frederick A. Stokes Co.

Nancy, Jean-Luc and John Paul Ricco (2015), 'The Existence of the World is Always Unexpected', in Heather Davis and Étienne Turpin (eds), *Art in the Anthropocene: Encounters among Aesthetics, Politics, Environments and Epistemologies*, 85–92. London: Open Humanities Press.

Nixon, Rob (2018), 'The Anthropocene: The Promise and Pitfalls of an Epochal Idea', in Gregg Mitman, Marco Armiero and Robert Emmett (eds), *Future Remains: A Cabinet of Curiosities for the Anthropocene*, Chicago: University of Chicago Press.

Nixon, Rob (2013), *Slow Violence and the Environmentalism of the Poor*, Cambridge, MA: Harvard University Press.

Noyle, Zak. (n.d.), *Dede Trash Barrel in Java*, Photograph. Indonesia Java. A-Frame.

Nyerere, Julius K. (1967), 'Education for Self-Reliance', *Africa Report*, 12 (6): 72–9.

Personal photograph (January 2018), *Construction of Hurricane-Proof Eco-Dome Homes*. Source Farm, Jamaica.

Robin, Libby, Dag Avango and Luke Keogh (2014), 'Three Galleries of the Anthropocene', *The Anthropocene Review*, 1 (3): 207–24. Available online: https://journals.sagepub.com/doi/abs/10.1177/2053019614550533.

Seawright, Gardner (2014), 'Settler Traditions of Place: Making Explicit the Epistemological Legacy of White Supremacy and Settler Colonialism for Place-Based Education', *Educational Studies*, 50: 554–72. Available online: https://www.tandfonline.com/doi/abs/10.1080/00131946.2014.965938.

Steffen, Will, Asa Persson, Lisa Deutsch, Jan Zalasiewicz, Mark Williams, Katherine Richardson, Carole Crumley, Paul Crutzen, Carl Folke, Line Gordon, Mario Molina, Veerabhadran Ramanathan, Johan Rochström, Marten Scheffer, Hans Joachim Schellnhuber, and Uno Svedin (2011), 'The Anthropocene: From Global Change to Planetary Stewardship', *AMBIO: A Journal of the Human Environment*, 40 (7): 739–61. Available online: https://doi/abs/10.1007/s13280-011-0185-x.

Stromberg, Joseph (2013), 'What is the Anthropocene and Are We in It?' *Smithsonian Institution*, January 1. Available online: https://www.smithsonianmag.com/science-nature/what-is-the-anthropocene-and-are-we-in-it-164801414.

Theriault, Noah (2015), 'Principles of Tsawalk: An Indigenous Approach to Global Crisis', *Inhabiting the Anthropocene*. Available online: https://inhabitingtheanthropocene.com/2015/03/02/principles-of-tsawalk-an-indigenous-approach-to-global-crisis.

Todd, Zoe (2015), 'Indigenizing the Anthropocene', in *Art in the Anthropocene: Encounters among Aesthetics, Politics, Environments and Epistemologies*, 241–54, London: Open Humanities Press.

Toffler, Alvin (1970), *Future Shock*, New York: Bantam Books.

Tsing, Anna (2013), 'Dancing the Mushroom Forest', *PAN: Philosophy, Activism, Nature*, 10: 6–14. Available online: https://doi.org/10.4225/03/5851eb3943a1a.

Velez, Bronté and Ayana Young (2018), 'Bronté Velez on Embodying the Revolution', *For the Wild (blog and podcast)*, February 15. Available online: https://forthewild.world/listen/bront-velez-on-embodying-the-revolution.

Vertovec, Steven and Robin Cohen (2002), 'Introduction: Conceiving Cosmopolitanism in Conceiving Cosmopolitanism'. *Theory, Context, and Practice*, 1–22, Oxford: Oxford University Press.

Woods, John (n.d.), *Forest and Mine Site*, Photograph. Fort McMurray Alberta Canada. Greenpeace.

Index

Abdi 30, 33
academic philanthropy
    assumptions about Dadaab 135–7
    collaborative student learning in 143–4
    concluding thoughts 148–51
    introduction 133–5
    science and special needs courses 142–3
    teaching in Dadaab 147–8
    working from Vancouver 137, 139–42
Academic Writing Centre, Toronto 124
Adelman, E. 82
afterword 185–8
Agamben, Giorgio 29
Agier, Michel 29
Alia 30–2
Ali-Dhere 24–7
Al-Shabab terrorist group 21–3, 61, 137
Amos 26, 32
Anthropocene epoch 15, 167–8, 171–4, 176–84
Anthropocene Gallery 172–3
Arendt, Hannah 4, 172
Arte (student) 102–5, 108–9, 111–13
Atkins, Salla 131
Australia 159
Avango, Dag 172, 174

Bailey, F. 55–6
banditry 22
Beck, Ulrich 181
Bellino, M. J. 53
BHER Commons 6, 190n.8
BHER Learning Centre
    construction and equipping of 28, 51
    and images from Anthropocene Gallery 173
    introduction 9
    KU instructors visit to 55
    students' access to 95, 111, 120–1
    teachers at 181
    technical and administrative support 126–7
    and UBC instructors 140
BHER project
    collegiality at 63
    and commitment to admissions equity 58
    cost-recovery funding model 53–4
    and DAAGU 86–7
    and digital platforms 88, 92
    and English language fluency 155–6
    four universities involved in 94
    funding by SSHRCC and Mastercard 51–2
    and gender equity 42, 48, 97–8
    inspiration of Jomo Kenyatta 148
    introduction 3, 5, 7–9, 11–15, 189n.2
    and LLTD 150
    and local Kenyans 28, 34
    need for 19–20, 95–6, 187
    and *Place and Learning* course 169–71
    and refugees 49–51, 82–3, 141
    and registration 54–5
    religious rights in 59–60
    relocation of 23, 62
    and Somalia 185–6
    and students 57–8, 167–9, 182
    and teachers 39, 84–5, 90, 135–6
    teacher-student relationships 180
    teaching assistants at 101–13
    teaching geography at 115–31
    and tripartite agreement (2013) 61, 63–4
    university courses 35–6, 45–6, 65–6, 69–70, 72, 74–6, 191n.1
    and WIK 134
Biology Curriculum (course) 142
Bishop, Danielle E. 12
Blessinger, P. 50–1, 62
Boškić, N. 133, 140
Bourdieu, P. 155–6
Brannelly, Laura 11

Bridi, Robert 92
British East Africa 21
Burundi 26

Cameroon 146
Canada 159–60, 168, 185–6
Canada education partnership 51, 55–9
   communications with Kenya 75
   degree courses with York University 101, 108, 126–30, 137, 139–42, 155
   Diploma in Teacher Education 135
   intercultural learning 115, 119, 122, 193n.1
   and production pedagogy 93
   special needs 143
   teaching methods range 144
Canadian Coalition for Global Health Research 68
capital 155–6
CARE 20, 102
Carlson, Sharon 44
change agents 84, 96
Charter of Rights and Freedoms (Canada) 59
Chernikova, E. 3–4
Children of the Camp (Grayson) 47
Chilisa, B. 151
collegial community 62–4
colonialism 3, 11, 153–4, 157, 160, 170, 183
Comic Life (graphic text-making tool) 88, 90–1
Commission for University Education standards (CUE) 57
community health education degree programme
   challenges 73–4
   collaborative research 70–2
   communication issues 75
   Development of BSc CHEd degree 72–3
   financial issues 74–5
   introduction 65–6
   key lessons 77–8
   security issues 75–6
   success 69, 76–7
   theoretical foundations 68–9
community health workers (CHWs) 6–98, 66, 70–2, 78, 192n.2

competence-based curriculum (CBC) 95–6, 99
Connected Learning in Crisis Consortium (CLCC) 63
contested terrains 20–9
cost recovery model 53–4
COVID-19 7, 188
Cozza, B. 50–1, 62
credit transfer/recognition 58
Crutzen, Paul 171
Cultivating Creative Communities (research project) 145
cultural barriers 41–2
Cultural Studies of Technology for Education (York University) 85–6

DAAGU (discussion board system) 85–8
Dacia (student) 103
Dadaab refugee camps
   context 8–9, 11, 135–7, 139–40
   courses in 140, 142–3, 169, 174–5
   degree programmes in 65–6, 69–70, 72–3, 75–7
   English language learning in 151–65, 194n.2
   and gender relations in 36, 96–8
   historical/political situation 19–34
   importance of 171
   introduction 1, 3, 6–7, 12–15
   and Kenyan government policy 41, 61
   learning experiences 101–13, 146–7, 149
   primary schools in 62, 64
   projects in 175–6
   protest in (2017) 29
   relationships in 145–6, 193n.6
   and religious rights 59–60
   security issues 50
   students in 58, 143–4, 188
   teaching in 84, 115–31, 133, 135, 147–8, 186, 193n.1, 193n.3
   and technology 86–7, 88–91, 93–4
   and UN 181–3
Dadaab town 9, 23, 25, 34, 174
Dagahaley refugee camp 9, 27, 152, 175
Dahya, N. 82, 90–1
Darfur village 27

Decolonising the Mind (Ngugi) 159
Democratic Republic of Congo (DRC) 153, 160
Dewey, John 170
digital games 99–100
digital media ecologies 81–2
'Digital media and forced migration' (Dahya) 90–1
digital storytelling 86, 90, 93–4
Dippo, D. 65–6, 94–5, 172, 186
Djibouti 21
Dolan, A. 55–6
Downes, G. 51
Dryden-Peterson, S. 82
DU Recorder 85

East African Certificate of Education (EACE) 57
education
  girls and women 4
  internationalizing 118–27
  neo-colonial forms of 11
English language learning (ELL)
  conclusions 163–5
  context 157–9
  introduction 151
  journeys 152–7
  language power 159–63
environmental degradation 27–8
Equity Enhancement fund (UBC) 145
Eritrea 9
Ethiopia 9, 21, 37–8, 86
Excel 117

Fatuma 30–1, 190–1nn.2,5
female genital mutilation (FGM) 71
flexible learning 109
focus group discussions (FGDs) 70–1
food security 26–7
forced migration 4, 83–4, 90–1, 123, 155–6, 183
Freire, Paulo 11, 109–10, 147, 170

Three Galleries of the Anthropocene (Robin et al.) 172
Garissa County 62
Garissa Cultural Center, Kenya 145
Garissa University attack (2015) 23, 31, 61–2, 75, 137

gender
  disparities in 35–48
  and language power 160–3
Gender, Population, and Migration (course) 123, 127, 130
Geographic Information Systems (GIS) 119
geography teaching
  and the BHER Project 118–27
  conclusions 130–1
  introduction 115–17
  lessons learned 127–30
Geoinformatics 117, 119, 123, 126–7
Gichiru, W. P. 150
Giles, W. 65–6, 82–3, 172
GIS companies 120
Global Affairs Canada (GAC) 51–4, 56, 74–5, 186
global capitalism 183
Global Environmental Change 123, 126–7
Global North 127–8, 188
Global North-South partnerships 3–4, 13, 113, 171, 189n.3
Global South 26, 50, 113, 188
Gmail 92
God 179–80
Goldsmith, Erin 105
Google Docs 87
Google Maps 174
Grace 42
Grayson, Catherine-Lune 47
Greenwood, David 170
Gross Enrollment Rate (GER) 161, 194n.7

HaEun Kim 156
Hagadera camp 9
Haraka Haraka Haina Baraka (haste makes waste) 146–8
Harber, Clive 1–4
Harrell-Bond, B. 40
Hassan, Arfon Bishar 175
'Hasu de Kulturen de Welt' (HKW) (poster series) 177
Hawa (student) 103
Hayba, Erin 105
hearing disabilities 143
Hecht, Gabrielle 168, 172, 182–3
Helsinki University, University Finland 186

Horn, Rebecca 41, 44
Humanitarian NGOs 23
Hure, M. 53
Hyndman, J. 83

ICT skills 102, 105, 108
IDPs (Internally Displaced Populations) 186
Ifo camp 28, 102–3, 163–4
incentive teachers 141, 193n.4
Increased Access and Skills for Tertiary Education Program (InSTEP) 102
InSTEP programme 102–3
International Development Research Centre (IDRC) (Canada) 67–9, 74, 77, 192n.4
International Rescue Committee 70
Introduction to Special Education (course) 93, 142–3
Introduction to World Geography (course) 123
InZone 36–7, 46
Ishengoma, J. M. 51

Jensen, Bram 33
JWL programmes 43, 46

Kakuma refugee camps
 context 8–9, 11
 financial support systems in 53
 gender and university access 35–48, 191nn.1, 5
 and Grace Nshimiyumukiza workshop 177
 harsh local community in 26
 introduction 1, 3, 7, 12–13
 learning experience of teaching assistants 101, 106–7
 relocation to 61, 120, 124, 126–7
 teaching geography in 124, 126
Kakuma town 38
Kalobeyei Township 9, 38
Kambioos camp 28
Kasarani Stadium, Nairobi 23
Kennedy, John F. 148–9
Kenya
 and BHER project 13, 52–4
 curricular system in 99
 education policy of 152, 194n.1
 health care in disadvantaged communities in 69
 human rights abuses in camps 40
 and Konza city (game) 100
 the language of schooling in 157–8, 160, 194n.6
 national exams in 93–4
 policy towards refugees 41
 refugee camps in 9, 12, 19–34
 teacher certification in 6–7
 and tripartite agreement (2013) 61
 university/student religious needs 60
Kenya Certificate of Secondary School Education (KCSE) 56–9, 192n.3
Kenya Ministry of Health (MoH) 76
Kenyan National Examination Council (KNEC) 57–8
Kenya Red Cross 70
Kenyatta, Jomo 148
Kenyatta University (KU)
 and BHER project 34, 49–50, 61, 94
 and ComicLife 91
 diploma/degree programmes of 58
 financial systems of 54–5, 192n.2
 introduction 6–7
 and refugee education 63
 and religion 59–61
 requirements for graduation and funding 56
Keogh, Luke 172, 174
Khalif 24–6
Kikuyus 25, 159
Kimonyo (student) 163–5
Kinyarwanda 46, 191n.6
Kismayo town 33
Kiswahili language 24, 32, 152–4, 158, 160, 163–4
Konza city (game) 100

land settlement 26–7
Larkin, D. B. 150
Lavia, Jennifer 11
learning disabilities 143
Learning Management Systems (LMS) 87
Lingard, Bob 3
Living, Learning and Teaching in Dadaab (LLTD) 145–6, 150, 194n.8

Local Engagement Refugee Research Network (LERRN) 63
Lutheran World Federation (LWF) 7, 62

marriage 42–4, 97
Mastercard Foundation 51
Mengistu Haile Mariam 38
Milner, James 29
Misoy, Philomen 76, 172–3
Mitchell, G. J. 87
mobility 31–2
Mohamed, Abdi Abdirahman 175
Moi University (MU)
    and BHER programs 34, 49, 94
    degree programmes of 56, 58, 65, 68, 70, 72–5, 78, 192n.4
    Diplomas of 135, 193n.1
    introduction 6–7
    student feedback 141
Montessori, Maria 170
MOOC *fantasy* 12, 82, 190n.10
Moodle 87–8, 101–2, 106–7, 119, 141, 172–3
Moser-Mercer, Barbara 105
Munene, Esther 172–3
Muslims 23–4, 59–60, 121
Mwalimu Nyerere mobility programme, Tanzania 55

new beginnings 29–34
Ngara refugee camp, Tanzania 37
NGOs
    adequacy of support from 40
    Christian staff in 59
    and degree programme in community health 68, 70
    making films 92
    minimal assistance to local communities 28
    and provision of basic health services 66, 69
    and security in Dadaab 75
    and service provision to refugees 24–5, 27, 83
    and WIK 76, 134
    workers in Somalia 137
    working for, in camps 43, 64, 98, 120
Ngũgĩ 159

Nixon, Rob 182
Njogu, Marangu 134
Nkrumah-Young, K. K. 53
Northern Frontier District, Kenya (NFD) 21
North/South partnerships
    and community health education degree 65–78
    financial arrangements 53–6
    funding assumptions 51–2
    and human rights 59
    introduction 49–50
    knowledge of 50–1
    and local social/political contexts 61
    political and pedagogical vision of 62–4
    student access 56–9
Norwegian Refugee Council 102
Nshimiyumukiza, Grace 177
Nyerere, Julius 170
nywele ngumu (hard haired people) 22

Ochan (student) 106–7, 110–11, 113
ODEL centres 60
Orgocka, A. 65–6
Oywer, Elizabeth 76

Partnership Assessment Toolkit (PAT) 68, 74
pedagogy
    and course delivery 140–2
    critical 110–11, 170
    and curricular adaptation 150
    and disabilities 143
    flexible 120–5, 128–9
    innovations 117
    participatory 111–12
    resilience 134
    scalar tensions 181
Place and Learning course 169–75
postcolonialism 3
Powell, P. 53
Problem-Based Learning (PBL) 142
production pedagogy 86, 93, 95
projects
    goats and garbage 178–80
    the greenbelt 175–7
    introduction 175
    youth and beauty 177–8

Rebecca 43–4
refugee camps
    academic conceptualizations of 29
    an option in a larger scheme 33–4
    gendered experiences in 40
    in Kenya 9, 12, 19–34
    living and working conditions in 120
    nature of and domestic violence 44
refugee incentive workers (CHWs) 66, 192n.2
refugees
    and BHER 49, 186–7
    crisis of 1990s 26
    CR training at Dadaab 70
    and digital technologies 81–4
    economic and political integration of 28–9
    education at Kenyatta University 63
    employment in camps 30–1
    and English language learning 151–65
    and female employment opportunities 41
    and health services 69
    and humanitarian support 24
    integration of 21, 26–7
    in Kakuma and Kalobeyei 38
    and Kenyan government policy 41
    leadership and assistance on education 146
    and NGO film making 92
    and primary education 89
    resettlement as a goal 122
    Somali 25–6, 28, 36
    South Sudanese at Kakuma 42
    students in Dadaab 58
    and teachers 66, 84
    and UNHCR 27, 31, 89–90
Refugees Respond (Wikimedia site) 86, 88–90
religious rights 59–61
repatriation 28, 61, 105, 118
'Researching the Gap' (feasibility study) 72
Rights in Exile (Verdirame/Harrell-Bond) 40
Rizvi, Fazal 11
Robin, Libby 172, 174

Salvation Army 143
Sam (student) 107
Sawhney, N. 90
scaffolded approaches 165
Scherer, C. 55–6
secondary teacher education diploma programme 134, 137, 140, 193n.4
Seventh Day Adventists (SDA) 59–61, 121
Shahow, Deko Gaiye 175
Shifta War 21–2, 190n.1
Skype 94, 97, 107, 111, 117, 124–6, 128–9
Small Grants for Innovative Research and Knowledge-Sharing programme 69
smartphones 81, 85, 92, 108
social capital theory 46
Social Sciences and Humanities Research Council of Canada (SSHRCC) 51
Somalia
    Bantus 26
    and clan conflict 26
    and digital games 99–100
    during colonial era 21–2
    emergent civil society in 64
    faltering government in 31
    farmers from 27
    introduction 8–9
    Kenyans 28–9, 33–4
    language use 158, 164
    learning in 95–9
    and the Moodle idea 88
    and returning refugee teachers 84
    schools in 30, 150
    significance of BHER project for 185–7
    teaching in 137
    and tripartite agreement (2013) 61
Somali Federal Government 22–3
Somali National University (SNU) 62
South Africa 1, 4
South New Hampshire University (SNHU) 36, 191n.2
South Sudan 8, 42
Stoermer, Eugene 171
Sudan 9, 38
Sullivan-Owomoyela, Joan 11
Sunni Muslims 24
Sustainable Development Goals (UN) 105, 192n.2
Svalbard 174
Swahili 147

Tanzania 26
Teachers Service Commission (TSC) 25
teaching assistant learning
    conclusions 112–14
    flexible learning approaches 109–12
    and innovative communication tools 106–9
    introduction 101–2
    and refugee education 103–6
    the students 102–3
Toronto 169
Tsing, Anna 176
Turner, Simon 29

Uganda 9, 26, 40
UNESCO 11, 133–4
UNHCR
    compound in Dadaab 174
    and English language usage 160
    introduction 8–9
    and post-secondary education initiatives 118
    and refugees 27, 31, 89–90
    and tripartite agreement (2013) 23, 61
    and UBC instructors 140
    and worldwide displaced people 145–6, 149
United States 159
University of British Columbia (UBC) 6, 94, 134, 136, 140–1, 145–8, 150
university programmes, gender disparities/access to 40–5

Verdirame, G. 40
vocational training 24
'Voices beyond walls' (Sawhney) 90

warya ('boy') 22
Webct 87
Westgate Mall, Nairobi attack (2013) 23
WhatsApp
    aiding connection between TAs and students 107–8
    discussion forum usage 169
    as a teaching communication 92
    use by instructors 140–1
    use by women 98, 121
    use in classroom interactions 85, 88
    for video clarification 124
Windle International Kenya (WIK) 6, 20, 34, 76, 134
Woldegiorgis, E. T. 55–6
women
    access to technology 140
    BHER participation versus family demands 121
    and collective childcare in Kakuma 44
    as community health workers 68
    in Dadaab refugee camps 96–7
    and domestic violence 43–8
    and education of 4
    and female genital mutilation (FGM) 71
    and gender disparities 35–48
    and higher education 35–7, 45–8, 105
    importance of education for girls 153
    married and attending classes 40
    political subjugation of 4
    refugee employment opportunities 41
    refugee girls in Kakuma 39–40
    and separate WhatsApp groups 121
Word 117
WordPress 141
World University Service of Canada (WUSC) 6, 159
The Writers Club 90

York University (YU)
    and BHER programs 94–6, 98, 102
    Certificate Program 162, 194nn.8–9
    degree programmes 65, 67–70, 73–4, 101–2, 119, 124, 192n.4
    delivery of higher education approach 112
    face-to-face courses 85, 88–9
    graduate programmes on site 150
    introduction 6–7, 13
    labour dispute at 92
    partnership functioning 50, 53–5, 57
    place-based learning 168
    and *Place and Learning* course 169–71
    use of Moodle 106
YouTube 88

Zoom (video) 5, 87–8, 94, 97–8, 107, 111